365 MEDITATIONS *for a* peaceful heart *and a* peaceful world

Marcus Braybrooke

365 MEDITATIONS *for a* peaceful heart *and a* peaceful world

To Mary,
With deep gratitude for her love
and her dedication to peace.

First edition for the United States and Canada
published in 2004 by Barron's Educational Series, Inc.

First published in Great Britain in 2004
by Godsfield, a division of Hamlyn Octopus Ltd.

Project Editor: Sarah Doughty
Project Designer: Michael Whitehead
Page Makeup: Nicola Liddiard
Picture Research: Lynda Marshall

Designed and produced for Octopus Publishing Group by The Bridgewater Book Company

All inquiries should be addressed to:
Barron's Educational Series, Inc.
250 Wireless Boulevard
Hauppauge, New York 11788
http://www.barronseduc.com

International Standard Book Number 0-7641-2765-9
Library of Congress Catalog Card Number 2003096197

Printed and bound in China

Picture acknowledgments: The Bridgewater Book Company would like to thank Corbis for the permission to reproduce copyrighted material: pp. 17, 29, 32-33, 35, 40, 65, 70, 74, 79, 80, 86, 96-9, 118, 122, 128, 135, 149, 152, 158, 161, 172, 174, 194, 198, 210, 218-219, 227, 244, 247, 249, 255, 257, 266, 288-289, 294, 316-317, 323, 351, 360, 366, 378.

Contents

PEACE MEDITATIONS 6

part one

PEACE IN OUR HEARTS 10

part two

PEACE IN OUR LIVES 64

part three

PEACE IN OUR HOMES 118

part four

PEACE IN THE COMMUNITY 172

part five

PEACE BETWEEN FAITHS 226

part six

PEACE IN THE WORLD 280

part seven

PEACE IN THE UNIVERSE 334

SOURCES 382

THE SEARCH FOR PEACE IN SOCIETY *and the world cannot be separated from the quest for inner peace in the heart. If you wish for a more peaceful world, the first step is to resolve to become a more peaceful person yourself. This is a commitment to a lifetime task. In the beginning, you have to learn how to quiet the body and still the mind. This is not just outer silence, which is difficult in a noisy world, but inner silence, which is even more difficult with a hectic schedule and many pressing concerns to think about. Yet without inner silence, you will not come to know yourself nor discover your deep rootedness in the Soul of All Being, to whom people have given many names.*

As you get to know yourself better, you may not like what you find. You may have a low opinion of yourself or a lack of self-worth. You may be plagued by feelings of guilt from childhood memories. You may feel bitter about an unresolved argument or you may still be hurt by a broken relationship. You may be struggling with pain or sadness. But as you look deeper you will find forgiveness for yourself and all those around you. Like cleaning a tarnished vessel of silver, you will gradually discover the original brightness of a pure heart. A peaceful heart is one without regret about the past or fear for the future. You are free to live wholly in the present—at peace with yourself and at one with life.

My own perspective is that of a Christian. As a Church of England vicar, I have learned much from my parishioners. Throughout my ministry I have also, on a voluntary basis, been active in the interfaith movement, as a member of the World Congress of Faiths. I spent a year before ordination studying Indian religions at Madras University. Subsequently, I have traveled widely and learned about world religions both from sacred scriptures and from practitioners, many of whom have become personal friends. Recently, I was a cofounder of the Three Faiths Forum of Jews, Christians, and Muslims.

The relationship of religions to each other has been much discussed by scholars. In my view, each religion is "unique and universal." Each religion has a distinct identity and is to be valued in its particularity, but each religion also has a message for all people. This means we can learn from the wisdom of great spiritual teachers, even if we do not belong to the same religion. Many of the meditations are based on the insights of a particular religious tradition. Similar themes, however, can be found in several religions—such as peace itself. It can be illuminating to juxtapose quotations from different traditions, as I have tried to do in some of the meditations.

When you meditate, you may experience timeless moments of total stillness and peace. But most of your days are spent interacting with other people or with the natural world. You can radiate peace to all you contact, but you will also pick up vibrations from others whom you meet. It was not until I developed a form of angina that I realized how the body, especially the heart, reacts to the anger, jealousy, and resentment of others, even if it is not focused on you. You are interrelated with life at every level of your being. Just as smoke may make it hard to breathe, another person's depression may dull your spirit.

To be a peaceful person means learning to respond peacefully to the ever-changing demands of life—at work, in the home, and in the community. Do not be discouraged if you are not transformed overnight. The lost keys, the delay on the way to work, your teenage daughter's loud music, your own mistakes will still be annoying. But gradually you will learn to react more creatively while maintaining an inner tranquillity.

The search for a peaceful heart is not, however, a selfish pursuit. It does not require you to live cocooned from the pain and conflict of the world. In fact, as your inner peace develops, you will feel more acutely the anguish of those who suffer. You will become increasingly aware of the changes necessary to create a more harmonious community. There are many ways in which you can help: by your attitude, by what you say to friends, by donations to charity, by campaigning for a cause, by overcoming prejudice, or by challenging injustice. You cannot do everything. But everyone can do something. Your most important contribution is not what you do but who you are—a person with a peaceful heart. You will become aware that you are part of a great network of people who, in a wonderful variety of ways, care for the sick, feed the poor, bring reconciliation to areas of conflict, and share in the healing of the world. You can find renewal in your search for peace in the example of people from many countries and faiths who have dedicated their lives to the service of others and the search for peace.

The ever-changing beauty of the natural world is another source of renewal. Many people feel most at peace when they are quiet in the hills or valleys or beside still water or churning waves. Many come in touch with the sustaining Source of Life through the experience of nature. The awareness of the preciousness of all life on this planet imposes a responsibility on each person to protect it for future generations.

The search for peace in the heart and the world is a daily calling and this book provides a quotation, a thought, and a suggestion for meditation and reflection for each day of the year. Many religious people, although not Buddhists, speak of "God," so the word appears in many of the meditations, but if you find the word a hindrance, you may prefer to use a term such as "the Real," "the Inner Light," "the Light Force," "the Soul of All Being," or your own choice of words. It may be that all words are inadequate. There is an old saying—"Pray as you can, not as you can't." Use what works for you without allowing religious disputation to distract you from your quest for peace. Of course, you can read more than one page a day if you wish and you may want to return several times to favorite passages.

The book is arranged under themes suggested in a prayer written by George Appleton, who was committed to the search for understanding and friendship between people of all religions and who longed for a more peaceful world.

O God of many names,
Lover of all people,
Give peace in our hearts,
In our lives,
In our homes,
In our community,
Between our religions,
In the world
In the universe,
The peace of our need,
The peace of your will.

part one

PEACE IN OUR HEARTS

You have it in you to become a more peace-loving and peace-giving person. The first step is to learn how to quiet the body and the mind. This chapter provides guidance on how to begin.

Art, music, flower arranging, and other traditional ways have helped people to give attention to the present moment. Certain times of day are also especially beneficial for developing inner peace. As awareness of your inner life grows, you become more sensitive to the Mystery at the heart of all life.

Peace in the Heart

If there is to be peace in the world. . .
There must be peace in the home.
If there is to be peace in the home,
There must be peace in the heart.

—LAO-TZU, CHINESE PHILOSOPHER (b. 604 BCE)

Like most people, you probably long for peace. But when you turn on the television or pick up the newspaper, you are bombarded by stories of violence and conflict. Your daily routine is hectic, with little time to stop and reflect. You may not feel at peace with members of your own family or may face conflict at work. Though you may feel that you can do little to influence international affairs, you can do something about yourself and your immediate surroundings. Just as a pebble thrown into a pond causes ripples that reach the bank, so your cultivation of inner peace can create harmonious vibrations that will spread all around.

PRACTICE *Make a resolution to live a more peaceful life. Telling someone about your intention will strengthen your resolve. Take some time to identify areas of tension in your life. Are you in conflict with someone at work or with a member of your family? Think of what you could say to ease the tension or what act of kindness you could perform to help resolve the situation: Can you offer help to a coworker? Can you listen to a family member without speaking or judging them? The road to peace starts with a single step.*

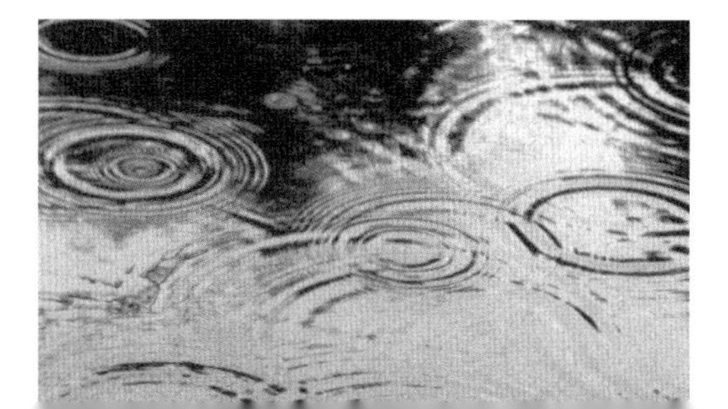

day
2 Quiet the Body

The first thing to be done is to procure silence.

—SOREN KIERKEGAARD (1813–1855), DANISH RELIGIOUS THINKER

Some trains now have "Quiet Zones" where you can get away from the constant buzz and chatter of mobile phones. You might find it helpful to create a "Quiet Zone" in your life as well. Spiritual writers stress that learning to be quiet is an essential means of discovering inner peace. Many spiritual paths suggest that the search for peace begins with the body. Stilling the body is a means of quieting the mind. We have always known the mind and body are linked. The Roman satirist Juvenal (55–127) said, "You should pray to have a sound mind in a sound body." (*Satires* no. 10.I.356.) Taking care of your body by exercising regularly, eating a healthy diet, and getting enough sleep are important preliminaries.

PRACTICE *Set aside time each day to be quiet. Decide on a place where you will not be disturbed. It should be warm and well ventilated. It is important to get comfortable. An upright chair that supports the back is best, or you can sit cross-legged on the floor. Now relax any tension in your body by clenching your hands and then opening them. Then relax any stiffness in the shoulders by moving your head gently in a circle. Stretch your legs and feet. Place your hands on your lap and close your eyes. Listen to your breathing and repeat the words: "As I breathe in, I quiet my body: As I breathe out, my body is calm." As you continue to breathe slowly and deeply, your body relaxes and your mind begins to quiet.*

Quiet the Mind

Like weary waves
thought flows upon thought
but the still depth beneath
is all thine own.

—George MacDonald (1824–1905), Scottish writer

Once you have stilled your body, try to quiet your mind. Father Keating, a Trappist monk who teaches the technique of Centering Prayer, once said to me that it is worthwhile to sit still for 20 minutes if only to have 1 minute of real silence. So do not give up. Our minds are full of plans for the future or memories of the past. Learning to still the mind means concentrating on the present moment. Living in the present helps you to be more attentive to tasks and to other people.

PRACTICE *Here is a simple way to quiet the mind. Sit comfortably, relax your body, and start to breathe deeply. Half close the eyes and focus them on a flower or a candle. You may find quiet music helpful. Soon you will find that the mind starts wandering. Do not get upset. Instead, gently bring the mind back to the focus of your attention. It helps to repeat a short sentence slowly to yourself, such as Kierkegaard's prayer, "O Lord, calm the waves of this heart." Slowly, just as the sea grows calm after a storm, your mind will become still.*

day 4

In Touch with Mystery

By What Name shall we call You, You who are Beyond All Names?

—Gregory of Nyssa (c. 330–395), Christian mystical writer

As you go deeper into peace, you discover your true self. Hinduism teaches that the inner self is one with Spirit of All Life—*atman* (the Self) is *Brahman* (the Divine). Many people have sensed a moment when they are at peace with the universe. The explorer and mystic Francis Younghusband (1863–1942) described a moment in Tibet when he "felt in touch with the flaming heart of the world—in touch with a mighty joy-giving Power." Some people speak of this Power as God. Others prefer to talk of the Inner Light. And for some, the Mystery is too wonderful to be named.

PRACTICE *There is no shortcut to stilling the mind. Just as a great pianist still practices the scales, so you need to remember to still the body, to listen to your breathing, and to focus the mind. The deeper you go into yourself, the more in tune you will feel with the Spirit of All Life. Do not get distracted by wondering what you believe about Ultimate Reality. Choose the term you find most helpful, otherwise the mind can start whirring again and distract you. You can fall in love without knowing why the other person attracts you. Instead of thinking, let yourself rest in the joy of deep inner peace.*

Follow the Breath

Your breathing is your greatest friend. Return to it in all your troubles and you will find comfort and guidance.

—The teaching of a Buddhist master

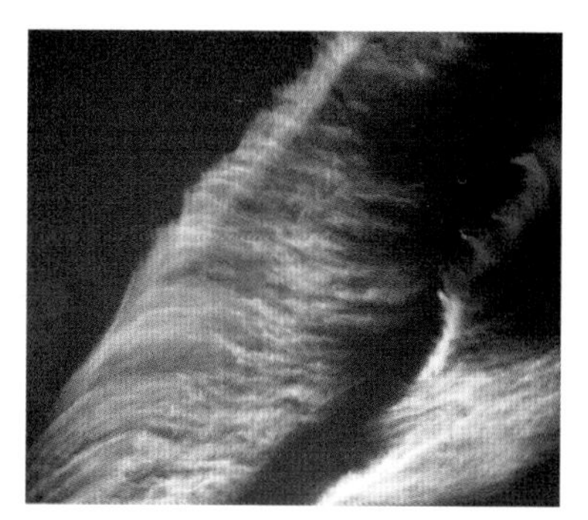

I learned the value of the breath in prayer and meditation at theological college—not from a spiritual director but from a woman whose usual job was to teach pregnant women how to relax before childbirth. She taught us to breathe deeply to help free our voices for speech and song. As part of the preparation for stilling the mind, you may find it useful to focus on the breath. This helps to relax the body. Attention to the breathing is also used by some Buddhist teachers to encourage awareness.

PRACTICE *This exercise may help you gain awareness of the natural rhythms of the body. Awareness of the body will help you to concentrate on the present moment. The aim of this exercise is to pay attention to the air as it passes through your nostrils. Do not try to control your breathing or to deepen it. Just let it come and go naturally. Concentrate on the sensation of air passing through your nostrils. If you find your mind has wandered, bring it back to the sensation in your nostrils. If you practice this for five minutes, it will have a calming effect. You can return to this practice when you are stressed and tense.*

day 6

Open Hands

Jesus said, "If I, your Lord and Master, have washed your feet,
You also ought to wash one another's feet. I have set you an example:
You are to do as I have done for you."

—BIBLE: JOHN 13.14

Your gestures can serve as an expression and reminder of your intention. Gesticulating is an essential part of expression in everyday life. You can also use your hands in expressing yourself to God. After his conversion, St. Oswald (c. 605–42), King of Northumbria, prayed with open hands, palms upward on his knees. He was ready to receive God's grace. He was also open-handed to the poor. Once, as a royal banquet was about to begin, Oswald was told that the crowd outside was begging for food. Oswald, pointing to a silver dish, ordered that the food on it should be distributed to the peasants and the dish sold so that money could be given to the poor.

You can use your hands to hurt or to heal the wounds of others, to fight or to make peace. Picture how Jesus used his hands:

Healing pain and sickness, blessing children small,
Washing tired feet and saving those who fall.

FROM A HYMN BY MARGARET CROPPER (1886–1980)

PRACTICE *Think of some of the ways you can use your hands. You can use them to push people away or to stretch out a hand of friendship. You can clench your fist so that you neither receive nor give, or open your hand to accept presents and to bestow gifts. Be mindful of your gestures. Ask yourself: Are they causing harm or bringing peace?*

Awareness of the Body

There is no better way of staying in the present than getting out of your head and returning to your physical senses.

—ANTHONY DE MELLO, CONTEMPORARY SPIRITUAL WRITER, *SANDHANA*

Many Buddhist teachers stress the importance of living in the present moment and cultivating total attention to our immediate activity. One helpful exercise is awareness of our bodies. When you sit quietly, relaxing the body helps to quiet the mind. There are forms of meditation where attention to the body is the meditation, not just a preparation.

PRACTICE *Try to become aware of the sensations of your body. Sit comfortably and close your eyes. Start with the touch of your clothes on your shoulders. What is the nature of the sensation? Do your clothes feel light or heavy? Can you sense their texture? Do not react. Just observe. Now become aware of the weight of your body pressing against your seat. Become aware of your sitting posture. This simple exercise relaxes the body and eases nervous tension. It also helps heighten your awareness of the present.*

Washing Your Hands

As imperfect beings, we often fail to recognize our mission. These failures come about because we have lost some of our natural purity. Purification enables a person to cultivate spirituality and to restore his or her natural greatness.

—REV. YAMAMOTO, SHINTO HIGH PRIEST, *THE WAY OF THE KAMI*

Everyday activities can lead you to inner contemplation. You place memos on your desk to remind you whom to call. When making memos to organize your busy day, why not use them as a reminder of your search for inner peace? When you rise each morning, do you welcome the gift of a new day? When sitting down to a meal, do you pause to give thanks before you eat? Do you pray for the safety of yourself and your fellow travelers as you set off for work each day?

PRACTICE *Muslims perform ritual washing before times of prayer. Hindus say prayers as they take their morning bath. In Japan, some members of the Shinto religion perform a ritual of purification by entering a waterfall (*misogi*). After preliminary rituals, participants enter the waterfall and chant a request to the spirits to wash away all impurities. Consider your daily routine. You can find many reminders of the sacred in your ordinary activities. How many times a day do you wash your hands? Each washing can serve as a reminder of your wish for purification.*

Equal Before God

"Humankind was but one nation." (Qur'an 10.19)
All people were created one and Allah's message to humankind
is in essence one, the Message of Unity and Truth.

—From the commentary on the English translation
of the Qur'an, the Custodian of the Two Holy Mosques

The movement of your body can express joy and reverence in God's presence. In Islam, movement of the body is part of the prescribed ritual of *Salat* (worship). After ablutions, a Muslim stands facing toward Mecca. After silently offering the prayer to God, he makes a deep bow in adoration and then touches his knees and forehead to the ground. Although Salat can be performed alone, it is often conducted with other worshippers at times of prayer. Such prayer helps bind the community of the faithful (*umma*) together in peace. The straight lines of worshippers affirm that before Allah, all Muslims are equal.

PRACTICE *On pilgrimage to Sikh holy places in the Punjab, I was expected to prostrate myself on entering a Gurdwara before the Sikh scriptures (the* Adi Granth*). From that experience, I came to appreciate how the body's position can express a relationship to the Divine. You may want to experiment—perhaps in private—at least to discover how your feelings over reverence can be expressed through the body. Some people lie back to feel their utter dependence on God. Others prostrate themselves to express their adoration. Some like to raise their arms above their heads in rejoicing. Dance in some religions celebrates the gift of life. Circle dancing and movements shared with others can create a strong sense of fellowship and peace.*

Tea Ceremony

Enable us to perfect the way of our living by completely submitting to the Laws of Nature.

—A PRAYER FROM THE MODERN JAPANESE ITTOEN RELIGION

Many activities can become a form of meditation if they encourage concentration, awareness of the present moment, and harmony with the laws of Nature. The Japanese tea ceremony (*cha-no-yu*) is one such activity that has been refined into a meditative art. Tea drinking was introduced to Japan from China by Zen monks to help them stay awake during meditation. It became part of Zen ritual, when friends would meet to discuss aesthetic or philosophical topics. The tearoom is so constructed that you have to enter humbly on your knees. The ritual is designed to encourage simplicity, quiet, and absence of ornament.

PRACTICE *You can take the opportunity of your family meals to foster mindfulness. Traditional societies recognize that meals are part of the rhythm of family and community life. Preparation and serving of food is an act of devotion, requiring concentration and care. Attention to the ceremonial details encourages recognition of the present moment. The food you eat is grown, harvested, and transported to you thanks to the labors of many others. Even in today's fast-paced world, you can come more in touch with the harmony and rhythms of nature and community by developing your own mealtime ritual.*

"Nearer God's Heart in a Garden"

The kiss of the sun for pardon,
The song of the birds for mirth,
One is nearer God's Heart in a garden
Than anywhere else on earth.

—"GOD'S GARDEN," BY DOROTHY FRANCES GURNEY (1858–1932), ENGLISH POET

Flowers are used in the rituals of many traditions. Their intrinsic beauty calms the spirit and induces a sense of harmony with nature. Attention to arranging them encourages mindfulness and an unspoken outpouring of praise. Gardening and flower arranging can encourage inner peacefulness and a sense of being in tune with the world. The Japanese developed tea gardens to provide an appropriate spiritual atmosphere for guests approaching the tea ceremony. The gardens suggested the "lonely precincts of a secluded mountain shrine." Japanese abstract gardens have a sense of space and balance in the relationship of objects to each other.

PRACTICE *You can use the beauty of a garden to encourage a spiritual atmosphere. Parks and nature preserves can bring an appreciation of the wider workings of the world. Ponds and water can encourage stillness and peace. Tending plants in your home and office can serve as a reminder of your place in nature. By attending to nature and appreciating its beauty, you can develop the mindfulness that leads to a calm and focused mind. In this way, you attune yourself to the rhythms of life. A sense of harmony with the world around nurtures inner peace and tranquillity.*

day 12 Living in the Present Moment

Grant to our eyes wide horizons,
Increase our vision to see
Beyond the obvious and into the depths.

—David Adam, contemporary English author of *Prayers in the Celtic Tradition*

When I am painting a watercolor of the sea or mountains, I become so absorbed that I lose all sense of time. The practice of painting requires such concentration that only the changing light makes me realize that evening has come and I will be late for my meal. Such "one-pointedness" of the mind, as some Japanese spiritual traditions call it, is a form of meditation. While engaged in painting, I am living totally in the present moment. Many other crafts, such as pottery, photography, or woodworking, require the kind of attention that helps increase your awareness.

PRACTICE *Acquiring skills is helpful and makes the end product more satisfying, but it is the mindfulness required to do the task well that makes it a spiritual exercise. Give yourself an opportunity to experiment. Many retreat centers offer weekend or short courses in "Prayer and Painting" or "Prayer and Calligraphy." Many people today live mainly in their minds. Pursuing a craft can help you become more aware of the body. Through this practice, you can rediscover your innate creativity. You will also find that artistic or craft activities are a helpful way to let go of the tensions of a hectic life.*

Music

Today, like every other day, we wake up empty and frightened.
Don't open the door to the study and begin reading.
Take down a musical instrument. Let the beauty we love be what we do.

—Jal al-Din Rumi (1207–1273),
also known as Mawlana, Sufi mystical poet

Music plays an important part in religious life. It can be an aid to meditation. It can stimulate ecstatic behavior, express worship, and create feelings of awe and wonder. For the spiritual practitioner, music may be a sacred activity that unites the player with the Divine. Music can bind people together in harmony. It can uplift the downhearted. As a Japanese prisoner of war wrote, "Man need never be so defeated that he cannot do anything. Weak, sick, broken in body, far from home, and alone in a strange land, he can sing."

PRACTICE *I sometimes prepare myself for a time of quiet by listening to music. Many people find it a helpful way of putting to one side the worries and preoccupations of the day. Attentiveness to music can help the mind become still. You may wish to listen to the music of your faith, but there are many traditions of spiritual music available that encourage quiet and reflection. Some people find that listening to recordings of birdsong or flowing water quiets the mind. You may like to sing softly to yourself or play an instrument. There are many ways in which music can help you become more peaceful. Experiment to find which forms help you most.*

day 14

Can People Read Your Writing?

Read; and your Lord is the most generous,
He who has taught with the pen
Taught man what he did not know.

—FROM THE MESSAGE OF THE ANGEL GABRIEL
TO THE PROPHET MUHAMMAD, BUKHARI, *SAHIH* I.3.

Can other people read your writing? Calligraphy, the art of beautiful writing, has been practiced in many cultures to enhance the dignity of sacred scriptures. Muslims believe that the very words of the Holy Qur'an are inspired by God (Allah). Copying the Qur'an was regarded as a meritorious act, and calligraphy was accorded a high rank among the arts. Because Islam forbids visual representation of animate forms to avoid the dangers of idolatry, calligraphy is used to decorate mosques and public buildings. Like painting, the concentration that calligraphy demands encourages mindfulness.

PRACTICE *I was surprised recently when I received typewritten letters from two friends on the same day thanking me for my* handwritten *letters. Modern methods of communication have made the old fashioned art of letter writing a rarity. Carefully written letters can bring a special gift of peace to both the writer and the reader in times of illness or bereavement. How often do you send handwritten letters? Do you take the time and care to make your writing readable? It is said that sending an illegible letter steals the time of the person who receives it. Learning to write beautifully is also a way of learning to concentrate and is itself a form of meditation.*

T'ai-chi

Think of the contrasting energies moving together and in union,
in harmony, interlocking, like a white fish and a black fish mating. . . .
If you identify with only one side of duality, you become unbalanced.
Movement and stillness become one.

—AL CHUNG-LIANG HUANG, A T'AI-CHI MASTER,
EMBRACE THE TIGER, RETURN TO THE MOUNTAIN

Do you go regularly to the gym for a workout? Exercise is important for our physical health, but several spiritual traditions recognize that physical movements also help to bring inner peace. T'ai-chi began as a martial art. It is still practiced by many Chinese every morning and evening and has become quite popular in the West. Its graceful motions speak of a sense of inner contemplation. They are intended to stimulate the unobstructed flow of the life force (*chi*) through the body. It is also a way of becoming one with the eternal relationship of movement and stillness.

PRACTICE *T'ai-chi instruction is becoming widely available in the West. Its gentle rhythmic movements are beneficial to the body and the spirit. You may wish to take an introductory course to experience the calming effect the focus on its movements brings to the mind. As a t'ai-chi text says, "In any action the entire body should be light and agile and all of its parts connected like pearls on a thread." Try to move more gently and gracefully. It will calm the mind as well as the body.*

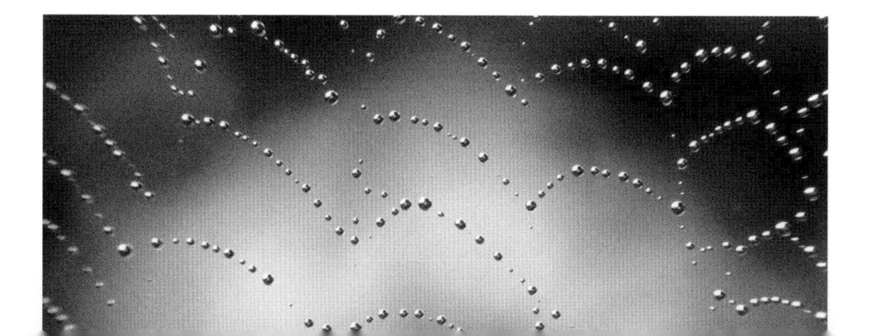

day
16 Yoga

Let the wise man vigilantly restrain his mind as he would a chariot yoked to bad horses.

—SVETASVATARA UPANISHAD. II.9

Yoga, which originated in India, is now widely practiced in the West. Although some people take it up for physical health, yoga is also a spiritual discipline. The word means "joining." Yoga's techniques aim at the transformation of consciousness and the attainment of liberation from the law of *karma*—the moral law of cause and effect—and the endless cycle of rebirth. Although the mind is constantly fluctuating, it can be brought under control and become one-pointed through the practice of yoga. Yoga can ultimately lead to higher states of consciousness, but even beginners find that it clears the mind and encourages a state of serene, detached awareness.

PRACTICE *Although there are many books available, yoga is best learned from a qualified teacher. There are a variety of practices covered by the term* yoga. *Hatha yoga is now often taught to promote physical and mental health. Raja yoga, which is based on the teachings of Patanjali (second or third century* CE*), emphasizes the importance of physical postures and of breathing. This practice teaches techniques of regulated breathing that calm the nerves and increase the body's supply of invisible life energy.*

Walk with Your Eyes Open

Your enjoyment of the world is never right until every morning you awake in heaven, see yourself in God's palace, and look upon the skies and the Earth and the air as celestial joys.

—THOMAS TRAHERNE (1637–1674), ENGLISH MYSTICAL POET

If yoga and t'ai-chi are not for you, consider a simple walk outdoors to exercise the body and steady the mind. Take your time and pay attention to your pace. Walking has a natural rhythm. Be aware of beauty all around—the majestic height of the trees, the changing light, the song of the birds. Donald Nicholl (in his book, *Holiness*) asked the students in his class on mysticism to go into the forest and see if a particular tree caught their attention. Then each week they were to go back to that tree and stay there quietly and carefully observe it, noticing any changes. For some, snails, dewdrops, or blades of grass stood out, each in its glorious individuality.

PRACTICE *Go for a walk by yourself. Pay attention to your surroundings. Notice how many different sorts of trees, bushes, or grasses you see. In the fall, pick up some leaves and look closely at their varying colors. You could do the same on the seashore, picking up the shells. Notice how, as you focus your attention, you become aware of the infinite and delicate variety that exists in the natural world and of your place in it. To be in harmony with life is to become more in tune with yourself.*

day 18

Pilgrimage

On a huge hill,
Cragged, and steep, Truth stands, and he that will
Reach her, about must, and about must go.

—JOHN DONNE (1572–1631), POET AND PRIEST, SATIRE NO. 3. L.79

Solitary walking is a meditative exercise, but the faithful in many religions walk together, often long distances, on pilgrimage to reach a holy place or shrine. Muslims are expected, if at all possible, to journey once in their lives to Mecca. For centuries, Christians have traveled to Jerusalem and Bethlehem. There are many Hindu and Buddhist pilgrimage centers. Pilgrimage is an act of devotion. It also strengthens your beliefs by deepening your sense of the history and tradition of faith. It links you in spirit with fellow believers of previous generations and with the faithful who live in other lands. Pilgrimage can help overcome the divisions in the world and can be a path leading to truth and lasting peace.

PRACTICE *Many cities contain cathedrals and other sacred spaces where generations have worshipped. Visiting a holy place, even if you are not a member of the religion, can give you a deeper insight into your own beliefs. Such places have been invested with the silence of reverence. Visiting them can put you in touch with this sense of stillness. Remember that your physical pilgrimage is the outward manifestation of your journey inward to the Truth.*

The Supreme Mystery

There is something beyond our mind which abides in silence within our mind. It is the supreme mystery beyond thought.

—HINDU: MAITRI UPANISHAD 6.19

Silence is a gateway to the inner life. As your mind becomes still, you enter more deeply into yourself. As you do so, the sense of your individual self fades and there is an awareness of oneness. You sense a Presence greater than yourself. This sense of Presence is a gift. It is like discovering water deep down in a well. Most people live their lives at a superficial level, occupied with the business of daily affairs. If you can empty your mind of these concerns, you gradually discover an inner peace and oneness with life. It is, as the Hindu scriptures say, "a supreme mystery." There is no need to name this reality. It is enough to taste the calm refreshment that this awareness offers.

PRACTICE *You will not experience inner peace if you are straining to achieve it, because then the sense of your individual self is dominant. It is a matter of letting go. Imagine you are about to make a parachute jump. At some point you have to let go and trust yourself to your parachute and to the air.*

day

20 You Are Accepted

O for a closer walk with God,
A calm and heavenly frame . . .
Return, O holy Dove, return
Sweet messenger of rest.

—HYMN BY WILLIAM COWPER (1731–1800), ENGLISH POET

The experience of a peace that passes all understanding is at the heart of every great religion. "You are accepted" was the subject of a famous sermon by the Protestant theologian Paul Tillich (1886–1965). He describes how meaningless many people find their lives. "We walk through a dark valley . . . we have violated another life, a life which we loved. Our disgust with our own being has become intolerable." But then, "Sometimes at that moment a wave of light breaks into our darkness, as though a voice were saying, 'You are accepted, accepted by that which is greater than you. Do not ask for the name now. Simply accept the fact that you are accepted.'" (Paul Tillich, *The Shaking of the Foundations.*)

PRACTICE *Do Paul Tillich's words resonate with your own experience? Have you had times when you felt life was empty and meaningless—perhaps when you split up from your partner or you lost your job or could not get another? Can you also recall moments when the clouds parted and a shaft of sunlight brightened up your life? For some people, those moments are so transforming that their life is changed. They may struggle at times, clinging on when life seems bereft of the hope that the clouds will break and the sun will shine again. But those memories of those transforming moments are the assurance that even in your darkness you are accepted.*

Unlocking the Riches of Religion

Catch the bird of heaven
Lock him in religion
Look again tomorrow
And he will be gone.

—SYDNEY CARTER (b. 1915), TWENTIETH-CENTURY HYMN WRITER

The experience of "being accepted," and the sense of Mystery or Presence, suggest that there is a deeper dimension to life. The great faiths, each in their own way, point their followers to this Reality. Just as some people pore over railway timetables but never catch a train, so there are those so absorbed by rituals and discussion of doctrines that they never reach the Fountain of Life. Others, alienated by the trappings of religions and the behavior of their followers, deprive themselves of the spiritual riches held in trust by the guardians of the sacred way. But these riches can be a resource for peaceful living, if you can find the key.

PRACTICE *Take time to assess your feelings about organized religion. Did your parents belong to a faith community? Were you, as a child, expected to go to the mosque, temple, synagogue, or church? What are your memories? Examine your feelings. Be honest in your assessment. Do you still go to a place of worship occasionally or regularly? If so, how does it nourish your spiritual life? If not, do you think worship with others would help you? Perhaps you have tried a New Age group? The spiritual path can be a lonely one, and fellowship with other explorers can encourage you on the journey.*

day
22
God of Many Names

God's name is hidden. God's name is secret to all God's children.
God's names are many, no one knows the number of them.

—AN ANCIENT EGYPTIAN VERSE

Islam speaks of 99 beautiful names for God. Hinduism has thousands of images of God. Although Hindus insist there is only one Supreme Being, some say that each person has his or her particular focus of devotion (*istadevata*). Christian worship is centered on Jesus Christ, but he has been pictured in many different ways, from stern judge to "Gentle Jesus, meek and mild." Many people see their relationship with Ultimate Reality in personal terms. That is the relationship we understand most intimately. The sense of union with the Divine is compared to a child's dependence on a parent or the joyous union of lovers. In mutual self-giving there is peace.

PRACTICE *When you consider God, do you have an image in your mind? Don't worry whether it is an "orthodox belief." If you have sisters and brothers, each would have different memories of your mother and father, although you would be thinking about the same two people. What matters is that your belief is real for you. Do you think of God in personal terms? This helps some people, but if you had an abusive or violent father, speaking to God as "Father" may be a problem. A Native American prayer addresses God as "Grandfather." However, do not get hung up on language. One of my teachers referred to God as "Boss," which nearly put me off for life! Find a name that is meaningful for you.*

Can You Put Your Beliefs Into Words?

The Tao that can be told of
Is not the Absolute Tao.

—THE OPENING VERSE OF THE TAO-TE CHING,
ATTRIBUTED TO LAO-TZU (C. 604 BCE)

You do not have to be "religious" or belong to a faith community to sense a Mystery at the heart of the universe. You may find it difficult to put into words what you believe. The ancient Chinese teaching of Taoism held that the eternally real is unnameable. "Nameless is the origin of Heaven and Earth," says the *Tao-te Ching* and adds,

The Names that can be given
Are not Absolute Names.

The twentieth century philosopher Ludwig Wittgenstein thought much the same, saying, "Whereof one cannot speak, thereof one must be silent." Many mystics have sensed that the Spirit of Life is too wonderful to be described in words.

PRACTICE *Do not worry if you have difficulties with religious language. Many people feel the same and find it easier just to be quiet in the presence of the Eternal. Could you truly describe falling in love other than in poetic terms? The world contains a wealth of poetry about love. Even so, it is difficult to convey the experience to someone who has not known it. It may help you to view the sacred scriptures of the world as poetry, which points to a Mystery that is also impossible to express directly. Try reading a sacred text with the sense of its poetry in mind. Use this feeling of poetry to find a way of meditation that helps you to discover a deeper reality and a sense of inner peace.*

day
24

You Are Enough for Me

My Lord, whatever share of this world you bestow on me,
bestow it on your enemies, and whatever share of the next world
you give to me, give it to your friends—You are enough for me.

—RAB'IA (c. 713-801), MUSLIM WOMAN MYSTIC

When many people first begin to pray, they do so because they want help from God, either for themselves or for a friend who is ill or in trouble. Others pray because they hope for reward in another life. Some people want to enjoy inner feelings of light and peace. The deeper your relationship, the less you will want from God. Your chief desire will be to wait in God's presence. As the Psalmist wrote, "With my whole being I thirst for God, the living God" (Psalms 42.2). In God's presence, all thoughts of enmity disappear and you long for all beings to enjoy the same bliss.

PRACTICE *There is nothing wrong in asking God for help. Jesus encouraged his followers to think of God as a loving parent and told them, "Ask and you will receive." As your trust in God grows, you will be more confident that God knows what you and your loved ones need. Instead of expressing wants, you will come to use your time of quiet to rest in God's presence. This Hindu prayer may be helpful.*

I desire neither earthly kingdom,
nor even freedom from birth and death.
I desire only the deliverance
from grief of all those afflicted by misery.

—FROM *PRAYERS FOR PEACE*, ED. B. MARTIN PEDERSEN

Longing for God

Do not feed your spirit on anything apart from God.
Cast away all cares and let peace and reconciliation fill your heart.

—St. John of the Cross (1549–1591), poet and mystic

What do you want more than anything else? Advertisers offer the chance of winning vast fortunes in competitions or lotteries. Spiritual teachers in every generation, however, recognized that the deepest longing of the human heart is to see God and to wait in God's presence. Jal al-Din Rumi (1207–1273), a great Sufi poet and founder of the Whirling Dervishes, compared this longing to a lover's desire for her beloved. He wrote:

There is some kiss we want
with our whole lives,
the touch of the Spirit on the body.

PRACTICE *The more you seek the Divine, the greater your yearning will become. If you were taught to pray, you were probably made to repeat set words. However, the deepest prayer is to be quiet in the Divine Presence. When lovers embrace, they need no words. So, too, the soul that seeks God loves to wait quietly for its Beloved. Sit still, and let the mind be quiet. Let your words, doubts, and thoughts go. Be still. Let the soul rest in harmony with the Spirit of the Universe.*

day 26 The Self

The Self is One. . . . Out of Self comes the breath that is the life of all things.
Of a certainty the person who sees all creatures
in himself, himself in all creatures, knows no sorrow.

—HINDU ISHA UPANISHAD, TRANS. BY W.B. YEATS AND SHREE PUROHIT SWAMI

For some people, the experience of union with the Real is so overwhelming that all sense of separate identity disappears. As a teenager, Sri Ramana Maharshi (1879–1950) was suddenly seized by the fear of death and had feelings similar to a near-death experience. Wanting to solve death's mystery, Sri Ramana imagined what it was like to die. He concentrated on this question until he became convinced that he was one with the deathless Self. "Absorption in the Self," he said later, "has continued from that moment right up to the present." All sense of an individual ego is illusory. The teaching of the Advaita (not-dual) tradition of Hinduism stresses the unity of all that is.

PRACTICE *Even if you do not agree with all the teachings of Advaita Hinduism, they may help you question your sense of ego, which often gets in the way of relationships. Some people think Western secular society places too much emphasis on individuality and forgets our shared humanity. If someone plans to build a new house nearby, do you protest that this will disturb your quiet and lower the value of your property or do you recognize that other people also need homes? Sensing our oneness with all beings, the divisions in the world appear illusory and we share the sufferings of other people.*

Mindfulness

You are asked to apply mindfulness to your sitting, walking, standing, looking, and speaking and to remain fully conscious in all your activities.

—ASHVAGHOSHA (C. 100 CE), BUDDHIST TEACHER AND POET

The Buddha taught that a mistaken sense of ego is the cause of all suffering. The Buddha denied that there is any permanent self or center of consciousness, unlike Advaita Hinduism, which says that the self is one with the Self of all things. To what extent, the Buddha might ask, are you the same person that you were 20 years ago? Much of your physical body has been renewed. Your self-consciousness has changed. The Buddha taught that there is no permanent subject. We are like an ever-flowing river—constantly changing. The hopes, fears, and disappointments of the self are illusory. If we recognize this, we can live lives that are detached, peaceful, and free from suffering.

PRACTICE *The Buddhist emphasis on mindfulness, or living in the present, reflects the teaching that there is no permanent ego. Whether or not you agree, Buddhist meditation techniques can lead you to a greater sense of calm and detachment. Try drinking a glass of water with total concentration. You could begin with paying attention to filling the glass. Notice the feel of the glass, the sound of the water. Then notice its touch on your lips, its taste, its coolness. Be aware of swallowing the water. Focusing your attention on what you are doing calms the body and gives you inner peace.*

day
28

One with Nature

Wisdom and Spirit of the universe!
Thou Soul that art the eternity of thought,
That givest to forms and images a breath
And everlasting motion.

—WILLIAM WORDSWORTH (1770–1850), ENGLISH ROMANTIC POET,
THE PRELUDE, BOOK I.1.401ff, EDS. S.GILL AND J.P. STERN

Have you ever experienced an overwhelming sense of oneness with nature, of being a part of a vastly larger organism? Master Mirihei Ueshiba, a Shinto teacher, looked at the stars one night and suddenly realized he was united with the universe. He burst into tears, covering his face with his hands. He sensed that human beings, indeed everything in this world, are cells that form this great universe. The theory of evolution indicates that we are related to all life. Author Donald Nicholl, descending the Grand Canyon and seeing evidence of different forms of life that have inhabited this planet over millions of years, recognized that he was the beneficiary of all their struggling for life. Scientific discovery confirms the mystical insight that life is a unity.

PRACTICE *Dinosaurs are quite popular with children. But have you reflected that human beings trace their descent to the earliest forms of life? Do you keep your scientific and religious understanding of the world in separate compartments? Have you considered how the mystic's sense of the unity of life and the scientist's recognition of the interdependence of living beings points to the same truth? Try spending an afternoon meditating in the prehistoric section of the local museum or some place in nature where the wealth of life is evident. It will make you marvel at the miracle of existence. Ponder these words of Donald Nicholl from* Holiness*: "What an incredibly hard-won privilege it is to be a human being; and at the same time it is an awesome responsibility. Every human being has a responsibility toward all those creatures whose agony and groaning has given him birth."*

The Name of God

There is One God
Whose Name is Truth,
The Creator, without fear, without hate,
Eternal being,
beyond birth and death,
Self-existent
realized by the Guru's grace

—THE JAP JI, THE FIRST MORNING PRAYER OF SIKHS

Repetition of the name of God not only instills peace but also can bring the devotee into the presence of God. Just as lovers whisper each other's name into the ear of the beloved, so lovers of God fondly repeat the divine name in meditation. Hindus and Sikhs believe that by repeating the name of God, they come to constantly be aware of God's presence and to reflect on the character of God. The "Nam," akin to the "Word" in Christianity, makes the Divine Reality present. "God, who is being himself, became manifest in Nam."

PRACTICE *Have you tried sitting quietly and repeating a name for God? You could use a word like "Peace" or "Love" in a similar way. Say the name quietly, slowly, and lovingly. You do not need to dwell on the name's meaning, but you will become aware of the different characteristics of the one whom you are worshipping. As you repeat the name, you will feel close to the Divine.*

Images of the Divine

We should believe in the Divine Presence filling the images of the deity.

—Sri Ramakrishna (1836–1886), Hindu ascetic and mystic

Do you have pictures of your family around the house? Just as the name of God may help some people realize God's presence, others like to use pictures and icons to remind them of their relationship to the Divine. Some faiths, such as Islam and Judaism, reject any representation that might lead to idolatry. However, Hinduism has numerous images of God, and Orthodox Christians treat icons—paintings of Christ, his mother Mary, and the saints—with great devotion. Judaism, Christianity, and Islam have all traditionally relied on words to communicate the divine, whereas Hinduism is a more visual religion.

PRACTICE *In your time of meditation, try focusing on a picture or statue. Rembrandt's famous painting* The Return of the Prodigal Son *is a good example. The picture shows the elderly father welcoming back his penitent son. It reflects the Christian belief in God's forgiving love—a theme echoed in other religions. Resting your eyes on a statue of the Buddha can bring a sense of the Buddha's serenity and a feeling of peace in yourself. Spend some time at a bookstore or museum looking at famous paintings and images. The landscapes of Cézanne, the calm interiors of Vermeer, or the work of other great artists may help you find a deeper peace.*

Inner Retreat

Oh that I had the wings of a dove to fly away and be at rest.

—BIBLE: PSALMS 55.6

Do you look forward to getting away from the city to spend a weekend in the country? Surprisingly, research has shown that vacations often are a time of high stress. Long ago, Roman Emperor Marcus Aurelius (121–180), a Stoic philosopher, warned that it was foolish to travel miles to a hideaway when you can find inner peace wherever you are. He admitted that like others, he looked for "cottages in the country, lonely seashores, and mountains." However, he added, "This is the very commonest stupidity; for it is in your power whenever you will, to retire into yourself."

PRACTICE *The real causes of stress relate to lifestyle and a lack of inner resources. Just as regular exercise is better than occasional sudden bouts of activity, so it is best to spend some time each day in quietness. Otherwise you may find you are taking your problems with you when you go away for a weekend or for a vacation. If you do go away, do you take a mobile phone and laptop with you? If so, ask yourself why? Is it because you still want to be in control? You need to learn how to escape the pressures that come from your hurried existence. Escaping from stress is much easier if you practice seeking a time of quiet every day.*

Let the Thoughts Pass By

When some first enter into the Prayer of Quiet they have many misgivings—
they wonder if they are really praying, or if anything
at all is going on, or if they are not just falling asleep.

—ST. TERESA, QUOTED BY M. BASIL PENNINGTON IN *CENTERING PRAYER*

Imagine you were in a business meeting on the ninth floor of a building and suddenly there was a noisy disturbance in the street. You got up, left the meeting, took the elevator to the lobby, and told the people outside to be quiet. By the time you got back, you would have done far more to disturb the meeting than the people who made the noise! In a similar way, do not get too bothered if thoughts suddenly distract you as you try to still your mind. If you follow these thoughts like a puppy that chases after anything that moves, you will never have peace. Try to take the attitude of a person looking through his or her window at passersby in the street. Observe your thoughts, and let them go by.

PRACTICE *You may find it easier to still the mind if you keep your eyes slightly open. Let them rest on an object a few feet away but do not focus on that object. It also helps to keep your back straight rather than to slouch. So sit on the floor or find an upright but comfortable chair. Then, if distracting thoughts come, acknowledge the thoughts as thoughts—"I am thinking what to have for supper," "I am thinking that I should phone my aunt"—and let them pass by. There will come a moment when you are no longer aware that you are thinking and your mind is still.*

Do Not Worry about the Lifeguard

O Love that wilt not let me go . . . I give thee back the life I owe
That in thine ocean depths its flow
May richer, fuller be.

—GEORGE MATHESON (1842–1906), BLIND SCOTTISH HYMN WRITER

Before swimming underwater, you take a deep breath. From time to time you surface to take another breath, but you do not climb out each time and start again. In the same way, when you have entered into quiet meditation, if you suddenly catch a thought, do not climb out of the deep silence. Gently return to the still water—and do not worry about what the "lifeguard" is thinking. There is a temptation to watch your own meditation and get anxious that you are not doing well. Some swimmers say to themselves, "The lifeguard must be thinking what a poor swimmer I am." Probably he is watching someone with a more attractive figure!

PRACTICE *Do you say to yourself at the end of quiet reflection, "That was good" or "I did not concentrate today"? If you do, you will find yourself observing yourself, and that becomes a distraction. Instead of letting go, part of your mind is still thinking. Meditation is not an achievement. It is a practice. Meditation does more than still the mind. It is a method for moving beyond a false sense of ego—which is a distraction—to sense a deeper unity. If the body and mind are really still, you are not conscious that you are meditating. You are one with the present moment.*

day
34
Do Not Hurry

There is a time for everything and a season for every activity under heaven

—BIBLE: ECCLESIASTES 3

Are you always in a hurry? I have a friend who ends every letter, "I must dash now." Sometimes I puzzle why she is always in a hurry. I hope I do not give the same impression to other people. You are more likely to offend other people and to make mistakes if you are always in a hurry. There is a saying that goes, "God gives you time for what you need to do." The Bible also says there is a time to rest and a time to enjoy life.

PRACTICE *Instead of hurrying and worrying about what you should do next, give your best energy to your present activity. If you have a lot of things to do, imagine telling them to "stand in line." Concentrate on each task, one at a time, and then move on to the next in line. If you multitask like so many of us today, you are likely to make a mistake and waste time—the time you supposedly saved—by correcting it. Carpenters have a saying, "Measure twice, cut once." If you concentrate on the task at hand, it can be surprising how quickly some things are dealt with and how calm you feel.*

Concentration Frees You from Worry

When I discover a form of prayer in which there is no distraction, I am no longer involved in the measurement of life, but in living it.

—FROM AN ANONYMOUS PRAYER, *1,000 WORLD PRAYERS*, ED. MARCUS BRAYBROOKE

Do you find yourself easily distracted? Any good sportsman or sportswoman must develop great powers of concentration. The champion tennis player learns to ignore shouts from the crowd, wrong line calls, and undue worry about the result. Michael Chang, who won the French Open championship at age 17 said, "As long as my priorities are straight, I'm able to go out with the mentality to leave the winning and losing up to God." (M. Chang and M. Yorke, *Holding Serve.*) Spiritual writers say that a similar detachment and focused concentration on what you are doing in the present moment reduces stress and encourages inner peace.

PRACTICE *Try this exercise to still the mind and help you to concentrate. Sit comfortably, relax the body, and breathe deeply. Then still the mind by repeating a sentence or looking steadily at a flower. As the mind wanders, gently bring it back to the focus of your attention. You may remember something you should have done or need to do. Make a mental note—some people even have a pad beside them to jot down stray thoughts—and then bring your mind back to the sentence or the flower.*

Concentrate on What You Are Doing

Make my heart open to you Lord and my task an easy one.

—BASED ON THE QUR'AN 20.25-26

"If you can't stand the heat," the saying goes, "get out of the kitchen." A busy kitchen is not the place you might expect to find peace, but that is where Brother Lawrence discovered it. After 18 years in the army, Brother Lawrence (1611–1691) entered a monastery in Paris and became the community's cook. After his death, a letter was found in his cell; it said, "The time of business does not with me differ from the time of prayer, and in the noise and clatter of my kitchen, while several persons are at the same time calling for different things, I possess God in as great tranquillity as if I were upon my knees at the blessed sacrament." His writings are collected in the book *The Practice of the Presence of God.*

PRACTICE *Concentrate on what you are doing and live in the present moment. It also helps to view every activity—even washing up—as a service to others and a gift to God. When you are tired of housework or the other routines of the day, repeat this verse, written by George Herbert (1593–1633), who abandoned life at court to become a country clergyman:*

Teach me, my God and King
In all things thee to see;
And what I do in anything
To do it as for thee.

Eating an Orange

What is the use of practicing meditation,
if it does not have anything to do with our daily lives?

—THICH NHAT HANH, A VIETNAMESE ZEN MASTER
AND PEACE ACTIVIST, *BEING PEACE*

How do you eat an orange? An American traveling in Vietnam with Thich Nhat Hanh ate a picnic lunch. Thich Nhat Hanh asked the American, "Shall I teach you how to eat an orange?" "But I've just eaten one," the American replied. "No," said the Zen master. "As soon as you peeled the orange, you put a segment into your mouth, and before you had swallowed it, you immediately grabbed the next segment. You were in such a hurry to eat the whole orange that you never noticed a single segment of it." (Donald Nicholl, *Holiness.*)

PRACTICE *One Zen practice, which encourages people to live in the present, is the walking exercise. The aim of the walking exercise is to be aware of the act of walking. As you walk, be conscious of the movement of your ankle, then of the feel of the ground as you put your foot down. Be aware of the sensations as you lift the foot and put it once more to the ground. As you concentrate on your walking, your mind becomes totally focused on the present moment. Zen monks spend many hours on such exercises, but you could also try it in daily life. If you walk mindfully to your next appointment, chances are you will arrive feeling more relaxed and peaceful.*

day 38

Waking Up

I slept and dreamt that life was joy,
I woke and saw that life was service
I acted and behold! Service was joy.

—RABINDRANATH TAGORE (1861–1941), INDIAN POET, *GITANJALI*

When the alarm goes do you turn over and wish it were not morning? Can you remember when you were a child, perhaps on your birthday, and morning could not come soon enough? Sir John Templeton, a well-known businessman and philanthropist now in his nineties, once told me that as soon as he woke up he said, "Thank you." A young man with severe rheumatoid arthritis told me the same. When he woke he was grateful for the gift of another day. When you recognize that life does not last forever, you realize how precious each new morning is.

PRACTICE *Do you wake up tired? It may be that you do not have a sense of purpose in your life. Your work seems "boring" and you have no "meaningful relationship." Rather than asking for sleeping pills, spend time examining your lifestyle. It may be lack of exercise, but it may also be that your life seems empty. Try to find Tagore's admirable quality of service in your work. Besides work, society offers many possibilities for voluntary service. Even the physically inactive can support charitable work by their prayers and interest. Service of others brings joy to each new day.*

Early Morning

O dawn, you shine forth with the eye of the Sun.
You wake the worshipper and inspire his heart.

—THE HINDU RIGVEDA, 1.113. 8,
FROM RAIMUNDO PANIKKAR, *THE VEDIC VISION*

Are you an early riser? The Brahma Kumaris World Spiritual University in Mount Abu, India, teaches meditation and spiritual values. Their day begins at 4 A.M. with meditation. In many traditions, the very early morning is considered a good time for quiet reflection. Your body and mind should be relaxed after a night's rest and your brain has not yet revved up for the day. In hot countries, the air is cool and fresh. Nature itself is often still. As the light rises, the birds sing their greetings to the dawn. At these times, you may sense the harmony of the Universe.

PRACTICE *It is not easy to find quiet in the busy modern world. Young children may call out early in the morning. You may have an invalid to care for. Or you may have a long commute to work. However, if it works for you—perhaps on vacation—the early morning is a good time for meditation. It may not be too much of a hardship to get up 15 minutes earlier. Find a place to sit where you look out at nature through the window and, if the weather allows, breathe in the morning air. You will take the stillness and sparkle of the dawn with you through your day.*

day 40 Count Out Your Plans for the Day

We should pray with the Bible in one hand
and our newspaper in the other.

—GEORGE MACLEOD (1895–1991), FOUNDER OF THE IONA COMMUNITY

People sometimes make a false distinction between the search for inner peace and the search for world peace. Those who were most active in twentieth century peace movements were people with a profound inner life. Perhaps only those who purify their vision see through the false images of the media and public relations industry to catch a glimpse of God's vision for the world. Thomas Merton (1915–1968), a Trappist monk whose writings were very influential, said, "It is the contemplative person who unmasks the illusion and the falsehood of the world and sees the world as God would have it be."

PRACTICE *Before you set out in the morning, you probably check that you have enough money with you. George MacLeod suggested that we should count out our plans for the day, like dollar bills, before we start, in the presence of God. Is what you are going to do useful to others, beneficial to yourself, and pleasing to God? You may see that some of your planned activities are a waste of time or self-indulgent. You may find this prayer a good way to start the day:*

This day, Lord, may I dream your dreams;
This day, Lord, may I reflect your love;
This day, Lord, may I do your work;
This day, Lord, may I taste your peace.

PRAYER BY ANGELA ASHWIN, *THE BOOK OF A THOUSAND PRAYERS*

Gandhi's Talisman

God has created me to do him some definite service. He has committed some work to me he has not committed to another.

—JOHN HENRY NEWMAN (1801–1890), CARDINAL

Setting out for a meeting, you may rush to be on time, but do you take time to pause and wonder what good the meeting will do? For many years by our front door, we have had a copy of Gandhi's (1869–1948) *Talisman*:

Recall the face of the poorest and weakest person you may have seen. Ask yourself if the step you contemplate is going to be any use to him. Will he gain anything by it?

PRACTICE *Stopping to check the purpose of what you are doing helps you to concentrate and calm down. It may not be obvious that your work does much for "the hungry and spiritually starving millions," which is Gandhi's challenge, but thinking about the needs of your clients or customers may make you more sympathetic and helpful and put your worries in perspective. If I have to conduct a funeral service but have a bad headache, it helps to know I have to concentrate on the needs of the mourners. Work, if it is to be satisfying, is not just about earning a living but about being of service to others. If you remember this, then as Gandhi has said, "You will find your doubts and yourself melting away."*

day
42 Keep Your Cool

They who believe and whose hearts are stayed in the recollection of God:
Is there not serenity of heart in the recollection of God.

—QUR'AN: 13.28

Do you find it hard not to "lose your cool" when you encounter difficulties at work or at home? Before the battle of Edgehill in the English Civil War, the royalist commander Sir Jacob Astley (1579–1652) prayed, "O Lord! Thou knowest how busy I must be this day: if I forget thee, do not thou forget me." (Sir Philip Warwick, *Memoires*.) In many traditions the faithful are encouraged to pause in the middle of the day to remember God's care. Muslims are expected to say prayers five times a day. You probably need spiritual refreshment just as much as you need physical nourishment. You may have no problem finding time for a coffee break, but it is just as important for your soul that you take a spiritual break.

PRACTICE *You may find the traffic light exercise helpful. At certain times of the day at the Brahma Kumaris World Spiritual University, soothing music is broadcast over the sound system. Everyone stops for a couple of minutes to renew their inner peace. The music is a spiritual traffic light—telling you to stop, to pause, and then to move forward. You could do this, instead of getting irritated, when you are waiting for someone who is late for an interview. Mothers with young children might encourage them to join her for an occasional pause, perhaps by listening to some calming music. Learning to pause is a good habit that can serve one throughout life.*

Evening

The day is no more, the shadow is upon the earth.
It is time that I go to the stream to fill my pitcher

—RABINDRANATH TAGORE (1861–1941), INDIAN POET, *GITANJALI*

Are you in touch with the natural rhythm of life? Driving along a country road in North India as dusk was falling, I noticed that one by one lamps were being lit in the simple homes along the road. In traditional societies, the coming of evening was a time for quiet and prayer. Even in cities that never sleep, it is a good time to pause and unwind. Evening is a time to be grateful for the day's achievements and to be sorry for what has gone wrong.

PRACTICE *Even driving home from work—if you keep your eyes open—you can let the body and the mind become quieter. You could play some meditation music, which will be more restful than listening to the news. If there is an argument your mind keeps replaying, resolve tomorrow to say that you are sorry, if necessary, and then let go of the disagreement, so that you feel at peace as the day draws to a close. Although it is true, as the saying goes, "not to put off to tomorrow what should be done today," there is no need to anticipate tomorrow's anxieties. As Jesus said, "Don't worry about tomorrow; it will have enough worries of its own." (Matthew 6.34.)*

day

44 Do Not Go to Bed Angry

Do not let the sun go down while you are still angry.

—BIBLE: EPHESIANS 4.26

If you are upset, especially after an argument, it can be difficult to go to sleep. Thomas Ken (1637–1711), a saintly Bishop of Bath and Wells, recognized that people sleep soundly only if their conscience is at peace. He wrote in a well-known evening hymn,

Forgive me, Lord, for thy dear Son,
The ill that I this day have done,
That with the world, myself, and thee,
I, ere I sleep, at peace may be.

It might seem dramatic to say it, but no one knows what is going to happen next. You might never forgive yourself if your last word to someone killed in a car crash was spoken in anger.

PRACTICE *You will not rest quietly while your conscience is troubled. After a quarrel, you will probably keep going over what was said, trying to justify your behavior. Instead, try seeing what happened from the other person's point of view. If possible, decide to make it up and to say that you are sorry at the first opportunity. If you still cannot sleep, instead of feeling sorry for yourself, radiate kind thoughts to others who are awake, because they are working or are in pain. You cannot be at peace with yourself if you are not at peace with other people.*

Lie Down in Peace

Drop thy still dews of quietness,
Till all our strivings cease;

—FROM A HYMN BY JOHN G. WHITTIER (1807–1882)

The mind, at times, is like a storm-tossed sea. You cannot relax or go to sleep until it is calm. One time Jesus and his disciples were in a boat on the Sea of Galilee. A great storm arose threatening to swamp the boat. Jesus continued to sleep peacefully, but the disciples were terrified and woke him up. At once, he told the waves, "Be still," and all was calm. If you trust in God's unfailing care, even when there are "rough seas," you know you will come safely to shore. Sleep can be a symbol of such a trusting relationship in God.

PRACTICE *There are times when you may feel too tired, anxious, or ill to say a prayer. It is enough to remember God's care and perhaps to repeat the words, "Underneath are the everlasting arms." You may also like to use this prayer of Amy Carmichael (1868–1951), who served as a medical missionary in South India. After a long, hot day caring for the sick, she was sometimes too tired to pray. She wrote,*

I am too tired to look for words,
I rest, O Lord, upon thy sympathy . . .
I know thou hearest me because
A quiet peace comes down to me,
Though waves are tossing outwardly.

—AMY CARMICHAEL, *LEARNING OF GOD,* EDS. S. AND B. BLANCH

Sleep

O sleep! O gentle sleep!
Nature's soft nurse.

—WILLIAM SHAKESPEARE (1564–1616), *HENRY IV*, PART 2, ACT 3, SCENE 7

One of my favorite prayers begins, "I don't like the man who doesn't sleep," says God. God goes on to say, "Sleep is perhaps the most beautiful thing I have created." The prayer was written by the French poet Charles Péguy (1873–1914). Péguy stressed the need for silence and trust. Picture a small child asleep, relaxed and trusting. Only when you are silent will you be ready to listen both to the deep desires of the heart and to the whisperings of the Eternal. Silence is not emptiness but a trust too deep for words. "Faith and love and hope are all in the waiting." (*God Speaks.*)

PRACTICE *There may be good reasons why you go to bed too late, but if you are overtired, you become irritable. Rest is important in spiritual practice. Otherwise, you become less sensitive to beauty and less spiritually aware. Are you overtired because you are trying to do too much? Does this cover up a hidden anxiety that you are not coping at work? Inner peace grows from a childlike trust that your life is surrounded by love. As Péguy wrote,*

He whose heart is pure, sleeps.
And he who sleeps has a pure heart.

Do Not Skip Your Quiet Time

Lord, I have time. . . . All the time that you give me.

—MICHAEL QUOIST, FRENCH PRIEST AND AUTHOR, *PRAYERS OF LIFE*

If you are late for work, do you skip breakfast? Then halfway through the morning do you wonder why you feel lethargic? Georges Vanier, when Governor General of Canada, always knew if he had missed his "half hour of reflection." Long before, he had picked up a book by an abbot in a Trappist monastery in Ireland that "changed his life." After his death, his son, Jean Vanier, found that his father had underlined these words: "There is no use arguing about it, give an hour to reflection and prayer no matter how busy you are. No one is too busy to eat, nor too busy to feed his soul." After his death, Cardinal Léger said of Georges Vanier, "God's presence was his habitual dwelling place."

PRACTICE *How often do you say, "I'm too busy?" It's really an excuse, not an explanation. Most people have some freedom to decide their priorities. If a time of quiet is really important, you will find time for it, just as if you are really hungry you will find time to eat. If you keep skipping your quiet time, ask yourself why. Was it an unrealistic decision? If it is always a mad rush in the morning to get to work or the kids to school, would it be better to find time in the evening or before you go to bed? Were you overambitious? A regular 15 minutes is better than an occasional 30 minutes.*

day 48 Buy a New Dress

Dance as though no one is watching you
Live as though heaven is on earth.

—FROM AN ANONYMOUS POEM, *1,000 WORLD PRAYERS*, ED. MARCUS BRAYBROOKE

Some people find it disturbing to be in the presence of a holy person. Have you ever felt their penetrating eyes look into your heart? A visitor to Ma Jaya Bhagavati's Kashi ashram was fixed by Ma's gaze. Ma, aware of the pain in the woman's chest, asked what she felt. "Nothing," was the reply. "You don't eat enough," Ma said. "You are always giving. As each person comes to you, you dip your cup into your pot of water but you never refill it. The pot will soon be empty. Take the pot and place it in the ocean and it will remain full. From time to time do something for yourself. Go out and buy a dress." (Toinette Lippe, *Shambhala Sun.*)

PRACTICE *Kashi ashram does an enormous amount for people in desperate need, but the ashram also has "Fun Days." If you forget to fill up the gas tank, the car will eventually grind to a halt. If you never stop working or looking after other people, you will dry up. Remember that in caring for people, you are a person to be cared for as well. Take time for yourself—time to be quiet or to go out for a walk in the country or a park. You may start to notice that the birds are singing or you may marvel at the majestic beauty of the trees. Nature abounds with renewable energy for the spirit. Take time, too, to relax and to enjoy your family and friends.*

Letting Go

If we let him, God can write straight with crooked lines.

—JOSEPH BERNARDIN (d. 1996), CARDINAL OF CHICAGO,

THE GIFT OF PEACE

"Prayer can't be done 'on the run,'" wrote Cardinal Bernardin, a few weeks before his death. Devoting the first hour of the day to God, the Cardinal struggled to let go, allowing God to take charge of events. Despite urging other priests to pray, he had fallen into the trap of "thinking that good works were more important than prayer." Looking back, he realized God was preparing him for his final trials. In November 1993, he was falsely accused of sexual misconduct. Less than two years later, he was operated on for pancreatic cancer. When, a year later, he announced the cancer had returned, he added, "I can say in all sincerity that I am at peace."

PRACTICE *It is not easy to let go, as the Cardinal discovered. You want to keep control of your life, whereas God wants you to let Him take charge. Start by emptying yourself both of the large plans for your life and the distracting little details. When you start the day's work, you know what you hope to achieve. Are you good at letting go and changing your plans? The Cardinal discovered that "God can write straight with crooked lines." In emptying himself, the Cardinal came to concentrate on the essentials of Jesus' message. Do you make what really matters to you a priority? Do you know what is most important? Do you need to let go of "the trivial pursuits" that take up so much time?*

day
50 Water

Water conquers by yielding; it never attacks but always wins the last battle.

—TAO CHENG OF NAN YEO, AN ELEVENTH-CENTURY TAOIST SCHOLAR

Have you wondered why water is a symbol in so many religions? The Sikh scriptures point to its humility, comparing the way it flows downhill to the deep humility of a person who serves rich and poor alike. Yet for all its gentleness, it has great strength. As a Taoist scholar said, "Water is yielding but all-conquering. Water extinguishes fire. . . . Water washes away soft earth or when confronted by rocks, seeks a way round or even wears them away. . . . Water gives way to obstacles with deceptive humility, for no power can prevent it following its destined course to the sea." It is a good symbol of the nonviolent strength to change the world of the person who has discovered inner peace.

PRACTICE *Let your mind recall pictures of mountain streams rushing past big boulders or great rivers slowly wending their way to the sea. Over time, water can move mountains. Then think about the softness and gentleness of water. Water cleanses and refreshes all people. How can you combine in your own life the humility and clarity of water with its strength and determination? Such are the qualities required of a servant of peace. Imagine yourself with others refreshed by the sea yet carried along by the wave. You are part of a great movement for renewal and peace.*

Change Is Possible

Unless we face the evils of the past, "Long since rusted knives stab us from behind, and revengeful dust rises up to haunt us."

—FROM "THE WHEEL," BY EDWIN MUIR (1887–1959), POET

Are you haunted by memories of some long past cruel or treacherous act? Bobby Bates, an Ulster loyalist paramilitary prisoner said that when he was locked in his cell, he was never alone. For 20 years he was shut up with the memory of the people he had murdered. One day the full horror of what he had done overcame him and he begged God for forgiveness. On his release, he visited many schools urging young people not to get involved with the gunmen but to work for peace. Sadly, Bobby Bates was himself shot dead in 1997.

PRACTICE *You do not have to go to prison to be locked up with your memories. Remembrance of past wrongdoings can suddenly recur to haunt you. The only escape is to face them honestly and recognize your bad behavior. Then ask God to forgive you. You may need to talk to an experienced counselor or spiritual guide to help you find your way. Then resolve to put the situation right or to make amends by helping other people. Your new way of life will gradually convince others that you really have changed, especially if you put up patiently with their distrust and prove that it is possible for people to change.*

day 52

Never Despise

We will not love body and life
But only care for the Supreme Way.

—FROM THE LOTUS SUTRA, QUOTATION FROM REV NIKKYO NIWANO, *A BUDDHIST APPROACH TO PEACE*

A young Buddhist monk used to greet his seniors with great respect, saying, "I revere you because you are to become Buddhas." Never Despise, as the monk was nicknamed, irritated some of the older monks, who chased him away with sticks. When the Buddha told the story he said, "I was really Never Despise." Rev. Nikkyo Niwano retold the story to emphasize a teaching of Rissho Kosei Kai, the lay-Buddhist movement which he founded, that every person can travel the road to Buddhahood by leading a moral life and serving the weak and suffering. It may seem an impossible dream, but it is a simple fact that the longest journey starts with a single step.

PRACTICE *Do you despair of becoming more peaceful? Have you been tempted to give up on this book and its practical suggestions? Maybe you begin the day with a time of quiet, but almost immediately become really angry because of something at work. Do not despair. Spiritual teachers say it is a long journey. Some in the East even think it will take many lives to become a* bodhisattva, *or pure soul dedicated to serving others. Never Despise was confident that eventually every soul would attain this high destiny. Even if that seems a long way off, as you become more peaceful, you radiate peace at home and at work and make the world a more peaceful place.*

Dream of Becoming a Better Person

Dream the Impossible . . . Then live so that the dream is fulfilled.

—MAIREAD MAGUIRE, IRISH NOBEL PEACE PRIZE WINNER,
THE VISION OF PEACE

Have the dreams and hopes of youth begun to fade? The Irish writer Eva Gore-Booth said, "We are not a being, but a becoming." We are meant to live "something we not yet are as that is the only way to become it." If you want to be more peaceful and in tune with nature, start living as if you were in tune with nature. Your intention will become the reality. If you dream of a more peaceful world, start behaving as if you had no enemies. Do not give in to the prevalent cynicism that things cannot change for the better.

PRACTICE *How many times a day do you climb the stairs or use an elevator? I like this modern prayer from Jerusalem which suggests that every time you climb up stairs, you could imagine that you are becoming a better person.*

By gradual steps I rise to the topmost attic of this house,
from which the views are spectacular.
I could rise to the palace of heaven if there were steps enough.
Let me take two or three steps to the palace of heaven each day.
Let me think of being a little better, a little kinder,
a little more grateful to you for your gifts,
each time I climb the stairs.

—FROM *THE BRIDGE OF STARS*, ED. MARCUS BRAYBROOKE

part two

PEACE IN OUR LIVES

As you become more at peace with yourself, you will find you can cope with changing situations with greater freedom and equilibrium. It is important to nourish your inner resources for peace as you face life's continuing demands. Work and family responsibilities, illness, loss, and the natural process of aging all will test your sense of inner peace. This chapter suggests how you can maintain your inner calm while responding to life's many challenges. If you are successful, your peace can enrich not only your life but also the lives of those around you.

Who Is in Control?

Look at the birds of the air; they do not sow and reap and store
In barns, yet your heavenly Father feeds them.

—BIBLE: MATTHEW 6.26

Do you like to be in control? Even politicians are much more at the mercy of events than they like to admit. President Abraham Lincoln said, "I claim not to have controlled events, but confess plainly that events have controlled me." The wise farmer knows that although he prepares the soil, sows the seed, and tends the plant while it grows—the harvest is not in his hands. It depends on forces beyond his control. People who work on the land often sense not only the rhythm of the seasons but also their dependence on a Loving Power at work in nature.

Read this prayer by a young African man and imagine what it is like to wonder each day whether there will be work and food.

Can't you make work for me in the harbor
Dear Lord,
So that I can buy food for my wife and children?

—FROM AN ANONYMOUS POEM, *1,000 WORLD PRAYERS*, ED. MARCUS BRAYBROOKE

PRACTICE *If you have a secure livelihood, that's a good reason to be grateful. But could you live with the young African man's uncertainty? All of us are dependent on the goodness of Life, which we cannot control. The next time you are challenged by adversity, ask yourself how much of it is in your power to change and how much is not.*

day 55

What Is the Use of Worrying?

Who sends his smile out to the dwellings of the suffering . . .
Yes, it is God himself who . . . redeems all from need.

—THE WHITE LOTUS ODE, ASCRIBED TO HUI YUAN (334–416), FROM *THE TEACHINGS OF THE COMPASSIONATE BUDDHA*

Do you worry too much? The Dalai Lama says he finds the teaching about suffering by the Indian scholar-saint Shantideva (eighth century CE) very helpful. You should not let suffering paralyze your faculties. Critically examine the cause of your suffering. If there is some means by which you can put it right, then there is no need for worry. Exert all your energy on tackling the problem. If there is no possible solution, then worry cannot change anything except to make it worse. (Dalai Lama, *Ancient Wisdom: Modern World.*)

PRACTICE *If you are anxious, it is good to take time to be quiet and to reflect. Try to be clear on what it is you are worrying about. Consider what you can do about the situation. Maybe your daughter is in the midst of a divorce. You can give her help and support. You may wish it had never happened, but there is no point worrying about the past. Our own suffering can awaken our empathy for others. Try to free yourself of negative thoughts toward people involved in causing the problems. No doubt, they too are suffering. Try to feel compassion for them and see if there is anything you can do to improve relations. If not, let go of the situation and look to the future.*

Go with the Flow

day 56

Water is the softest thing on earth, yet its silken gentleness will easily wear away the hardest stone. Everyone knows this; few use it in their daily lives. Those of Tao yield and overcome.

—FROM THE TAOIST SCRIPTURES, *THE WAY TO LIFE: AT THE HEART OF THE TAO-TE CHING*, TRANS. BY BENJAMIN HOFF

Taoists believe that there is an unnameable reality at the heart of all things. Known as Tao, it is the principle of harmony. It is like flowing water, which is a metaphor for human behavior. Water bypasses or gently wears away obstacles rather than fruitlessly attacking them. So when difficulties arise, the sage does not panic, but gently finds a way through the problem.

PRACTICE *How do you cope with opposition? If you're on the highway and you hear there's been an accident, do you complain about the stalled traffic? Or do you take the first exit and find another route home even if it means following winding country roads? If you are heading for a showdown at work or there is an argument in the family that you cannot resolve, stop and ask yourself how important the issue really is. Is there a way around it that would meet both your concerns and those with whom you are arguing? Would it not help to become more flexible—more like a river that may curve around the hills but always finds its way to the sea?*

day

57 Find Your Own Balance

The ten thousand things carry yin and embrace yang
They achieve harmony by combining these forces.

—LAO-TZU, CHINESE PHILOSOPHER (c. 604 BCE)

Have you ever felt the need to balance work and life? For centuries, Chinese teachers have recognized the need for balance in all things. They believed that the cosmos is the manifestation of a self-generating force called *Chi*, which has two aspects *yin* and *yang*. *Yin* is the dark, receptive, "female" aspect. *Yang* is the bright, assertive, "male" aspect. The creative rhythm of the universe is called *Tao,* or the "way." Wisdom lies in recognizing their ever-shifting but balanced patterns and moving in harmony with them.

PRACTICE *Try this exercise to reflect on your "work-life" balance. Draw three concentric circles. Name the inner circle "self," the middle circle "family," and the third circle "work." Consider each circle in turn. Do you feel at peace with yourself, your family, and your work? Are there problems in your personal relationships? Do you feel you neglect your family or do they feel that you neglect them? If your perceptions differ, can you see why this is so? Is your work fulfilling or is it dreary and exhausting? Do you have space for personal growth and renewal? Are there adjustments you need to make to restore a proper balance in your life?*

Dropping Out

O God of creations and transformations,
Who constantly begets new beginnings,
Inspire me by your personal creativity.

—Father Edward Hays, former director of a contemplative center, *Prayers for a Planetary Pilgrim*

Have you ever been tempted to chuck it all and move to a simpler life in the country? Dropping out, according to the press, is becoming increasingly popular. Because of long, demanding work hours and a tedious commute, many working parents see their children only on the weekends. A number of couples are giving up their jobs to run a small farm or craft center in the countryside. Although the desire for a simpler life closer to nature, with your own organically produced food, may be attractive, it is hard work. But a change of scene will not make you more at peace unless you are at peace with yourself.

PRACTICE *The decision to change your lifestyle, your job, or where you live may be helpful, but it is easy to transfer problems from the old situation to the new one, because they really lie within. Think carefully about your present work. If the work is unfulfilling, why do you think this is so? Is it because making money is no longer the most important goal in your life? Is it the competitive atmosphere and the pressure that you dislike, or is it the time spent commuting or the fact that you are often away from home? How will an external change alter the way you live and the pattern of your behavior?*

Follow Your Conscience

This above all: to thine own self be true;
And it must follow, as the night to the day,
Thou canst not then be false to any man.

—WILLIAM SHAKESPEARE (1564-1616), *HAMLET* ACT 1, SCENE III

Are you willing to follow the call of your conscience? How far would you go? Dietrich Bonhoeffer (1906–1945), a distinguished German theologian, had a good position at Union Theological College in New York, but he gave up his comfort and security to return to Germany to oppose Hitler. It was a decision that would cost him his life. The Jewish leader Leo Baeck (1873–1956) also refused to leave Germany and was arrested and survived 2 years at Theresienstadt concentration camp.

PRACTICE *As others have shown, once you hear the call of your conscience, only by following it will you be at peace with yourself. Sometimes, accepting danger or difficulty is the price of remaining true to your own ideals. Shakespeare, in* Henry VIII, *describes "a still and quiet conscience" as "a peace above all earthly dignities." (Act 3, Scene 2.)*

Choosing and Changing a Career

A little sleep, a little slumber, a little folding of the hands to rest,
and poverty will come upon you like a vagabond, and want like an armed man.

—BIBLE: PROVERBS 6.6-11

How often have you changed jobs? Social scientists predict that in modern society, career changes may occur as often as ten times in a lifetime. Circumstances may require you to learn new skills. Religions recognize the importance of work, not only as a way of supporting yourself and your family but also as an expression of human creativity and a contribution to the welfare of the community. The Sikh Guru Nanak did not encourage beggars, saying that, "He whose livelihood is earned through work and part given away in charity . . . truly knows the way of God." (Guru Nanak, *Adi Granth, Var Sang.*)

PRACTICE *Many people have little choice about their work and are glad to find any employment. However, because work takes up much energy and time, you will not be at peace with life if you cannot find satisfaction in your work. If you are experiencing difficulties and feel it is time for a change, you will need to carefully balance the advantages and disadvantages. Would a change mean uprooting the family? Would the new work be more fulfilling? If change is not possible, can you modify the situation or alter your attitude? If your colleagues are irritating, can you find ways of improving your relationships? A generous word or gesture can go a long way.*

day
61 # No Work Is Demeaning

He who says, "It is too hot, too cold, too late!"
Leaving the waiting work unfinished still,
Lets pass all opportunities for good.
But he who reckons heat and cold as straws
And like a man does all that's to be done,
He never falls away from happiness.

—BUDDHIST TEXT: DIGHA NIKAYA III. 185, SIGALOVADA SUTTA

If you cannot change your situation, you can alter your attitude to work. No work that is necessary for human welfare is demeaning. Gandhi insisted on cleaning his toilet himself to exemplify that belief. Regardless of its nature, if work is done with concentration, it can encourage mindfulness and happiness. (R.K. Prabhu and U.R. Rao, *The Mind of Mahatma Gandhi.*)

PRACTICE *Getting started on an unwelcome chore can often take as long as the task itself, as the Buddhist text suggests, but even the most routine task can become a form of meditation, if you give to it your total attention. Do you remember the Zen technique of Walking Meditation, when you were asked to concentrate on every step? Sweeping a room, washing the dishes, or doing any mundane task offers an opportunity for concentration. You will find that the more attentive you are to the task, the more satisfaction you will feel with your results.*

The Gospel of Work

My Father is always at his work to this very day,
And I, too am working.

—BIBLE: JOHN 5.17

Gandhi emphasized the importance of work, quoting from the *Bhagavad Gita* (3.23) where the Lord says, "If I did not remain ever at work, sleeplessly, I should set a wrong example to humankind." He even said that if he were to meet the Buddha, he would ask him why he did not teach the gospel of work instead of contemplation. He insisted that we should be ashamed of resting until everyone has enough to eat. Like Bernard Shaw, he thought everyone should be paid the same, whatever their job, because sanitation is as important as surgery. All work should be an offering to God and of service to other people.

PRACTICE *Do you see your work as an offering to God? People of faith often bring gifts of produce or money to a shrine. In many Christian churches, money collected from the worshippers is presented at the altar. When you offer your work and the whole of your life in thanksgiving to God, you give added meaning to any task that you undertake. By giving some of your money to charity, you also recognize that your work is not just for yourself and your family but is a contribution to a fairer and more peaceful world. If your work is of benefit to others, it is a fitting offering and will leave you with a sense of fulfillment and peace with yourself.*

day 63

Expose Yourself to the Suffering

The believer who participates in human life, exposing himself to its torments and suffering, is worth more than the one who distances himself from its suffering.

—A SAYING OF THE PROPHET MUHAMMAD, *HADITH OF IBN MAJAH*

Do you see your work as a service to others? Jesus, who set an example of service by washing the feet of his disciples and by touching those with the disease of leprosy, said to his followers, "The greatest among you will be the servant of all." (Luke 22.26.) Edith Brown, one of the first women science students at Cambridge in 1881, was such a follower. She dedicated her life untiringly to the service of the sick in India. The program she started for training Indian midwives eventually became the Ludhiana Christian Medical College, known internationally for the highest standards in medical care and training. (Cyril Davey, *50 Lives for God.*)

PRACTICE *A life of service has its own rewards. Not everyone is called to work among the poorest of the poor. Perhaps you could spare some of your "leisure" time to help at a local hospice. Take time to reflect on your pattern of life. In most communities there is a great need for volunteers. There may be lonely neighbors who need company or practical help. The effort of service is seldom wasted and, if done wholeheartedly, always enriches the one who serves.*

You Are Valuable for Yourself

The problem of unemployment compels us to re-examine the priorities in our society. What will convince humankind willingly and joyfully to sacrifice its impetuous need for consumption?

—PATRIARCH BARTHOLOMEW I, ECUMENICAL PATRIARCH OF CONSTANTINOPLE, *YES TO THE GLOBAL ETHIC*, ED. HANS KUNG

Unemployment is a severe test of your inner resources. Because human beings are naturally creative, being out of work is frustrating and undermines self-esteem. Submitting countless unsuccessful job applications saps self-confidence. To be unable to provide for your family diminishes you in your eyes and in theirs. Bartholomew I, a leader of the Orthodox Churches, has highlighted the tragedy of unemployment. Reflect on the words of Edward Hays:

I'm naked, so please don't look:
I've been stripped of my identity by the loss of my work.

—FROM EDWARD M. HAYS, *PRAYERS FOR A PLANETARY PILGRIM*

PRACTICE *If you have been unemployed, you will identify with this feeling. If you have not, it will help you to be more sympathetic. Remember that in God's eyes you are not important because of what you do or how much you earn. You are valuable for yourself. Being stripped naked may be the way for you discover this truth and learn to see through the false values of society.*

day
65 Coping with Failure

Of all plans of ensuring success, the most certain is Christ's own,
Becoming a corn of wheat, falling into the ground and dying.

—RAGLAND, A MISSIONARY TO SOUTH INDIA,
LEARNING OF GOD, EDS. S. AND B. BLAND

How do you cope if something in which you have invested much effort comes to nothing? Bob Dylan sang, "She knows there's no success like failure," long before public confession of failure became almost a television cult. The social psychologist Martin Skinner says, "When celebrities fail, they become real people." (*The Daily Telegraph*, July 29, 2003.) Failure can paralyze and bring despair or it can motivate people to learn from their mistakes. Stuart Blanch, a former Archbishop of York, said to me once that "all true ministry starts on the other side of failure." He meant that knowledge of your own weakness makes you more sympathetic with others.

PRACTICE *Do you blame other people for your failures? Are you honest enough to admit your own mistakes and learn from them? This may mean recognizing that you do not live up to your self-image. Fear of failure may be a sign of pride. It is said that, "The person who never makes a mistake, never makes anything." Failure can make you more humble and more sympathetic to others and more willing to accept help. Many who themselves have felt failures have been acclaimed by history.*

A New Chapter

Deprive me of my home,
Of children, wealth and land. . . .
If you, O Lord, I gain.

—Tukaram (c. 1607–1649), Hindu poet and saint

If your business went bankrupt, you might feel sorry for yourself. However, Tukaram, who was a Hindu poet, saw that his misfortunes had brought him closer to God. "It is well, O God, that I became bankrupt and was crushed by famine; this is how I repented and turned to thee. . . . It is well that my wife was a shrew, I sought your protection, O God." (Roger Lesser, *Saints and Sages of India.*) Tukaram's misfortunes prompted him to turn closer to God. No one wants misfortune, but if it comes, rather than wallow in self-pity, you can use it to find out more about your inner being.

PRACTICE *When things go wrong, do you get angry or depressed? After a divorce or business failure, you have to close a chapter of your life. It is too late to rewrite it, just as when the bell goes at the end of an examination, you have to hand in your test. Rather than looking back with regret, say to yourself, "This is the first day of the rest of my life." Start to make positive plans, but also ask yourself, "What do I really want out of life?" You may find your misfortunes have been a spur to help you discover your true self.*

day 67

Use Your Bad Experience

Everything can be taken from a person but one thing: the last of human freedoms—to choose one's attitude in any given set of circumstances, to choose one's own way.

—VIKTOR FRANKL, A CONCENTRATION CAMP SURVIVOR

Misfortune can also be used to help others, as Mary Verghese was to discover when an accident nearly destroyed all she had worked for. As a house surgeon at Vellore Christian Medical College, she worked with leprosy patients. One day, the car she was in hit a bridge. Mary's back was broken. Her career seemed at an end. Operations eventually enabled her to sit in a wheelchair, held upright by a metal support. Despite constant pain, she learned to operate again. Her example encouraged her patients to overcome their own disabilities. (Dorothy Clark Wilson, *Take My Hands*.)

PRACTICE *If you've had a disaster in your life, do you still look back with resentment or have you moved on? Self-pity is destructive because it ties you to the past. No one knows why misfortune hits some people. Tragedy challenges you to call on your inner resources to find ways of using the experience. Consider if there are ways that you could use your bad experience to help other people. This will also help you feel more at peace with life.*

A Friend in Need

I have been ill so long that I do not count the days . . . I meet a friend who is coming to see me . . . Tranquil talk was better than any medicine;
Gradually the feelings came back to my numbed heart.

—TRANSLATED FROM THE CHINESE BY ARTHUR WALEY

When you are suffering, it helps to talk to someone who has gone through the same thing. No one chooses pain, but suffering can give you a deeper understanding of your own and other people's humanity. It makes you vulnerable and perhaps willing to accept the grace and strength God offers. Learning to cope with deafness has made me more aware of other people's problems, and I wish I had shown more understanding of my father's deafness.

PRACTICE *The following words of Martin Buber (1878–1965), a Jewish philosopher, may help when you feel disheartened, "If we could hang all our sorrows on pegs and were allowed to choose those we liked best, everyone of us would take back his own, for all the rest would seem even more difficult to bear." Many people I have visited in the hospital have said that they had no idea what others had to go through until they faced their own suffering. It makes them less resentful of their own misfortune, more aware that they are not alone in their pain, more able to help others who suffer. Ponder these words of Pete Seeger: "By the broken, I will mend you. Tell me which one is which."*

day
69 Save Me from Fame

My heart is troubled when I hear my praise—save me from fame.

—TUKARAM (1607–1649), HINDU POET AND SAINT

How well do you handle praise? Success has its own temptations. Unless you are careful, you become pleased with yourself and look down on others who are less successful. Holy people are not free from this temptation. Tukaram, a Hindu poet, gained a reputation for holiness. He admitted, "Because the saints have praised me, I feel an internal arrogance—that I alone am a wise man." He countered this temptation by recognizing he was a sinner in God's eyes and dependent on divine mercy.

PRACTICE *It is gratifying to know people think you have done a good job, but it is dangerous if it makes you too proud or reluctant to listen to other people. If you are honest with yourself, you will know how far you still have to go to be free from the pride that steals your inner peace. Tukaram said, "For a real saint, no enemy can exist. . . . For me there are neither friends nor foes; for wherever I look I see the vision of God."*

Forget about Success

Learning to be still and peaceful is our daily work, a lifetime's work.

—MAIREAD MAGUIRE, IRISH NOBEL PEACE PRIZE WINNER,
THE VISION OF PEACE

At work, do you have to meet targets set by your managers? The monk and peace activist Thomas Merton warned peace workers not to make the mistake of becoming "success orientated." Worrying about results can distract you from the truth of the work itself. "The big results," Merton said, "are not in your hands or mine." (William Merton, *The Hidden Ground of Love.*) In the end, Merton said, personal relationships matter most. If you can learn to be at peace with those closest to you, then you can help to create a climate of peace. As Mairead Maguire has written, "The real struggle starts in my own heart."

PRACTICE *Take time to be quiet, and learn to be still. Do not forget to relax the body and to listen to your breathing. Then spend a few minutes reflecting on your lifestyle. Do you rush from one activity to another or do you have a calming influence on other people? Do you work so that others will admire your efforts? If you want people to praise you and are upset by criticism, you are still "success orientated." Spiritual guides teach us to act with detachment by concentrating on the importance and worth of what you do, not on what people think of you.*

day
71 A Concentration Camp of the Mind

Every one who does evil hates the light, and will not come into the light, for fear his deeds will be exposed.

—BIBLE: JOHN 3.20

If you have been robbed or attacked, you probably think of yourself as the victim, but perhaps it is the criminal who is the real victim of evil. During the cruel fighting in former Yugoslavia, of the 45,000 Bosnian Muslims who lived in Banja Luka, all but 3,000 were killed or expelled. More than 200 mosques were destroyed. The leading Muslim, Mufti Halilovic, personally witnessed the suffering and destruction. He said, "We are not the greatest victims of this evil, the Serbs are. They are living in a concentration camp of the mind, and they do not even know it." (P. Belz and D. Reeves, *A Tender Bridge*.)

PRACTICE *If you have been victimized, you are likely to feel sorry for yourself. Self-pity easily turns to hatred of your attacker and may lead to further violence. When you feel the urge toward self-pity, spend some time in silence and examine your reactions. Think about the people who hurt you. What drove them to it? Are they not controlled by their own anger and hatred? If so, it is they who are in a prison of the mind.*

The Test of Faith

The true test of faith is the hour of misery.

—GURU ARJAN (1563–1606), FIFTH GURU AND FIRST SIKH MARTYR

Do you hope your beliefs will not be put to the test—at least not by imprisonment or physical violence? History has many examples of those jailed for their faith or their work for peace. The Sikh Guru Arjan Dev, although on good terms with the Emperor Akbar, was tortured by his successor. Arjan Dev told his followers that he endured this to set a good example. Otherwise, people of weaker faith would not stand up to oppression. "The body," he said, "is perishable, the soul is imperishable." As he walked to his death, he repeated the verse, "Your will is sweet, O God."(Roger Lesser, *Saints and Sages of India*.)

PRACTICE *What would you be prepared to die for? You would probably risk your life to protect members of your family. Would you stand up against aggressors to protect innocent victims whom you did not know personally? No one knows for certain how he or she would react at such a moment, but the question focuses the mind on what is really important. Would you risk your life to prevent injustice or the suffering of others?*

day 73

It Is Best to Speak the Truth

Simply let your "Yes" be "Yes" and your "No" be "No."

—BIBLE: MATTHEW 6.37

How important is the truth to you? Franz Jagerstatter was an Austrian farmer who was conscripted into Hitler's army in February 1943. He refused to take the military oath of obedience and was beheaded in 1943. With his hands in chains, he wrote a last letter to his wife. "If I know in advance that I cannot accept and obey everything I would promise under that oath, then I would be guilty of a lie. I am convinced it is best to speak the truth, even if it costs me my life."

PRACTICE *I am sure you hope you are never put in this position, but say you know something illegal is going on at work and you are asked to take part in a cover-up. Do you have the courage to speak the truth? Consider whether other people would regard you as honest and a person of integrity. Are you truthful to your children? If you make a promise to your children, do you keep to it? True peace requires great honesty, because deceit destroys trust, which is essential for good human relationships.*

It Is Hard to Hate Little Children

Lord, teach us to forgive and to look deep into the hearts of those who wound us, so that we glimpse in that dark water not just the reflection of our own face but yours as well.

—SHEILA CASSIDY, A DOCTOR WHO WAS IMPRISONED AND TORTURED IN CHILE

Leonard Wilson was a prisoner of war under the Japanese. "Why don't you curse us?" one of his torturers asked him. "I am a follower of Jesus Christ, who taught that we are all brothers," he answered. Although he admits he hesitated to use Jesus' words on the cross, "Father forgive them," he found a way to see beyond the cruelty of his captors. "By the grace of God, I saw them as they once were before they were conditioned by false nationalist ideals—little children with brothers and sisters happy in their parent's love. It is hard to hate little children." (John Bowker, *Problems of Suffering in Religions of the World.*)

PRACTICE *Those who sell children to be sex slaves or who recruit youngsters to join cruel militias seem so vile that it is hard to recognize any common humanity. It is important to try to see the person, whose actions we deplore, as also a child of God. It is easy to pray for the victims, who need all the prayers and help they can get. Can you bring yourself to pray for the perpetrators? An unknown prisoner in Ravensbrück concentration camp left this prayer beside the body of a dead child. "O Lord… when the people of ill will come to judgment, let our fruits of courage and generosity that have come from our suffering be their forgiveness." (From* Oxford Book of Prayer.*)*

day
75

Falsely Accused

The truth shall set you free.

—BIBLE: JOHN 8.32

How do you react when people tell lies about you? In November 1993, Joseph Cardinal Bernardin of Chicago was devastated to be accused falsely of sexually abusing a young man. Although he knew he was innocent, he wondered "if the voice of truth could be heard in a culture of image making and distortion." In silent reflection, he heard the words of Jesus: "The truth will set you free." At the press conference, Bernardin said simply, "I have always led a chaste and celibate life." Months later the case against the Cardinal collapsed. Bernardin went to see his accuser, who was dying of AIDS. In prayer together they were reconciled and found peace. (Joseph Cardinal Bernardin, *The Gift of Peace.*)

PRACTICE *When someone falsely accuses you of saying or doing something wrong, you are likely to feel shattered. Reacting with anger only makes things worse. Try to find time to be quiet. Recall the words of Jesus: "The truth shall set you free." It can be difficult amid claim and counterclaim to hold on to these words. If your conscience is clear, you have nothing to fear.*

God's Child

May thy holy presence remove all dangers from my soul and body.
May thy many graces fill the inmost recesses of my heart
And inflame it with thy divine love.

—HENRY SUSO (c. 1295–1366)

Does your blood boil when you feel you've been falsely accused? The mystic Henry Suso, of noble birth, became a Dominican at age 13 and soon became famous for his sanctity. But a scheming woman placed her baby on the doorstep of his home, saying he was the father. Suso did not protest, but looked after "God's child." Even his friends ridiculed his claims to holiness. Only when she was dying did the mother confess that she had lied. (Donald Nicholl, *Holiness*.)

PRACTICE *By cultivating a peaceful approach to life, you become less irritable and better able to cope with life's annoyances. When overcharged in a shop or restaurant, you can politely say, "I think there has been some mistake." Give people a chance to apologize and rectify the matter before launching a rant at them. You could ask yourself, "Would I want to be doing their job all day? Why was I so angry? Are these people deliberately out to wrong me? Even if that were true, does my anger help me see and deal with the situation any more clearly?" As a sense of peace fills the inmost recesses of your heart, you will better cope with little and great injustices.*

Is That So?

(Holiness is) a condition of complete simplicity
Costing not less than everything.

—T. S. ELIOT (1888–1965), POET, *LITTLE GIDDING*

Are you tempted to want to be thought of as a spiritual person but not make the sacrifices that true holiness requires? The Zen master, painter and poet Hakuin (c. 1685–1768) experienced profound enlightenment, but in his eyes his "arrogance swelled like a tidal wave." (From *Orate-gama 3*.) Later his humility was put to the test. A wealthy young woman announced that Hakuin was the father of her child. A crowd soon surrounded the hermit's hut mocking and denouncing him. Hakuin simply said, "Is that so?" When the child was born, Hakuin looked after it. Some 18 months later, the woman confessed that in fact the father was a local fisherman. The villagers returned to the hermit to apologize. All Hakuin said was, "Is that so?" (Donald Nicholl, *Holiness*.)

PRACTICE *If you are a peace activist, you may find yourself the subject of false accusation from your opponents. You may even be accused of being in the pay of "the enemy." The tendency today is to take libel action, but this can make your reputation more important than the cause to which you are committed. Even at work you may be blamed for something that has gone wrong. You know it was not your fault, but is it your job to point the finger to get someone else into trouble? An ancient prayer asks that when we "are called to suffer reproach" we may be "valiant to abide still in God's commandments." (*The Primer, *1559.)*

God's Strength

The weakness of human means is a source of strength.

—Charles de Foucauld, from Jan Vanier, *In Weakness, Strength*

How well do you deal with physical affliction? No one would choose to have a chronic or life-threatening illness, but such affliction may make you more aware of your dependence on divine grace. When Georges P. Vanier, who was well aware of his physical weakness, became Governor General of Canada, his first words were a prayer, "In exchange for God's strength, I offer my weakness." In a private letter, he wrote that on many public occasions he had to put on a front to appear strong and sure of himself. Inside he felt overwhelmed with weakness and was dependent on God's grace. This taught him humility, which he said combines awareness of personal weakness with boundless confidence in God's strength.

PRACTICE *When I was diagnosed with a heart condition, a rabbi said to me, "Don't become an angina cripple." Everyone has to cope with illness in their own way, but to be overprotective of one's health may limit one's activities. When physical weakness has made me reluctant to carry out my responsibilities, I have prayed, "God give me the strength for what you want me to do." Illness can make you more dependent on divine strength and more grateful for the support of other people. If you suffer from illness, ask yourself whether you resent it and are feeling sorry for yourself. Try to accept your affliction and offer it up. You may discover hidden blessings.*

day 79

God Gives Strength to Bear Pain

I asked for power, that I might have the praise of men,
I was given weakness, that I might feel the need of God.

—FROM A PRAYER BY AN UNKNOWN SOLDIER, *THE LOTUS PRAYER BOOK*

How do you react to suffering? No one can be confident how they would react under torture, but the example of those who have not become embittered by it may be an encouragement for you in times of pain and difficulty. In a remarkable radio talk, Leonard Wilson, Bishop of Singapore, shared some of his spiritual experiences as a Japanese prisoner of war. He suffered cruel and repeated torture. "After the first beating," he said, "I was almost afraid to pray for courage unless I should get another opportunity for exercising it!" During one session, he was asked whether he still believed in God. "I do," he replied. "God does not save me from pain, but gives me the Spirit to bear it."

PRACTICE *When I conduct a healing service, I usually say that I am confident that God will answer prayer, but not always in the way people expect. Instead of physical healing, God may give the grace to bear pain without resentment. Look back at your own times of disappointment or difficulty. Has it turned out better for you that you did not get the job on which your heart was set? Did you learn anything from illness? Did you become more sympathetic to others who are unwell? An American Confederate soldier said, "I got nothing I asked God for—but everything I had hoped for." Is that true to your experience?*

I Cried Out and I Was Answered

Death is not our enemy. Just like our thoughts are not to be seen as enemies . . . and life is not an enemy. Life is something glorious, because in life we can awaken to who we truly are.

—RICK, AN AIDS PATIENT

Does meditation really help when you are ill? When Rick was diagnosed with AIDS and he thought he was dying, he said, "I cried out and I was answered." He had taken up Tibetan Buddhist meditation and found that it worked. First he realized he had to take personal responsibility. "There was no one else to blame—not that I blame myself." Then, he made a decision to be happy. "You must make a decision. . . . If you don't want to change, no one is going to do the work for you." He became grateful for life. As life was slipping away, Rick said, "I become so much more grateful for everyone and everything."

PRACTICE *Are you sometimes glad when your time of meditation is over? Rick warns that spiritual practice is not just the sitting. "When you stand up from your practice seat, that's when practice really begins." For example, when you see the sun, think of the radiance of Divine Light. When you are in pain, you can call out for the help of the Enlightened Being. Do not be swallowed up by fear. Fear, Rick says, is "just something passing through my mind." In meditation, you can keep the mind still and let go the thought of fear. Rick's final message was not to wait until you are ill before you take up meditation. Start now and keep up with the practice. You will build up a reservoir to refresh you in days of darkness. (Sogyal Rinpoche,* The Tibetan Book of Living and Dying.*)*

day 81

I Felt Your Suffering Presence

I have been ashamed of the scars I bear. . . . In the sunlight of your presence I was able to uncurl. For the first time I felt your suffering presence with me in that event.

—FROM AN ANONYMOUS POEM, *1,000 WORLD PRAYERS,* ED. MARCUS BRAYBROOKE

Healing for those abused in childhood, if it occurs at all, is a long process. The horrific experiences are often deeply buried and a person needs expert help to get in touch with their memories. Abuse often induces self-hatred because the abused child blames himself or herself rather than the parent. Trust in other people and in the "Father God" of many religions is destroyed, and a sense of abandonment becomes pervasive. Healing at best may be partial. "Life gets better," writes Rabbi David Blumenthal, "it never reaches the garden of Eden. Control, not absence of pain, is the goal." (David Blumenthal, *Facing the Abusing God.*)

PRACTICE *As you go more deeply into meditation, you may unlock painful memories that you had buried in your subconscious. If they are too painful for you to handle, you should get help from a therapist or spiritual guide. The healing of the memories, which is part of the inner purification that leads to deep inner peace, requires honestly facing past experiences. Try not to blame yourself. Try to accept yourself as you are, because your scars have made you.*

Moving to the Other Side of Horror

Though the heavens boom with thunder, though the sphere of my universe cracks into pieces, though fire devours the three worlds, yet will I wait on you, O Lord.

—EKNATH (1548–1600), HINDU POET AND SAINT

Some experiences are so shattering that you despair of ever recovering. One girl who was raped at age 16 struggled to leave it behind her. "As I began therapy," she wrote, "I learned that you also can't make sense of it, or resolve it, or forgive it, and you definitely can't 'make the best of it.'" "Healing," she says, "means looking deep into the evil, right in its face, and then moving through it to the other side." Gradually, as you face the horrific memory, you recognize that you have survived and that, although a lost innocence cannot be recovered, life is a blessing. (David Blumenthal, *Facing the Abusing God*.)

PRACTICE *It may be therapeutic to write down your painful memories. As you confront them, they begin to lose their power. The scars remain and bind you to the fellowship of suffering humanity. Life continues, and there is a place in it for you. The girl who was raped was, by age 21, able to write:*

And yet, the deep dark green of the trees
And yet, the running mountain water
And yet, the bliss of trusting again, of running through sprinklers
On a summer day, laughing and kissing and feeling complete.
A tear.
A promise.
Yes, Lord, I will still participate in
the PROCESS.

Illness—A Blessed Experience

Lord, Your strength and courage are in my spirit. . . . In my illness I have learnt what is great and what is small. I know how dependent I am upon you. My own pain and anxiety have been my teachers.

—A JEWISH PRAYER, *FORMS OF PRAYER FOR JEWISH WORSHIP*

Can you recall a time of illness? What did you learn from it? No one chooses to suffer, but many people have grown in character through it and demonstrated the indomitable strength of the human spirit. "Finally came illness—a truly blessed experience," wrote Kathleen de Beaumont in her privately published memoires. (Marcus Braybrooke, *A Wider Vision.*) Kathleen de Beaumont had been active for years in the Girl Guides in England before becoming housebound because of arthritis. Illness gave her time to entertain her many friends and to develop her interest in spirituality. Another friend, Thelma Bailey, suffered from a severe muscle-wasting illness. She used her time to pray for Mother Teresa's work, to write poems, and to raise money for charity. She even learned to use a computer so she could edit a magazine for prisoners.

PRACTICE *Suffering comes in many shapes and sizes, and only you can learn how to respond to your own trials. The stories of other people can encourage you not to dwell self-pityingly in the past, disappointed about what you can no longer do. Instead consider new possibilities. Can you do volunteer work? If you have always been too busy, you could use the extra time you have to read or to develop your inner life. Thelma Bailey wrote:*

Fill me, Lord, with your healing power.
My hands, my feet, my mind, my all
I give to you this day.
Prepare me for Thy service, Lord
That when you call, I say, "I will."

—FROM THELMA BAILEY, *MISCELLANY OF POEMS AND REFLECTIONS*

Challenged by Disability

Happiness does not mean a pair of legs, or eyes, or ears, but the will to take part and share with others, respecting them as human beings and being respected as such.

—CELIA LEAE

If you have a disability, ask yourself whether you give in to self-pity or whether you use life's opportunities to the fullest. Celia Leae of Brazil, in *A Letter to the World*, wrote, "It's important to look at disability, not as the best that ever happened to you, but not the worst either. It has been 18 years since I had my car accident. The wheelchair didn't prevent me from studying and becoming a lawyer, to work for disabled people. My social work with the poor took me to represent my state with a population of 36 million people in the National Congress. At 37, I am the proud mother of Diego and Rodrigo." (J. Potter and M. Braybrooke, *All in Good Faith*.)

PRACTICE *Not everyone has the courage of Celia Leae. But nearly everyone is challenged at some point in his or her life by physical illness or disability. If you are spared such disadvantages for now, are you developing the resources that will help you meet the challenges when they arrive? Are you willing to accept the inner strength that is available through prayer and meditation?*

day
85 God as a Mother of Comfort

So we struggle on
Myself and I
I take it on the chin
And I just cry.

—NORA LENEY, WHO NURSED HER SICK DAUGHTER,
CICELY SAUNDERS, *BEYOND THE HORIZON*

Do you pray expecting God to take away your pain and suffering? Although God sometimes grants miraculous healing, the German theologian Dorothee Sölle pictures God as more like a mother taking an injured child on her knee to comfort him. She cannot make the pain disappear, but her love sustains the child during his suffering. "I see the sun in the rain," she wrote, "How can we see darkness and light together if not in God who comprises both." (Dorothee Sölle, *Remembering for the Future*.)

PRACTICE *Has your experience of suffering affected your view of God? Some people abandon belief in God when they are not granted the healing for which they prayed. "How could God let me suffer?" they ask. We cannot explain natural disasters, but much suffering is caused by human actions, even if they are not our own. If there is real freedom in the world, then God will not save human beings from the consequences of their actions. Life loses its meaning if it is the playback of a prerecorded video. Your prayers may not make your suffering vanish, but you have the choice how you will face your hardship. Many people have experienced God's sustaining power in their suffering. Job, a righteous man who endured horrific suffering, although urged by his wife to curse God, said, "Though God slay me, yet will I trust him." (Job 13.15.)*

Do I Suffer for Your Sake?

Show me what this, which is happening to me at this very moment, means to me, what it demands of me, what You, Lord of the world, are telling me by way of it. It is not why I suffer that I wish to know, but only whether I suffer for your sake.

—LEVI YITCHAK OF BERDITCHEV, CICELY SAUNDERS, *BEYOND THE HORIZON*

The Holocaust, or *Shoah*—in which 11 million people were murdered, more than 6 million of whom were Jews—was an unspeakable crime and a challenge to all believers in God. My friend Rabbi Hugo Gryn was taken to Auschwitz when he was 15. On Yom Kippur, the Day of Atonement, in 1944, he spent the whole day fervently praying. Eventually, he dissolved into tears, but then was granted an amazing inner peace. "I believe God was also crying. And I understood a bit of the revelation that is implicit in Auschwitz. It is about man and his idols. God, the God of Abraham, could not abandon me, only I could abandon God." (Rabbi Hugo Gryn, *Chasing Shadows*.)

PRACTICE *It is impossible for those who were not there to imagine the horrors of Auschwitz, so reflect on the most painful experiences of your life. Did you blame God, yourself, or other people? Where did you find strength in your darkest moment? Looking back, did the experience weaken or strengthen your belief in the ultimate goodness of Life?*

day
87

Always White Ice Cream

I have a dream that one day on the red hills of Georgia the sons of former slaves and the sons of former slave owners will be able to sit down together at the table of brotherhood.

—MARTIN LUTHER KING (1929–1968), BAPTIST MINISTER AND CIVIL RIGHTS LEADER, FROM CORETTA SCOTT KING, *MY LIFE WITH MARTIN LUTHER KING*

Have you ever been the victim of discrimination? Many people have been treated as inferior because of the color of their skin, their nationality, or their religion. Discrimination humiliates and pervades everyday life. Coretta Scott King said she used to smile when white people talked nostalgically about the quaint old corner drugstore. "I remember," she wrote, "when I was a very little girl having to go to the side door of the white-owned drugstore to buy ice cream. I had to wait until all the white children were served and then, no matter what flavor I asked for, the man would give me white ice cream. Of course, I paid the same as the white kids."

PRACTICE *Constant humiliation undermines your human dignity and saps the human spirit. If you have experienced discrimination, reflect on your reactions. If not, try to imagine what it feels like to be treated as second class. Many react with anger, and it is right to challenge unjust laws; however, the aim of nonviolence is never to oppress the oppressor. It seeks justice for all. After Martin Luther King's assassination, his daughter asked, "Mommy, should I hate the man who killed my Daddy?" Her mother replied, "No, darling, your Daddy wouldn't want you to do that." It requires deep inner peace to follow the way of nonviolent action, which avoids both cowardly indifference to injustice and destructive anger.*

Religion Does Not Discriminate

It's really wonderful that I haven't dropped all my ideals, because they seem so impossible. Yet I still believe that people are really good at heart. If I look up into the heavens, I think . . . that peace and tranquillity will return again.

—ANNE FRANK, *THE DIARY OF ANNE FRANK*

Millions of Jews—including more than a million children—died in the Nazi death camps. Although the Nazis were anti-Christian, long centuries of Christian anti-Semitism was in part responsible. Pope John XXIII apologized for this when he visited Jerusalem, and said, "Religion is the enemy of discrimination and hatred." (*The Times*, March 27, 2000.)

PRACTICE *Tragically, the legacy of racial and religious hatred is handed down from generation to generation. If you are to help create a more peaceful world, you need to examine your conscience. Have you inherited the prejudices of your parents? Have you passed them on to your children? Is it time to apoligize and seek a new relationship with those you have despised? A new beginning is always possible. Some children whose parents were killed in the concentration camps have been willing to meet with children whose parents were Nazi SS officers. Children are not responsible for the behavior of their parents, but too often they perpetuate past prejudices. You can never hope to achieve peace when your heart remains the prisoner of prejudice.*

day 89

Do Not Judge Others

Why do you look at the speck in your brother's eye and pay no attention to the log in your own eye?

—BIBLE: MATTHEW 7.3

Do you find difference threatening? When visiting a gentle young Irish woman who was terminally ill, I asked if she would like communion. She said that in the hospital a priest had refused her this, because she was living in a lesbian relationship. I recalled that Annie Besant, who had left the church for the Theosophical Society, asked Arthur Stanley, Dean of Westminster Abbey (from 1863–1881), to give her dying mother communion. Two priests had refused because of Annie's views, but Stanley said, "It was folly to quarrel about words when dealing with the Divine mystery. . . . Communion was never meant to divide hearts that are searching after the one true God." (Hal French, *A Study of Religious Fanaticism and Responses to It.*)

PRACTICE *The behavior and beliefs of those who are different can make you question your own attitude. Each person is different. If you cannot accept this, it may be a sign of insecurity and that you do not really accept your own special identity. Spend time giving thanks for your own special gifts and good qualities. Even your faults may be the other side of your good qualities. If you get things done quickly, you may be impatient with those who are slower. Instead of criticizing the faults of others, concentrate on dealing with your own faults and improving your qualities so that your heart becomes more peaceful.*

Grow Old Gracefully

Before the gray descends on your cheek,
the wrinkles plough your chin
and the body becomes a cage of bones
Adore the Lord.

—BASAVANNA (C. 1106–1167), HINDU RELIGIOUS REFORMER

As you grow older, do you sometimes feel that life is passing you by? Your friends have died or are too infirm to visit you. You cannot keep up with new technology. Contemporary music seems too loud, and no one seems to be interested in what you think. Modern society is very different from traditional societies, where the old were regarded as a fount of wisdom. True wisdom is learning to let go, so perhaps modern society makes that easier. Hinduism traditionally encouraged couples who saw wrinkles in the skin and grayness in the hair to retire together to the forest, where they were free to explore spiritual pursuits before the final stage of renunciation.

PRACTICE *If you are young, imagine what it feels like to be old. It may make you more sympathetic. If you are old, it is time to come to terms with yourself, to put away past regrets, to heal broken relationships, and to prepare yourself for the next great journey. Be available to those who seek your help and advice, but do not keep telling people how to behave. Perhaps this prayer of a seventeenth century nun will be helpful:*

Release me from craving to straighten out everybody's affairs.
Make me thoughtful but not moody: helpful but not bossy.
Teach me the glorious lesson that occasionally I may be mistaken.
Give me the ability to see good things in unexpected places, and talents in unexpected people. And give me, Lord, the grace to tell them so. Amen.

day
91 God Is Forgiveness Itself

One of the criminals on the cross next to Jesus, said, "Jesus, remember me when you come to your kingdom." Jesus said, "In truth, today you will be with me in paradise."

—BIBLE: LUKE 23.42–43

A medical student, on her first day working at a large hospital went over to a lonely old man, who was staring at the wall. "Do you think God will forgive me for my sins?" he asked. She had no answer. Her medical training did not deal with spiritual questions. The Buddhist monk Soygal Rinpoche says he would have reassured the old man by saying, "God has already forgiven you, for God is forgiveness itself. The real question is, can you forgive yourself? Your feeling of being unforgiven and unforgivable is what makes you suffer." (Sogyal Rinpoche, *The Tibetan Book of Living and Dying*.)

As death approaches, you may worry what lies ahead. The poet John Donne (1572–1631), accepting God's forgiveness of his past sins, admitted:

I have a sin of fear, that when I've spun
My last thread, I shall perish on the shore.
But swear by thyself, that at my death thy Son
Shall shine, as he shines now and heretofore:
And having done that, thou hast done: I fear no more.

PRACTICE *Often, the real worry is not about what God thinks but your own fear and disgust at your past action. You have not forgiven yourself. If you overcome your pride and like the criminal on the cross ask for help, you will discover that God is merciful.*

Forgive with All Your Heart

Who takes vengeance or bears a grudge acts like one who, having cut one hand while handling a knife, avenges himself by stabbing the other hand.

—JERUSALEM TALMUD, NEDARIM 9.4

Do you experience a desire for revenge when someone dear to you has been injured? Parents are naturally protective of their offspring. Ghassibe Kayrouth, a young Maronite Christian theological student on his way home to his Lebanese village to spend Christmas in 1975, was well aware of the dangers. In his Arabic bible, he had written a note to his family urging them not to be sad if he died. "I have only one thing to ask of you: Forgive those who killed me with all your heart . . . and to my country I say, 'People who live in the same house can hold different opinions without hating each other. They can quarrel without killing each other.'" (Emmanuelle Cinquin, *Sister with the Ragpickers*.)

PRACTICE *How do you react when a loved one, especially one of your children, has been wronged? Though it is easy to feel the initial desire for revenge, what will retaliation achieve? Remember that forgiveness has to be total. As Gerald Jampolsky said, forgiveness "is like getting pregnant. Either you are pregnant or you're not. 'Sort of forgiving' doesn't work. It has to be total and complete." (Gerald Jampolsky,* Forgiveness, the Greatest Healer of All.*)*

Finding Peace After a Loss

There are people who suffer terrible distress and are unable to tell what they feel in their hearts, and they go their way and suffer and suffer. But if they meet one with a laughing face, he can revive them with his joy. To revive a person is no slight thing.

—NACHMAN OF BRATZLAV (1772–1811), HASIDIC RABBI AND ASCETIC, *FORMS OF PRAYER FOR JEWISH WORSHIP*

"How can I be angry at a dead friend?" asked a 15-year-old after a classmate had taken his own life. Any death creates a mixture of emotions and a suicide is especially likely to create guilt and anger. A family may feel ashamed, as if the death was their fault. These are natural reactions, best shared with friends or a counselor. Talking about the one who has died helps. Remember the enrichment he or she brought to others. All religions deplore suicide but teach that the real self lives on, regardless of what happens to the body. They also offer reassurance to friends and family. Anyone in despair also needs to talk to other people and to seek help. (Gerard Green, *Coping with Suicide*.)

PRACTICE *Some people have found it helpful to write a letter to the one who took his own life. See if this letter expresses some of your feelings. "As you read this letter, we want you to know that we miss you very much. Maybe you thought you were doing us a favor by taking your life. What hurts is that you never said 'goodbye.' We have cried as we have tried to understand your despair and misery. At times we've been angry and felt responsible. Somehow we failed you. We really miss you. We still cry for you, but we try to remember the good times. We pray that you are now at peace. One day, we shall be with you again." Expressing feelings of grief and dealing with the anger that can arise from loss goes a long way toward finding peace.*

Nothing Can Make Us Afraid

And now we are saved absolutely, we need not say from what, we are at home in the universe . . . there is nothing anywhere within the world or without it that can make us afraid.

—BERNARD BOSANQUET (1848–1923), BRITISH NEO-HEGELIAN PHILOSOPHER

The writer Winifred Holtby had been told that she might only have two years to live. Vera Brittain describes how one day Winifred was feeling tired and despondent. As she walked by herself through the farmyard, she saw some lambs trying in vain to drink from a frozen water trough. As she broke the ice, she heard a voice saying, "Having nothing, yet possessing all things." She looked around, but she was alone. Suddenly, her grief and bitterness disappeared and never came back. She walked down the hill with the exhilaration that can come from the sense of having abandoned the self and its possessions to the Mystery of Life. (Vera Brittain, *Testament of Friendship*.)

PRACTICE *Although you may not have had what you might describe as a "mystical" experience, can you recall a time when you felt at peace with life? In your meditation, as you go deeper into yourself, you will sense an inner calm and oneness with all that is. This liberates you from your possessions and achievements and gives you confidence that you are a part of life, which death cannot destroy. Ponder this Hindu text:*

He who has realized Eternal Truth does not see death, nor illness,
Nor pain; he sees everything as the Self, and obtains all.

day 95

Radiant Light

Light upon Light. God guides whom God wills to the Light

—QUR'AN: 24, 35

They will not need the light of a lamp or the light of the sun,
for the Lord God will give them light.

—BIBLE: REVELATION 22.5

When Mahatma Gandhi was shot, his immediate response was to call out, "Ram. . . Ram!"—a Hindu name for God. The Buddhist monk Sogyal Rinpoche describes a meditation that is an essential preparation for death. You may want to practice it for the sense of serenity and release it brings.

PRACTICE *Sit or lie comfortably. Picture your embodiment of truth in front of you in the form of radiant light. It could be the Buddha, Christ, Krishna, or just pure golden light. Focus your mind on that presence, and pray that blessing and grace may stream from that light into your inmost being. Now imagine that figure smiling in response and sending out rays of compassion that cleanse your inner self so that you know you are forgiven and at peace. Imagine yourself totally healed and purified by the light. Your body itself dissolves into light. Now your body soars up into the skies and merges with that blissful light. Stay in a state of oneness with that presence for as long as you can.*

A Peaceful Death

The day of death is when two worlds meet with a kiss:
this world going out, the future world coming in.

—JOSE BEN ABIN (FOURTH CENTURY CE), PALESTINIAN RABBI

Have you tried to live a peaceful life? Do you hope to die a peaceful death? You should try to ensure the same for your loved ones who are nearing the end. Accept that the time is coming to say goodbye. Most people would like to die at home, but even in hospital surround them with flowers and pictures of the family. If they can have some privacy, quiet music is helpful. Remember that the dying may be aware of what is said, even if they say nothing. Reassure your loved one that you love them and they have nothing to fear. Communicate your presence by holding a hand and perhaps saying a prayer. If you are peaceful, you will communicate this to your beloved.

PRACTICE *"Should she be told? Does he know?" are questions that relations of a loved one who is dying often ask medical staff. Those who are near death sometimes want encouragement to let go and reassurance that they will be all right. Spend time thinking what you would say to a dying relation. "Thank you for all your love. It's time to say goodbye. You won't suffer any more. I will miss you very much, but I will manage. You will never be alone. We shall always love you." If you share a faith, you could add, "God's love is always with you."*

day
97 # I Will Be Home

It is in dying that we are born to eternal life.

—FROM A PRAYER ATTRIBUTED TO ST. FRANCIS OF ASSISI

Eighteen months after facing the false accusation of sexual misconduct, the supreme test of Cardinal Bernardin's readiness "to let go" came when he was diagnosed with malignant cancer. His surrender to God's will and his trust in life after death gave him inner peace. "Don't try to control your destiny," he said to fellow sufferers, "The more we let God take over, the more we discover our true selves." When asked about the next life, he said that as a child he leafed through his mother's photo albums of her childhood home in Italy. When he eventually visited her village, he felt "I know this place. I am home." Crossing to the next life will be similar. "I will be home." (Joseph Cardinal Bernardin, *The Gift of Peace.*)

PRACTICE *Illness is a difficult test of your inner equilibrium. Do not be distressed if your concentration wavers. Bernardin admitted that physical discomfort meant he could not focus on prayer. He told visitors, "Remember to pray when you are well, you may not be able to do so when you are ill." Repeating a name for God or a single word like "Peace" or listening to spiritual music may help. Remember that others are thinking of you. Try to let go, trusting yourself to the care of medical staff and the renewing power of life. As a visitor, spare the patient your advice. As Bernardin wrote, "Be present as a silent sign of God's presence and love."*

I Need Love So Much

I would not mind if I grow old
As long as my true Love is near.

—Baba Farid (1169-1266), a Sufi saint

Do you dread the physical dependence on others that the weakness of old age may demand? Baba Farid, a Sufi mystic, lived to the great age of 93. When young, he was strong and independent but "now, white-haired, old and weak and sick," he wrote, "I need love so much." Shaky with age knowing the end was near, he was not afraid, provided God's love was near. (Roger Lesser, *Saints and Sages of India.*)

PRACTICE *Most of us would rather not think about growing old. Perhaps you try to disguise it by dyeing your hair or getting rid of your wrinkles. As you reflect quietly, acknowledge your fears. Recognize that physical dependence on others may make you more aware of the love of your family and of caregivers. Think, too, of elderly relatives and friends. Like Baba Farid they "need love so much." Even more than physical care, your reassurance that they are loved and valued will help them find inner peace.*

day 99 Rebirth

As a man abandons his worn-out clothes and acquires new ones,
so when the body is worn out a new one is acquired by the self,
who lives within.

—BHAGAVAD GITA: 2.22

Death is part of living, but it is hard to contemplate your own death with equanimity. It may be reassuring if you believe, as most religions teach, that death is not the end. No one knows what lies beyond the grave. The Qur'an (27.65–66) says honestly, "No one in heaven or on the earth knows the Unseen save God." Hindus, who believe that the soul is by nature immortal, see this life as one of a series of lives. If you live a good life, you will be born with greater opportunities for spiritual development.

PRACTICE *Whether or not you believe in rebirth, you are shaped by your genetic makeup and by your upbringing. Moreover, past behavior affects future actions. Those who drink to excess become alcoholic, and the more they drink the harder it is to break the habit. The same is true of addiction to drugs or gambling. However, although you are shaped by the past, you are not bound by it. You can change. The Hindu philosopher Sarvepalli Radhakrishnan (1888–1975) said that we are dealt a hand of cards, but we choose how to play them. You can begin today to discover your true self, which is a peaceful being. (Sarvepalli Radhakrishnan,* The Hindu View of Life.*)*

A Vestibule to Heaven

Love is as strong as death. . . . Many waters cannot quench love, neither can the floods drown it.

—BIBLE: SONG OF SOLOMON 8.6-7

"What happens when we die?" children ask. Traditionally, Jews, Christians, and Muslims picture this life as a preparation for the next world, where, after being judged according to their behavior, people go either to heaven or to hell (which some people believe is a place of purification rather than punishment). This belief, which affirms that human beings are precious to God, is comforting when a loved one dies. It suggests that this is a moral universe, even if this is not always apparent. It emphasizes the importance of how we behave.

PRACTICE *Hope of another life is not a matter of argument—it springs from experience in this life of love, which is inherently deathless. As you meditate and enter more deeply into yourself, you may discover an inner reality that is untouched by time. Many religions suggest, like this Rabbinic saying, that you should live this life as a preparation for eternity: "This world is like a vestibule before the World to Come; prepare yourself in the vestibule that you may enter the hall."* (From Mishnah, Abot, 4.21.)

day

101 A Message to Your Loved Ones

A ship sails to the morning breeze till at last she fades on the horizon. Someone at my side says, "She is gone." At that moment, others who are watching her come take up a glad shout, "Here she comes"—that is dying.

—BISHOP BRENT, CHIEF OF CHAPLAINS TO THE U.S. EXPEDITIONARY FORCE IN EUROPE, 1917–1919

A funeral service of a friend began with a recording of a moving talk that the person who had died had given a few weeks earlier. It was strange to hear his voice, but we were all vividly aware that his spirit was still with us. My mother left a notebook with some reflections for us to read after her death. Sometimes the bereaved almost sense that the loved one has returned to reassure them. A mother who was grieving for her son once told me that he had come back for a moment but said, "Don't make me stay, I am now so happy," which was all she needed to hear.

PRACTICE *None of us knows when death will come, which is why we should never part from another person in anger. It is also a good reason to have left a message for our loved ones to reassure them of our continuing love for them. Writing such a letter would be a good spiritual exercise and would deepen our appreciation of all that our loved ones mean to us while we are still here. This psalm by Father Edward Hays is an example:*

I leave my thoughts, my laughter, my dreams
to you whom I have treasured
beyond gold and precious gems . . .
after I am home in the bosom of God,
I will still be present
whenever and wherever you call me.

—FROM *PRAYERS FOR A PLANETARY PILGRIM* BY EDWARD M. HAYS

Grieving

Grief can be the garden of compassion.

JALAL AL-DIN RUMI (1207-1273), SUFI POET AND MYSTIC

There is no shortcut for grieving. Traditional societies know that it takes time to recover inner tranquillity, especially if the death was sudden. Jewish custom observes 7 days of intense mourning—*shiv'ah*. Mourning continues for a year, with children saying *Kaddish* for a parent for 11 months. Modern society has few accepted rituals and expects the bereaved to be "back to normal" after a few months. Judy Tatelbaum says that grieving requires you to honestly face your feelings and accept them for however long it takes to heal. "Grief experienced does dissolve. Grief unexpressed lasts indefinitely." (Judy Tatelbaum, *The Courage to Grieve.*)

PRACTICE *This Tibetan meditation is designed for people in deep anguish and grief. Imagine in the sky an enlightened being who radiates compassion—for example, the Buddha, the Virgin Mary, or Rama. Open your heart to them, and pour out your grief. Don't hold back your tears. Use, if you choose, the ancient Tibetan mantra* OM AH HUM VAJRA GURU PADMA SIDDHI HUM. *Imagine the Compassionate One responds with his or her love, with rays of light streaming to you, transforming your suffering into bliss.*

day
103 Let Go of All Anger

The protected heart that "is never exposed to loss, innocent and secure, cannot know tenderness; only the won-back heart can ever be satisfied: free, through all it has given up, to rejoice in its mastery."

—FROM "DOVE THAT VENTURED OUTSIDE," *THE SELECTED POETRY OF RAINER MARIA RILKE,* TRANS. STEPHEN MITCHELL

You may have unfinished business when a parent dies. You still harbor resentment for the way you were treated as a child or for the way your parents never made your partner feel welcome. When I conduct a funeral, I allow time for the mourners to let go both their good and bad memories and also to ask forgiveness of and to grant forgiveness to the departed. Then I invite them to say:

All our laughter, all our sadness,
Safe now in God's hands.
All our anger, all our gladness,
Safe now in God's hands . . .
Those we remember, those we love
Safe now in God's hands.

—FROM A PRAYER BY RUTH BURGESS

PRACTICE *This meditation, which builds on the previous meditation, allows you to be free from suppressed anger and guilt in relation to one who has died. Imagine again that you are in the presence of an enlightened one. Now visualize that the person who died is in the company of the saints, looking at you with a greater love and understanding than he or she ever showed you while alive. Put into words any feelings of hurt or anger or guilt you have been harboring. Let your complete forgiveness go out to the departed, and ask for his or her forgiveness. Ask yourself if now you can truly say farewell and be at peace with yourself and with the one who has died.*

The Death of a Child

Your pain is the breaking of the shell that encloses your understanding. Even as the stone of the fruit must break, that its heart may stand in the sun, so must you know pain.

—KAHLIL GIBRAN, *THE PROPHET*

There can be no greater grief than the death of one's child, whether from illness or misfortune. Mary Craig recalls her utter bewilderment when a doctor said her son Paul was "not normal." She tells of her struggle to care for Paul, who eventually died when he was 10. His passing was a release for the entire family, but Mary Craig says, "I owed him an incalculable debt. He opened my eyes to the suffering in the world. I had been broken, but I had been put together again. . . . He had handed me a key to unlock reserves buried so deep I didn't know they existed." (Mary Craig, *Blessings*.)

PRACTICE *With the loss of a child, there is no easy comfort. It is perhaps only years later that you will see the tragedy was not without meaning. That others have found a strength they did not know they possessed may help you to hold on in your grief. "Human beings have a deep need for stillness and harmony," writes Mary Craig. "In the standing still, in the acceptance of the unavoidable moment in all its bleakness, lies the possibility of salvation and growth for ourselves and for others."*

day 105 Near-Death Experience

Woe to me! . . . I am a man of unclean lips. . . . My eyes have seen the King, the Lord Almighty.

—BIBLE: ISAIAH 6.5

Have you ever spoken to someone who has had a near-death experience? A 1982 Gallup poll said that up to 8 million Americans have had such an experience. Bede (c. 673–735), an English monk and historian, tells of a man who "had risen from the grasp of death," who said, "A handsome man in a shining robe was my guide. . . . He soon brought me out of darkness into a clear light. . . . The light flooding all this place was greater than the brightness of daylight or of the sun's rays at noon." His guide warned him to keep "his words and ways virtuous and simple" so that he would "win a home among these happy spirits that you see." (*A History of the English Church and People*, trans. Leo Sherley-Price.)

PRACTICE *Near-death experiences are an encouragement but also a challenge. Jesus said, "Blessed are the pure in heart for they will see God." Suppose you are invited to meet the president or a queen or king. You would spend time choosing what to wear and wondering what to say. The hope of many devotees is that one day they will see God. How would you prepare for that meeting? Contemplating the holiness of the Almighty is an inspiration to purify our lives.*

Heaven

Pure it is, the Light of lights.
He who knows the Self knows it . . .
With the radiance of that Light alone all things shine.
That radiance illumines all this world.

—HINDU SCRIPTURES: MUNDAKA UPANISHAD

Heaven is beyond our imagination, but poets of many faiths and lands have dreamed of a place of unbroken peace and joy. If life is a journey, it helps to have some picture of its destination. It gives us confidence that life's experiences have meaning, that there is a fellowship that reaches beyond the grave and a peace beyond all understanding. Many visions speak of radiant light. Heaven is not so much a place as it is a presence—an unimpeded awareness of the reality of Divine Love and Peace. The vision should encourage us in this life to seek a foretaste of that radiant presence in the stillness of the heart.

PRACTICE *You may like to spend time quietly allowing your imagination to roam freely as you picture the life beyond. Then try writing a poem or painting a picture of your vision. I find this anonymous poem helpful:*

Oh! think of stepping ashore,
And finding it heaven;
To clasp a hand outstretched,
And to find it God's hand!
To breathe new air
And find that celestial air;
To feel refreshed,
And find it immortality;
Oh! to think to step from storm and stress
to one unbroken calm;
To awake and find it home.

—FROM AN ANONYMOUS POEM, *1,000 WORLD PRAYERS*, ED. MARCUS BRAYBROOKE

part three

PEACE IN OUR HOMES

A peaceful world requires every child to have a secure and caring upbringing. A peaceful and loving home and society provides the environment in which a child learns that he or she is loved and in turn learns to love others. To provide that environment, all concerned with children need to develop a loving and peaceful heart in the ever-changing circumstances of life. Everyone can help ensure that no child is without food, medical care, and education. All children should have the opportunity to grow up in a peaceful world.

Harmony in the Home

Where there is light in the child, there will be beauty in the soul. When there is beauty in the soul, there will be harmony in the home. When there is harmony in the home, there will be order in the nation. When there is order in the nation, there will be peace in the world.

—CHINESE PROVERB

A child first discovers his or her identity within the family. That is where we learn to relate to other people. If your first experiences of life are loving, chances are you will develop a sense of self-worth and will learn to relate to others in a loving way. This is why the quality of the home is important not only to the healthy development of the individual but also to the health of society and to the peace of the world. Most religions stress the importance of the family. The English puritan Richard Baxter (1615–1691) said, "Family is the seminary of Church and State, and if children be not well principled there, all miscarrieth." (Rosemary Dawson, *Something to Celebrate*.)

PRACTICE *The importance of family life in the healthy development of each member of society puts a heavy responsibility on parents. Its importance to a well-balanced society means that society should support and strengthen family life. Providing proper care for those deprived of normal home life is also essential. Take a moment to consider your responsibilities. If you are a parent, you are no doubt concerned about your children's physical and educational well-being. How much attention do you give to their moral and spiritual growth? Children learn by example. Time spent in cultivating a peaceful heart will help to create a harmonious atmosphere in the home.*

day 108 Children Share Our World

I believe the child should be taught from the very first that the whole world is his world, that adult and child share one world, that all generations are needed.

—Pearl Buck, *To My Daughters, With Love*

The welfare of children is a concern not just of parents but of the entire society. Education is an important aspect in developing a child's relationship to society. It is important that educational policy is not dictated primarily by the economic needs of the country but by a concern that each child develops his or her full potential. For this reason, it is proper for those who do not have children also to contribute to the cost of education through taxes, because the quality of the society as a whole is affected by the well-being of its children. Whether or not religious and spiritual education is provided in schools—the legal position varies from country to country—it is vital that young people learn the principles of ethical behavior. You can contribute to this through your faith community.

PRACTICE *Think back to your childhood. Who had the most influence on you? Which teachers do you recall with appreciation? Do you remember them more for their character than for what they taught you? Were there neighbors or relations who took an interest in you as a person rather than talking down to you? Reflect how you relate to children who live in your neighborhood. Do you resent their noise and games? Do you know their names and talk to them?*

The Eyes of a Child

God needs no pointing out to a child

—PROVERB FROM GHANA

Spiritual nature is a gift at birth, according to some Native Americans. Native Americans avoid hitting or shouting at children. Instead a child who behaves badly is brought before several elders who gently and kindly explain why the behavior was wrong. Afterward, no one refers to the matter again.

PRACTICE *Most young children, like great spiritual teachers, have a sense of wonder and joy and live in the present moment. In some societies, children are regarded as spiritual beings until age five. People can retain some of their inherent spirituality through prayer and ritual. A few people recover their childhood spirituality after special experiences. Some go on to become spiritual teachers and healers. Children and grandchildren can help you recapture this primal vision, but you need to communicate with them on their level, both physically and mentally. Can you remember what the world looked like when you were two feet high? What did you enjoy most when you were a child? Are you really too old not to try it again?*

day

110 Take the Children with You

Love your children and treat them with compassion.

—THE PROPHET MUHAMMAD

Would you take your children with you to a public meeting? The prophet Muhammad often did, and he used to carry his granddaughter Imama on his shoulders while performing his prayers. He wanted children to learn to be part of the community. He taught that every Muslim adult should help the young to uphold religious values and social responsibilities. This should be done through education not coercion. Muhammad insisted that children should be treated fairly. Once, a disciple enticed her daughter inside with the promise of a gift. When they sat down, the Prophet reminded the mother, "You'd better give her those dates or you will lose face with your child."

PRACTICE *Do you talk to your children or to young people you know about what is going on in the world? Do you explain your concerns for peace to them? Many people who get involved in peace work or social reform do so because they were encouraged to take an interest in the outside world as children. Muslim parents are encouraged to accustom their children to hearing at home quotations from the Qur'an and stories about the Prophet. They learn to pray and fast by observing adults in the house.*

Children in the Kingdom of God

Let the children come to me, and do not hinder them; for to such belongs the kingdom of heaven.

—BIBLE: MATTHEW 19.14

For Jesus, children were not adults in preparation, but full members of the kingdom of God. Their naturally open and trusting spirit often makes them seem closer to God than adults. Modern society tends to segregate people according to their age. But the daily routines of life can bring the family together. By their gradual acceptance into adult routines, children learn what is expected of them. The modern invention of "quality time" is, in the view of some social historians, a poor substitute for unstructured, meaningful interaction between adults and children.

PRACTICE *How much time does your family spend sharing in household activities, such as preparing meals, cleaning the house, or gardening? Some social scientists suggest that the modern emphasis on personal fulfillment means that members of a family concentrate on realizing individual needs rather than taking part in family life as a shared project. Gilbert Meilander, the Lutheran writer on ethics, says, "We seldom discover in the family anything more than an arena for our personal fulfillment and we fail to see it as a community that ought to transmit a way of life." Could you plan a family activity, such as preparing a meal together, in which everyone takes part? (H. Coward and P. Cook eds.* Religious Dimensions of Child and Family Life.*)*

day 112

The Buddha Nature

Every Being has the Buddha Nature. This is the self.

—BUDDHIST SCRIPTURE: MAHAPARINIRVANA SUTRA 214

Buddhists believe that all beings are endowed with "basic goodness," or the Buddha nature. This is an inherent indwelling enlightenment, which can be realized or awakened. Unlike some Western psychologists, Buddhists do not regard a newborn as a blank page. Buddhists believe in rebirth and think that each child is endowed with specific talents. These talents are the result of behavior in past lives rather than genetic makeup. Sometimes *karma*—the moral law of cause and effect—is used to explain the inequalities and injustices in life, but it also suggests that a person can shape his or her future.

PRACTICE *Do you at times feel dissatisfied with yourself because you do not live up to your ideals? Perhaps you complain that you had a deprived childhood. Buddhist ideas of karma, like the Christian doctrine of original sin, may tempt you to blame the past. But both religions really emphasize future possibilities and urge you to discover your Buddha or Christ nature. In your meditation, stop regretting the past. Instead recall your ideals, visualize the person you want to be, and turn your face to the rising sun.*

One World Family

Earth is but one country and all people its citizens.

—BAHA'U'LLAH (1817–1892), FOUNDER OF THE BAHI'I FAITH

According to the Baha'i, all people are members of one world family. In raising their children, they seek to overcome all racial and religious prejudice. Believing that the soul comes into being at the time of conception, Baha'i parents are encouraged to pray for the child even before he or she is born. They view the rational mind as a faculty of the soul, so intellectual and spiritual knowledge go together. As such, the child's spiritual education is a vital responsibility of the parents. Children, however, are not expected merely to imitate their parents beliefs, because it is important that each person discovers the truth for himself or herself.

PRACTICE *If you are a parent, how much attention do you give to your child's spiritual education? Do you want him or her to agree with your beliefs? The Baha'i leader 'Abdu'l-Baha said, "The education and training of children is among the most meritorious acts of humankind." Young people are most likely to share your outlook if they see that your life is fulfilled and enriched by your faith. Each person should be encouraged to find a faith to live by for himself or herself. Respect for each person's—including your children's—conscience and religious beliefs helps to overcome the prejudices that cause division in the world.*

day
114 Hands as Rough as Sandpaper

My father, thank you for petting me;
My mother, thank you for making me comfortable;
Thank you for robing me with wisdom, which is more important than robing me with clothes.

—FROM A NIGERIAN YORUBA NUPTIAL CHANT

A leaflet produced by the Indian charity "Child Relief and You" features a small piece of sandpaper. It compares the sandpaper to the roughness of the hands of many children in India, who are trapped in bonded labor. If children are to develop their full potential, then they require basic physical care as well as education. The health of children who are forced to work long hours is often damaged and their mental and spiritual growth stunted. If the next generation is to create a more peaceful world, the present generation has to ensure that children are free from poverty and deprivation.

PRACTICE *Are you aware of the poverty in which many children grow up? Do you support any charities that are trying to change the situation? Thanks to public opinion, several corporations that sell sporting goods now refuse to buy articles made by child labor. In several Asian countries, governments have banned the use of child labor in carpet manufacturing. Charitable contributions are one way to help. As a consumer or a tourist you can also help to change age-old abuses.*

Who Washes the Diapers?

You are all my children, and I am your Father. For age upon age, you have been scorched by multitudinous woes, and I have saved you all.

—From the Buddhist Lotus Sutra 3

The sharing of child-care responsibilities can still be a cause of disagreement between parents. Nearly 500 years ago, the reformer Martin Luther (1483–1546) encouraged fathers to wash diapers. If these fathers were ridiculed, Luther told them, "God with his angels would be smiling because the father was washing diapers as a sign of his Christian faith." (Martin Luther, *Luther's Works.*) Jesus washed his disciples' feet. The prophet Muhammad helped look after his children. If father and mother can agree on sharing the care for their children, it can help unite the family and serve as a positive example for the young.

PRACTICE *If you are a parent, do you share the work of caring for your children? Does your pattern of work allow both mother and father to spend enough time with the children? Have you discussed this with your spouse? Otherwise, it is all too easy for hidden resentments to develop. Pope John Paul II warned that "the absence of a father causes psychological and moral imbalance as do oppressive 'machismo' attitudes." If parents can communicate with each other, it will help them communicate with their children, thereby helping to create a more peaceful world.*

116 Parenthood—a Model of Self-Giving

Jesus, you are gentle with us as a mother with her children . . . You comfort us in sorrow and bind up our wounds: in sickness you nurse us and with pure milk you feed us.

—St. Anselm (c. 1033–1109), Archbishop of Canterbury

An increasing number of children are brought up in single-parent homes. More than 50 years ago, a World Health Organization report stressed the importance of continuity in child care. "In no other relationship do human beings place themselves so unreservedly and so continuously at the disposal of others. . . . This holds true even of bad parents—a fact easily forgotten by critics who have never had the care of children."

PRACTICE *Although the economics of modern society exerts pressure on mothers of young children to work full-time, the practice may be depriving the children of the loving and peaceful environment that will help them develop a peaceful heart. Although some activities outside the home may be stimulating, this need to work can put added stress on the mother. Just as the baby needs to feel that he or she belongs to the mother, the mother needs to feel that she belongs to her child. If you are a parent of young children, you need to balance both the economic and the emotional benefits. Unfortunately, there is no easy answer. Simply take a few moments to reflect on whether there are ways to balance the time you do have with your child.*

Wanted

Not flesh of my flesh nor bone of my bone, but still miraculous, my own. Never forget that you didn't grow under my heart but in it.

—An anonymous prayer for an adopted child, *1,000 World Prayers,* ed. Marcus Braybrooke

All children need to know that they are valued and wanted, regardless of who cares for and raises them. The experiences of adopted children, like those of children brought up by natural parents, vary. One respondent to a survey conducted by Alice Heim said, "To be adopted has no disadvantages." Conversely, another respondent wrote, "There are no advantages in adoption, rather the reverse." Several adoptees were glad they lived in a family rather than an institution. Others emphasized the value of knowing that they were wanted. As one person put it, "My adoptive parents had not got me by accident (though my natural ones very probably did!)" (Alice Heim, *Thicker Than Water.*)

PRACTICE *St. Paul speaks of all of us as being the adopted children of God, whom we can call Father. For Christians, the rite of baptism is a recognition of this. In your meditation, remember that you and all people are valued and loved for themselves as unique individual children of God, regardless of the circumstances of their birth. In the scriptures of the Japanese Tenrikyo religion (Oufudesaki 4.79), God says, "People of the world are all my children. All of you equally must understand that I am your Parent."*

Marriage as a Sacrament

Blessed are You, Lord our God, king of the universe, who created joy and happiness, bridegroom and bride, love and companionship, peace and friendship. May the sound of happiness and rejoicing be heard in our cities, the voice of bridegroom and bride.

—FROM *FORMS OF PRAYER FOR JEWISH WORSHIP*

A happy home helps all its members find inner peace and fulfillment. It contributes to a stable and peaceful society. The importance of marriage is recognized in most religions. The Bible says God intended husband and wife to leave the families in which they grew up and to "become one flesh." (Genesis 2.24.) St. Paul compared the relationship of husband and wife to the union of the believer and Christ. He urged husbands to "love your wives, just as Christ loved the church and gave himself up for her." (Ephesians 5.25.) Bodily union is seen by many Christians as sacramental—the physical expression of the union of mind and spirit.

PRACTICE *Are you tempted by the pressures of modern society to separate the physical pleasure of sex from personal relationships? Jack Dominian, a leading Christian psychiatrist and writer on marriage, points out that couples say, "Let's make love" not "Let's have an orgasm." Intercourse, he says, enhances our sense of personal worth and self-esteem. It affirms our identity, including our sexuality. It relieves the stress and tension of daily life. It can heal differences between the husband and wife, and it expresses gratitude toward and affection for the partner. Awareness of its potential enrichment to you and your partner helps you see its importance to your inner well-being. (Jack Dominian,* Marriage, Faith and Love *and* Let's Make Love.*)*

Sustaining a Marriage

They are not man and wife who only have physical contact;
Only they are truly wedded who have one spirit in two bodies.
Ask the happy one by what ways they have won the beloved.
They answer, by sweetness of speech and the beauty of contentment.

—GURU AMAR DAS (1479–1574), THIRD SIKH GURU

What is the secret of a happy marriage? Jack Dominian, a Christian commentator on marriage, suggests three main characteristics of loving: sustaining, healing, and growth. Sustaining involves being available for the other, which seems increasingly difficult in modern society. Couples need to reveal their private world to each other. Without time to talk, there can be inner loneliness and misunderstanding. Praise and signs of affection are a reminder that the partner is loved and valued. In an intimate relationship, disagreements are almost inevitable, but it is vital to make up as soon as possible.

PRACTICE *When you are courting, you cannot have enough time with your beloved, but when you settle down, the demands of work, commuting, and family responsibility mean you have little relaxed time together. Some couples even find that their main means of communicating is by leaving voice mail messages. However, real communication requires relaxed time together, otherwise conversation becomes an argument about who's going to do the shopping or pay a bill. You need time for your heart to become peaceful. You also need time together to develop a deeper and more loving relationship.*

day

120 Growing in Marriage

And among God's signs is this, that he created for you mates among yourselves, that you may dwell in tranquillity with them and God has put love and mercy between your (hearts). Verily in that are signs for those who reflect.

—QUR'AN: 30.21

"We emerge from childhood as wounded people." This is the rather depressing verdict of Jack Dominian, a writer on marriage. Our first intimate relationships are with our parents. These are seldom perfect, but in a loving adult relationship, these early hurts can be healed. In the security of the partner's accepting love, a person can let go his or her defenses and gain self-confidence. Real love overcomes a person's negativity and self-hatred. Couples can too easily forget that both are continuing to develop as human beings. Without good communication, partners can drift apart. Mature accepting love helps both husband and wife to develop his or her personality to the fullest.

PRACTICE *If you are in a loving relationship, ask yourself whether you have grown as a result. You may find it helpful to reflect on these words:*

Love one another, but make not a bond of love:
Let it be rather a moving sea between the shores of your souls.
Fill each other's cup but drink not from one cup . . .
Give your hearts, but not into each other's keeping
And stand together yet not too near together
For the pillars of the temple stand apart
And the oak tree and the cypress grow not in each other's shadow.

—KAHLIL GIBRAN, *THE PROPHET*

Marital Breakdown

The very altar weeps when a man divorces the wife of his youth.

—A Rabbinic saying based on Malachi 2.14

The breakdown of a marriage or a long-term relationship is almost always a painful experience. Although religions vary in their attitude about divorce, they all urge faithfulness in marriage. They recognize the distress divorce causes to the partners and to children. However, marital breakdown has become more common in Western society. It commonly occurs during the first five years of marriage. The increase in the number of marital breakdowns is partly because people have higher expectations of personal fulfillment in marriage, partly because the economic freedom of women has increased, and partly because people live longer and marriages last longer. Those whose marriages fail should be reassured that they are still loved and valued as persons by God.

PRACTICE *If you are in a long-term loving relationship, have you recently asked yourself whether your partner is finding the fulfillment he or she hopes for? It is easy to take the other for granted—not noticing his or her new interests or even a new hairstyle! The pressures of work, the business of daily life, and the demands of young children may mean you have little time to talk together. However, time together restores and renews your love for each other. Regular praise and signs of affection reassure your partner that he or she is loved and valued and will help to make your home a place of peace.*

day
122 Recovering from Divorce

May forgiveness heal injury and joy triumph over sorrow.

—FROM AN ANGLICAN WEDDING SERVICE PRAYER

If you are facing a marital breakdown, you are likely to feel a deep sense of failure. You might blame yourself, or you might blame your partner. You may be tempted to express your anger violently. Do not be surprised if your behavior becomes erratic and you become prone to physical and emotional illness. You may find if difficult to sleep and be reluctant to eat. This is a natural reaction, but excessive blame and self-pity may delay your healing. It is more helpful to see if you can learn from past mistakes. Maybe you were too young when you married or were too preoccupied with your career. This is a time when, if you let them, relatives and friends can be a great help by giving you their support.

PRACTICE *After a divorce you may find this prayer helpful:*

Heavenly Father we thank you for our friends and for all who have stood by us in time of trouble, who give wise advice when we need it, who are there when we want them, who teach us much by their quality of life. We thank you for those who have meant much to us and have now been called to their rest. Above all we thank you that again and again in our earthly lives you speak to us through your word, through the people we know or meet, through nature, through art and literature, of the lasting things which really matter.

—FROM *A FORM OF BLESSING ON A SECOND MARRIAGE*,
THE DIOCESE OF BATH AND WELLS, ENGLAND

Helping a Friend

O Lord of humankind, send suffering away and restore health.
You are the healer.

—From a prayer of the Muslim scholar Bukhari (810-870 CE)

If a friend in an unhappy marriage asks you whether he or she should leave his or her partner, how would you reply? It may help to encourage your friend to look at the five dimensions of marriage—emotional, intellectual, sexual, social, and spiritual—and see how much the two still share. Is there enough to rebuild a relationship? Ultimately, the individual concerned has to make the decision. Some Christian theologians suggest that if a relationship dies, the marriage is just as finished as if one of the partners dies.

PRACTICE *Do not impose your religious views about divorce on your friend. Tell him or her what you believe, but recognize that he or she has to make the decision. Even if you disapprove of divorce on religious grounds, assure your friend that God still loves and values him or her. Discourage your friend from assigning blame, which only adds to the pain and bitterness. Promise to support your friend in whatever he or she decides. The more peaceful you are, the easier it will be for you to help your friend find inner peace at a difficult time.*

day

124 Put the Children First

Give us grace, Lord, to tell our children nothing but the truth . . . and to expect from them no higher standard of honesty, unselfishness, and politeness than we are prepared to live up to ourselves.

—From a prayer by Joan Kendall, a contemporary writer

With the growing number of divorces, an increasing number of children spend some weekends with the other parent. The space between the curbside and the front door has been described as the no-man's-land that a child has to cross from one estranged parent to the other. A child may feel conflicts in his or her loyalties if one parent denigrates the other in front of the child. Separated parents need to overcome their own feelings of animosity to their former partner for the sake of their children.

PRACTICE *If a divorce has been particularly painful and messy, children are bound to suffer. But those involved owe it to their children not to use them as pawns in their battle. This is a time when the parents and other relations especially need to seek inner peace so as to reflect this in their home. When you start to feel anger or bitterness toward your former partner, think about what is best for your child. Try to remember the good times you had. Recognize that the faults were not all on one side. You still have a shared responsibility for the child's welfare. Try to put that first.*

Becoming a Real Family

Soon this modern family would be even more complicated, full of half-brothers and stepsisters. . . . But now I finally saw that it was up to us if we felt like a real family or not. Nobody else mattered. The labels they stuck on us meant nothing at all.

—TONY PARSONS, FROM *MAN AND WIFE*

In his novel *Man and Wife*, Tony Parsons describes the Sunday scene at a fast-food restaurant, which was packed with weekend dads making stilted small talk with their children. "We avoided eye contact, me and all the other one-day dads. When there were unpleasant scenes, we felt for each other." Tony Parsons speaks about "blended families," in which the new man in a woman's life moves into a semiparental role. It's easy for the natural father to compete with the new man for his child's affection. Harry, the father in *Man and Wife*, asks himself, "Did the new man Richard kiss my son good-night? I didn't ask and I didn't know what would hurt me more. The warmth that a good-night kiss would indicate or the cold distance implicit in the absence of a kiss."

PRACTICE *If you are in such a situation, ask yourself whether you are still trying to compete with your former spouse or scoring points against the new partner? What help is this to your child? It is important that the adults do all they can not to impose their hurt and anger on the child. You should not use a child as a pawn in your marital tug-of-war. If you have a friend or relation in this position, encourage him or her to put the child's interests first.*

126 Living Together

The moral person finds the moral law beginning in the relation between man and woman, but ending in the vast reaches of the universe.

—A Confucian teaching: Doctrine of the Mean, 12

In the view of several commentators, the increase in the number of divorces does not mean a decline in the importance or popularity of marriage. The U.S. census for the year 2000 (*USA Today,* September 18, 2003), showed that out of 105 million households, there are 54 million married couples. More unmarried couples, however, are living together. There are now nearly 5 million unmarried couples with opposite-sex partners, compared to 3 million in the 1990 census. Some 41 percent of these homes had children younger than age 18 living in them. Commentators differ in the effect that this has on the children, but Dorian Solot says, "Unmarried families can certainly thrive if they are loving, fairly stable and have set up rules and goals." (D. Solot and M. Miller, *Unmarried to Each Other.*)

PRACTICE *A growing number of homes, especially in the Western world, no longer fit into traditional patterns of family life, which have had the sanction of religion. Some religious groups think the best way to uphold the permanence of marriage is to reject those who do not conform to the norm. Other teachers emphasize that the quality of the relationship is more important than its legal expression. What do you think? What qualities do you consider are the most important in providing children with a stable and loving upbringing? How can these be best reflected in your home and in society?*

Same-Sex Relationships

Men and women who are homosexual need the opportunity to work out their own individual solutions without having to conform to stereotypes created for them.

—From *Homosexual Relationships, A Contribution to Discussion*

A Report for the Church of England

Would it disturb you if your son or daughter started living with a person of the same sex? The number of same-sex couples is increasing, and in some places they still face hostility. Although most religious teachers have condemned homosexuality in the past, the understanding of human sexuality is changing. Some spiritual guides recognize that a long-term faithful same-sex relationship has some of the characteristics of a marriage. Like husband and wife, same-sex partners share life's joys and sorrows. They express and strengthen their love through physical relationships. The quality of relationships may be more important than their legal status.

PRACTICE *Jesus warned his followers against judging other people. If you are confident in your own standards and ideals, then you can welcome and accept those who adopt a different lifestyle. Society is quickly changing. People should be free to choose the way they live, without facing hostility and prejudice. In your time of meditation, try to confront your own prejudices. They may be attitudes inherited from your parents or faith community but not questioned or examined. Remember what St. Paul said: "Love is the fulfillment of the law." (Romans 13.10.)*

day 128

Living Alone

Our hearts are restless till they find their rest in Thee, O Lord.

—St. Augustine (354–430), influential Christian thinker

Many people live alone. Some choose to do so, whereas others do so because their partner has died or because a relationship has ended. Dr. Martin Israel, a pathologist and a priest, distinguishes between aloneness, loneliness, and solitude. Aloneness is thrust upon you by the circumstances of life. You can no longer avoid confrontation with your inner self by outer companionship. Loneliness is a feeling of unhappiness and yearning for company, which you may even feel when you are surrounded by other people. It reflects a sense of inferiority that you cannot compete with the people around you. Solitude is a state in which you choose to be by yourself. It is necessary if you are to deepen your inner life.

PRACTICE *Recall the times when you have been by yourself. Was it by choice or necessity? When you have been alone, did you feel relaxed or uneasy? If you were not relaxed, you may not be in tune with your feelings and your inner self. Companionship may conceal an inner void. Loneliness is the feeling that you do not matter to anyone else. It can, as Dr. Israel suggests, help us "realize that there is One who alone can satisfy the soul—God. . . . Until we know the living God we will know neither ourselves nor our fellows." (Martin Israel,* Living Alone.*) If you reach beyond loneliness, you may come to value solitude as the pathway to a peaceful heart.*

Learn to Be at Peace with Yourself

I was shipwrecked on the ocean of life. . . . Sent by the winds of Thy mercy, a little raft of spiritual hope floated near me. . . . In Thy safe presence all hurt from my hardships vanished.

—PARAMAHANSA YOGANANDA (1893–1952),
FOUNDER OF THE SELF-REALIZATION FELLOWSHIP

Those who live alone may not have a deep relationship with one person, but they can find fulfillment in relating to a number of people, particularly through service to them. "One's chances of relating successfully to another person are remote until one has learned to relate effectively to oneself. Until I am at peace with myself, accepting the manifold elements of my personality—the dark and unpleasant as well as the light and attractive—I will never be at peace with anyone else." (Martin Israel, *Living Alone*.) Until you have done this, you will be preoccupied with your own emotional needs rather than available to the person you seek to help.

PRACTICE *Learning to know and accept yourself is not easy. In fact, it may be painful. Some people need expert help. But many spiritual teachers affirm that in the depth of our being there is an inner self, which is pure and beautiful, and which we can realize in meditation. Other teachers emphasize the love of God, who values and accepts us for ourselves, whatever we may have done. If you do live alone, by choice or necessity, it is a time to discover your inner being and, through self-acceptance, find healing and wholeness.*

day
130 Retreat

Once, read your own heart right
And you will have done with fears;
Man gets no other light
Though he search a thousand years.

—MATTHEW ARNOLD (1822–1888), FROM *EMPEDOCLES ON ETNA*

Those who live by themselves may experience considerable periods of silence. However, everyone needs to learn how to use silence in a positive manner. The first use of silence is to explore the depths of your own personality and to come to terms with your hidden fears and inhibitions. The second use of silence is to learn to listen to what people are communicating by what they say. The third use of silence is to listen to what our lives are telling us about ourselves. It means hearing the voice of the Spirit that leads us to that inner peace where God dwells.

PRACTICE *Have you ever been on a retreat? Some people look forward to going away once a year for a few days of complete quiet. Some retreats are conducted by a spiritual leader who provides guidance. There may be times of communal prayer. Other retreats include activities, such as painting or calligraphy. Some people prefer to be by themselves. Would you be afraid of 3 or 4 days of silence? If so, perhaps you have not come to terms with your inner self. Silence allows you to grow in self-knowledge and discover the presence of the Spirit in the center of your being. Perhaps you could begin by spending a half day in silence in a place where you will not be disturbed.*

If You Let Go, You Will Find Support

We are the weak ones, the failures, the second-rate redundant weaklings.
Help us, Christ, greatest of failures on Golgotha,
distil from the bitter, the elixir of life.

—SISTER MARY DUNNOCK, FROM *THE TABLET*

"It is an amazing paradox," writes Martin Israel, a member of the Royal College of Surgeons, "that until one can live successfully on one's own, one will never be able to live as a full person with anyone else." (Martin Israel, *Living Alone.*) Some people try to escape from themselves in a flurry of activities. Others enter a new relationship "on the rebound," only to find it no more satisfactory than previous relationships. If you face your loneliness, you will free yourself from your fears. Once you are no longer making demands on others to assuage your loneliness, you will find others are attracted to you because of your inner tranquillity.

PRACTICE *Dr. Israel says that in caring for the very weak and ill, you discover the face of a helpless child in people with a previously haughty demeanor. In your weakness, you become more willing to open yourself to the healing and upholding influences of life. When you are learning to swim, it is only when you let go that you find that the water supports you. Your struggle to be independent keeps people at arm's length. Acknowledging your human frailty is a recognition of your interdependence.*

day 132 Our Responsibility for the Young

A new child is born. While in the womb it was the woman's thing; Safely delivered, it is everybody's child.

—FROM AN NIGERIAN IGBO NAMING CEREMONY

Even if you have no children of your own, you can help to create a peaceful society through your concern for the welfare of children and young people. If you are a grandparent, aunt, or uncle you can befriend and support the children in your family. Perhaps you can help with the many voluntary activities your community arranges for children. As a voter, you can encourage politicians to devote adequate resources to education and child welfare services. Everyone needs to take part in ensuring the well-being of society's future—its children.

PRACTICE *If you are an employer, have you given thought to adopting family-friendly policies? Does your place of work provide a day-care center? Do you allow for part-time and flexible hours of work, to make it easier for parents to be with their children after school? Are the career prospects of women who take maternity leave affected? How concerned are you about children in other parts of the world who are exploited or who live in poverty? In your meditation, recall ways in which your life as a child was enriched by concerned adults. How can you help to ensure that the next generation is healthy and peace loving?*

Forgive Your Parents

One Companion asked, "O Apostle of God! Who is the person worthiest of my consideration?' He replied, "Your mother." He asked again, "And second to my mother?" The prophet said, "Your mother." The companion insisted, "And then?" The Messenger of God said, "After your mother, your father."

—SAYING ATTRIBUTED TO THE PROPHET MUHAMMAD

"We emerge from childhood as wounded people." This comment of Jack Dominian, quoted earlier, is rather discouraging for parents. Jack Dominian suggests that we emerge with wounds from our first intimate experience of life. Mothers know how difficult it is to find the right balance between smothering a child with love and being too strict or overprotective, which can lower a child's sense of self-worth. Remember that your parents were also hurt by their own experiences in life.

PRACTICE *Have you forgiven your parents? It may have been a shattering experience when you discovered that they were only human. This could have led to feelings of resentment, but as you mature, you should learn to accept the humanity of your parents. They may have made mistakes but probably tried to do their best. Many religions emphasize respect for parents. This means loving them as they are. Otherwise you may feel guilty if you cannot pretend they are perfect. Then you can look on them with sympathy, humor, and true affection. If you have not yet found this acceptance, even if your parents have died, try in your times of meditation to confront these feelings. Recall and then let go of painful memories by asking and offering forgiveness.*

day

134 Siblings

The regulation of the family depends on the cultivation of the personal life. . . . Few people in the world know what is bad in those whom they love and what is good in those whom they dislike.

—CONFUCIAN TEACHING: GREAT LEARNING, 8

Sibling rivalry is as old as creation. Adam and Eve's first child Cain murdered his younger brother Abel. Genesis, the first book of the Bible, is full of stories of brothers and sisters who were jealous of each other. Jacob tricked his brother Esau out of his inheritance. Jacob's wives, Rachel and Leah, were envious of each other. Joseph was sold into slavery in Egypt by his brothers. Joseph grew up to become that country's chief minister. When his brothers came to Egypt to buy food because of a famine in Canaan, he forgave them, saying: "Do not be angry with yourselves for selling me here, because it was to save lives that God sent me ahead of you." (Genesis 45.5.)

PRACTICE *Through his sufferings, Joseph learned to accept himself and to see a pattern and a purpose in his life. He no longer resented his brothers' cruelty; instead, he cared for them and his parents when they came to him in distress. If you have learned to accept yourself and to see a pattern in your life, then you will have come to terms with the happy and unhappy memories of childhood. Competition with brothers and sisters will have helped to shape your character. You may also now recognize that good parents love each child equally but in different ways. Learn to be yourself and not to judge yourself by comparison with your siblings.*

Strong Bonds

The family that prays together stays together.

—Motto devised for the Roman Catholic Family Rosary Crusade, 1947

Family bonds have a strength seldom found in other relationships. Our granddaughter Helen wrote a poem about her family:

I have a mum and a dad which makes me very glad.
I have three sisters, they can be a pain,
But I cherish and love them all the same
We are mostly happy but sometimes snappy
We chat and play almost every day
We share our toys and make a lot of noise
We say a prayer because we care
We'll stay friends until life ends.

Although she is only 10, Helen recognizes that the family ties forged in youth often sustain us in old age.

PRACTICE *Have you drifted apart from your brothers and sisters? My wife is a medical social worker. A critically ill patient once told her that before he died he would love to see his brother again, but he didn't know his address because they had not been in touch for 40 years. A search turned up the brother, however, and he visited the hospital. The patient died peacefully a few days later. No doubt you've seen pictures of a reunion of a brother or a sister who were separated more than 50 years ago by war or some other disaster. Their delight at meeting again is evidence of the sustaining strength of family bonds. Is it time for you to strengthen or renew these bonds and to remember your relations in your prayers?*

day 136 Gender Equity or Gender Equality?

The world of humanity has two wings—one is women and the other men. Not until both wings are equally developed can the bird fly.

—'ABDU'L-BAHA (1844–1921), A LEADER OF THE BAHA'I FAITH

Gender equality may not always be practiced in Western society but gender discrimination is illegal in many countries. Other cultures, however, still see men and women as having different roles. Hindu culture sees "a partnership between man and woman of 'gender equity' rather than 'gender equality,'" writes Werner Menski, of the School of Oriental and African Studies at London University. The Muslim writer Mavis Badawi says, "We are all equal in the eyes of God. . . . We are different in terms of ability, strength, and aptitude." (P. Morgan and M. Braybrooke, eds., *Testing the Global Ethic.*) Certainly, many women have been and still are oppressed, but it is important not to judge other communities by our own standards nor, in a plural society, to impose one pattern on everybody.

PRACTICE *Do you think it is better to treat people "equitably" or with "equal respect" rather than "equally"? Consider your own attitude toward gender identity. How do you react to the attitudes of other communities? Western women often feel sorry for Muslim women who are veiled, but some deliberately choose to wear the* hijab *(or scarf). One woman who converted to Islam said, "If another Muslim sees you in a* hijab *and you are in trouble, they step in and help." By the same token, many Muslims judge Western women from Hollywood stereotypes and think they are all addicted to alcohol and promiscuity. It is important to value your own identity while trying to overcome prejudice. That way you can appreciate other people's way of life as well as your own.*

Three or Four Acorns

Original energy is unified, yin and yang are one;
The spirit is the same as the universe.

—SUN BU-ER, A TWELFTH-CENTURY FEMALE TAOIST SAGE

Do you insist on doing things your own way? Does your own way make sense or is it a form of stubbornness? According to a Taoist story, a monkey trainer was handing out acorns to the monkeys. "You get three in the morning and four at night," he said. The monkeys were furious. "All right," he said, "You get four in the morning and three at night." (Thomas F. Cleary, ed., *Immortal Sisters: Secrets of a Taoist Woman.*) The monkeys were delighted. The wise person is concerned with what is useful and successful. Taoism avoids labeling actions as "good" or "bad" and seeks a harmony beyond moral judgments.

PRACTICE *Many parents seem to be more rigid than the trainer's monkey. How flexible are you with your children? Do you say, "This had better be the last story?" at your children's bedtime? Do you relent or stand firm when they beg for "just one more short story?" Do they settle down happily if you grant their request or do you spend another half hour calming them down after they burst into tears? Do you fear a loss of face or of authority if you give in to what others ask? Taoism suggests that harmony is more important than being proved right.*

day 138 Leaving Home

You, brethren, are released from all bonds, those that are divine and those that are human. Go forth, brethren, on your journey for the profit of many, out of compassion for the world and the welfare of mankind.

—SAYING OF THE BUDDHA, VINAYA PITAKA I.21

Many people are shocked when they read that, according to Luke's Gospel (14.26), Jesus said, "Unless a person hates his father and mother, his wife and children, he cannot be my disciple." The translation "loves me more than his father. . . ." is rather less extreme. But the Buddha, after seeing the "four signs" of an old man, a sick person, a corpse, and a monk, abandoned his wife and tiny baby to become a wandering ascetic. Religions may emphasize the importance of family life and filial obligations, but they recognize a higher loyalty to follow God's calling. Sometimes a person can only establish their own identity by breaking free from the family, even if later they return to it in a more mature relationship.

PRACTICE *Did you leave your family home when you got married? If an only son is living with a widowed mother, she may try to cling to him when he marries and leaves home. It is sometimes difficult for newlyweds to realize that their first loyalty is now to their spouse, not to their parents. If there is to be peace in the home, it is important that those who are married learn to balance the needs of their relationship with the demands of their parents.*

The Kitchen

Praised be God who gave us food and drink and took care of our needs and housed us and blessed us amply.

—A Muslim prayer, *Radiant Prayers*

The kitchen is often the heart of the home. The kitchen in the house where I grew up was tiny, but the whole family still congregated there. My mother hardly had room to cook. A family can find enjoyment in preparing a meal together or clearing up afterward. Packaged foods and dishwashers have made this less common in the more affluent homes in the West, but it is good for the family to share tasks together. It strengthens family bonds that make for peace in the home.

PRACTICE *Do you take food and its preparation for granted? This prayer by the American Sioux Indian John Lame Deer could help you recapture awareness of our dependence on the gifts of Life.*

I'm an Indian.
I think about the common things like this pot.
The bubbling water came from the rain cloud.
It represents the sky.
The fire comes from the sun
which warms us all, men, animals, trees.
The steam is living breath.
It was water, now it goes up to the sky,
becomes a cloud again.
These things are sacred.
Looking at that pot full of good soup,
I am thinking, how in this simple manner,
The Great Spirit takes care of me.

—John Lame Deer, *1,000 World Prayers*, ed. Marcus Braybrooke

day
140
The Bedroom

I remember, I remember,
The house where I was born,
The little window where the sun
Came peeping in at morn.

—THOMAS HOOD (1799–1845), ENGLISH POET AND HUMORIST

Does your childhood bedroom hold special memories for you? Was it a place where you could be on your own and have your private dreams? A sense of place can make a significant contribution to our inner peacefulness. In traditional societies, many people grew up and lived in the same village for most of their lives. This created a sense of stability, which is easily lost in a more mobile society.

PRACTICE *Have you had to move a lot in your life? Have you found it is important for your own inner tranquillity and that of your children to put down roots as quickly as possible? Do you try to get to know your neighbors? Joining a local church, synagogue, mosque, or temple can help you to make friends and give you a feeling of belonging. If you are a long-time resident, you can make a real contribution to the community by welcoming newcomers and helping them to settle. It will make them feel more at peace. In some traditions, the gods adopt the guise of a stranger, so those who welcome a stranger and invite them into their home are aware that they may have invited a god as their guest. That way, they welcome all guests with honor.*

The Dining Room

I saw a stranger today. I put food for him in the eating-place and drink in the drinking-place and music in the listening place. O oft goes Christ in the Stranger's guise.

—CELTIC RUNE OF HOSPITALITY

How often do you share meals together as a family? In many faiths, shared meals have religious significance. Sikh gurdwaras have a communal kitchen or langar attached to them, where food is freely offered to everyone, regardless of their caste or religion. Both the Bible and the Qur'an compare heaven to a banquet. A good way of making newcomers feel at home is to invite them to a meal. Despite the saying that "there's no such thing as a free lunch," true generosity has no ulterior motive. Meals shared in this way are for the mutual enjoyment of all. Both in the home and in the religious community, a meal together is a sign of fellowship.

PRACTICE *The busy demands of modern life may mean that you often eat "on the run" or wolf down a hurried sandwich at your desk. At home, the varied commitments of family members make it difficult to eat together. However, it is important to find occasions when a family can relax over a meal. Spend some time reflecting on how this can be accomplished in your home. Eating together strengthens family bonds and promotes peace in the home.*

day
142 The Sitting Room

In this family, may peace overcome discord, charity overcome selfishness, devotion overcome pride and the truth always be spoken.

—BASED ON A ZOROASTRIAN TEACHING

Is your living room dominated by the television? Do you find it brings your family closer together or do you shush each other when someone tries to speak during a program? Our granddaughter Sarah's description of a perfect day was of the family sitting round the fire, happily playing games, with a large sheepdog keeping them company. If the home does not have a center where the family can come and enjoy being together, teenagers will always be out and family relationships will become superficial.

PRACTICE *Parents sometimes complain that their teenagers are little more than lodgers. They sleep at home, where they return after everyone else is in bed. They raid the refrigerator when they are hungry. However, they are seldom seen and their conversation is even more rare. If this description has some resemblance to your life, is it because you have been too preoccupied with your own life to give time to your family? Modern life tends to encourage each age-group to do its own thing, but a peaceful home that brings the family together can help to bridge the generation gaps that cause unrest in society.*

The Third Age

We're too old to work,
We're too young to die,
So off we go,
Just Mum and I.

—A BUMPER STICKER ON THE BACK OF A CAMPER VAN

The development of a wealthy, healthy class of people in late middle age is a new phenomenon in Western society. Many are retiring earlier, often in their fifties, and living in fairly good health until their eighties. Members of the so-called third age may, therefore, have as much as 30 years to enjoy life. Many people in this category have money to spend. Another sticker read, "We are busy spending our children's inheritance." A leisure market of cruises and tours to exotic places has developed, but there is a certain unreality in the lifestyle of some people who are in their third age. (Richard Harries, *God Outside the Box*.)

PRACTICE *It is good to enjoy life, but to make enjoyment the goal of life is ultimately unsatisfying. If you are in your third age, there are many ways in which you can give a deeper significance to your life. Some people use their third age to study and increase their knowledge. Others take up charitable work. Some devote time to their grandchildren so that the parents can pursue their careers. If you are among this age-group, you have the time to give to reflection and meditation. Hinduism teaches that this is a period to learn detachment from your previous concerns and to prepare for the next stages of life.*

144 Afraid of Old Age?

Before the teeth fall off from your mouth,
the back bends to the earth
and you become a burden to others,
Adore the Lord.

—BASAVANNA (c. 1106–1167), A SOUTH INDIAN RELIGIOUS REFORMER

Do you look forward to growing old? Rabbi Ben Ezra, in Robert Browning's poem, said "The best is yet to be." But other poets are more chilling. In "Growing Old," Matthew Arnold describes the time "When we are frozen up within and quite the phantom of ourselves." No one knows how they will cope with illness and the physical indignities that old age may bring, but those who have been loving to others will find themselves surrounded by loving care. People of faith also have the confidence that their true self will survive physical death. As Rabbi Ben Ezra said in Browning's poem, "Earth changes, but thy soul and God stand sure."

PRACTICE *As you go deeper into yourself in meditation, you become more aware of the still center of your being and you may sense a deathless reality. People of faith can often face death without fear—even if they dread the process of dying. Lady Swan, a spiritualist who believed in reincarnation, said, "I regard each life as a term at school and dying as going home for the holidays." (Alice Heim,* Where Did I Put My Spectacles?*) Other people who have experienced God's love in this life are convinced that "neither death nor life . . . will be able to separate us from the love of God." (Romans 8.38.) You can also take comfort from looking back at all the good experiences of your life.*

Worried About Your Parents

When you die, you will be again with those you love who have gone before you. Again you will be young and strong. . . . You will be happy whether you were good or bad. So death is nothing to be afraid of."

—NATIVE AMERICAN YUMA RELIGIOUS TRADITION

Most elderly people don't want to be a burden to their families. Although they may prefer to stay in their own home and to die there, increasing physical and mental frailty may make this impossible. In such situations, the children worry how to best provide for their elderly parents. This is especially difficult if you live many miles away. If you visit too often, you may neglect your own family and other responsibilities. If you persuade your parents to come and live with you, you take them away from familiar surroundings and friends and disrupt your own family. If you encourage them to go into a home or sheltered accommodation, you may feel guilty.

PRACTICE *As you think quietly about this, recognize that there may not be an ideal solution. You certainly cannot reverse the aging process. Be honest about your own feelings, and recognize your limitations. Try to discuss the situation with all concerned. Encourage people to be honest. Try to agree on the best plan. It may help you to see old age and death as the natural conclusion to life—the final act of self-giving.*

An Open Door

O God, is there no one to listen?

—SENECA (4 BCE–65 CE), A ROMAN PHILOSOPHER

When I am working, I like to keep the study door open. Although interruptions can be irritating, this means our grandchildren—and our poodle—can come in when they want to. I do this because I once read of a college where all the European teachers kept their doors shut. The only door that was always open was that of an African professor. He explained that "people are more important than footnotes." It is easy to think your work is so important that you do not have time for other people, but many family disputes are caused by a lack of communication.

PRACTICE *Learning to listen is a skill. You may be tempted to dominate the conversation or tell the other person what he or she should do. If this is true for you, it is because your approach is still self-centered because you are thinking more about yourself than about the person to whom you should be listening. Real listening demands both attention and imagination. You need to put yourself in the other person's shoes. To achieve that, you need peace in your own life, which comes from the inner stillness learned by being quiet. A Japanese writer, Dr. Masumi Toyotome, said that "listening is the rarest form of love."*

Recognize Your Own Failings

If God loves us, we in turn are bound to love one another.

—BIBLE: I JOHN 4.11

Do you find it difficult to get along with some people? Is there a colleague at work who rubs you the wrong way? Have you stopped to think that that person may find it hard to get along with you? Self-awareness is an important step on the way to peaceful relationships. It may be that your daughter annoys you because her behavior is just like that of a sister with whom you always argued. Perhaps the colleague at work makes you feel inadequate, because he seems so efficient and successful. How does your behavior in these situations reflect on your own view of yourself?

The real problem may be that you have a poor self-image. It is easy to blame our faults onto our parents. It is said,

If children live with criticism, they learn to condemn.
If children live with hostility, they learn to fight.
If children live with tolerance, they learn patience.

—DOROTHY LAW NOLTE

PRACTICE *Your current behavior may be because you never felt totally loved and accepted as a child. Recognizing this helps you see that you are replaying old childhood tunes in your reactions to your colleague or your child. However, the needle does not have to remain stuck. Accepting God's love will make you more accepting of others.*

day

148 Humor and Forbearance

Laughter is the medicine of the soul.

—RABBI BERTRAM KLAUSNER, QUOTED IN *THE QUOTABLE AMERICAN RABBIS*

Sharing a home with other people can provide a wealth of daily annoyances. The newspaper is crumpled or left upstairs. The toilet seat is not put down, the television control is missing. The trip to school is a nightmare because one child is never ready on time or has forgotten her swimsuit when her brother particularly wanted to be early. At times it seems that you only open your mouth to criticize or complain. However, family life also gives you ample opportunity to practice forgiveness. As our daughter says, "It's not the end of the world."

PRACTICE *A regular time of quiet and meditation helps you keep your cool and put life's daily irritations in perspective. Remember to relax the body and to breathe deeply when you sit quietly. Listening to soothing music or repeating a simple phrase, such as "Peace be still," helps to still the mind. Then affirm your love for your family and think positively about them, remembering their good qualities. Why do you get irritated about little things? Is it because you want everyone to make you the center of attention? Do you have habits that irritate others in the household? Maybe you need to laugh at yourself a bit more and to be more relaxed.*

Forgiveness

May I forgive (first inwardly, then outwardly) those who have most deeply injured me. I would return love for hatred, sweet praise for sour complaints, and good for evil.

—PARAMAHANSA YOGANANDA (1893-1952),
FOUNDER OF THE SELF-REALIZATION FELLOWSHIP

Do you feel sorry for yourself? "For many years I saw myself as a victim," wrote Gerald Jampolsky in his book, *Forgiveness, the Greatest Healer of All*. "I blamed the world and everyone in it for my own unhappiness, but I am now convinced that only forgiveness can provide happiness." In 1973, after a 20-year marriage, he divorced and thrashed around in a mire of pain, blaming himself and his ex-wife for the mess he was in. However, in 1975, he studied *A Course in Miracles*. Instead of blaming others, he took responsibility for his thoughts and actions and asked for God's help in forgiving himself and his ex-wife.

PRACTICE *After he had turned himself around, Gerald Jampolsky said, "I woke up each day with a single purpose—to have peace of mind, peace with God, as my only goal." He added, "I realized how important it is to make forgiveness a continuous daily practice." This involves letting go past bad experiences. Otherwise you assume that someone who hurt you in the past is still out to get you and you project past negative feelings onto the present. Imagine a big garbage can. Put all your anger and guilt into it. Tie a giant helium balloon to the can and watch it go high into the air and disappear. You are free to face the future, no longer crippled by the past.*

Free for the Future

For the past is gone
And I have laid to rest,
For we both now know
We did our beautiful best.

—DIANE JAMPOLSKY, *FORGIVENESS, THE GREATEST HEALER OF ALL*

Would you go to the wedding of your ex-wife? Gerald Jampolsky, in deciding to forgive, found his bitterness toward his first wife Pat gradually changed. When he went to lecture in Seattle, Pat and her father came to hear him. The next morning they had breakfast together, but when Gerald Jampolsky heard that Pat and her husband-to-be were coming back to live in the same town, he had to practice forgiveness even harder. It worked and when Pat married, Gerald took the photos and his new wife Diane did the videotaping.

PRACTICE *Self-forgiveness and forgiving others frees you from the past so that you can get on with your the rest of your life. It also prevents new relationships from being overshadowed by memories of past experiences. As you let go of the past, you may recognize that you have learned from its difficulties as well as from its happy moments. Just before she married, Diane admitted feeling guilty that she had wished her father had been different. However, now she understood his anger and pain and was grateful that because they had shared so little, he forced her to look inward.*

To search and to find
The meaning of life,
Of love, and of time.

—DIANE JAMPOLSKY

Decide to Forgive

When I forgive, I am set free. I am no longer determined by the past.

—FATHER JENCO, WHO WAS HELD HOSTAGE IN BEIRUT

Every parent fears something terrible happening to their child. Marietta Jaegar and her family were on camping vacation in the mountains of Montana. Marietta's children were sleeping in their own tent. As she went to kiss them goodnight, she saw a hole had been slashed in the tent. Her daughter Susie was missing. It turned out she had been kidnapped. With natural feelings of anger and revenge, Marietta told her husband that even if the kidnapper brought Susie home, she wanted to kill him with her bare hands. Yet as soon as she had said this she knew she had betrayed the values she lived by. Marietta said, "I made a decision to forgive the man who had done this." (R. Enright and J. North, eds. *Exploring Forgiveness.*)

PRACTICE *If something terrible happens to you or your family, you are bound to feel angry and to want retribution, but if you get stuck in your anger, it will only add to the psychological damage. "Bitterness and resentment," Marietta Jaegar said, "are death-dealing spirits which destroy us." In your time of quiet, recognize that your anger will not help your loved one who has been hurt. Then decide to forgive. It is a matter of will-power. Let go of your anger. You will still want the criminal brought to justice so that he can no longer harm others, but your decision to forgive releases you from being imprisoned in hatred. Repeat the words of Paramahansa Yogananda, "I would return love for hatred and good for evil."*

God Is Crazy about Each One of Us

Lord, teach us to look deep into the heart of those who wound us.

—SHEILA CASSIDY, WHO WAS ARRESTED AND TORTURED FOR GIVING MEDICAL TREATMENT TO A CHILEAN REVOLUTIONARY

A year after Susie's abduction Marietta was awoken by a call from the kidnapper. By then, she says, "My heart had moved from fury to forgiveness. I kept reminding myself that in God's eyes the kidnapper was as precious as my daughter. I believe in a God who is crazy about each one of us, no matter what we've done." After listening to the man's taunts, Marietta asked, "What can I do to help you?" When he started weeping, she found herself trying to comfort him. Eventually, she visited him after his arrest, telling him she forgave him and hoped he would receive treatment. (R. Enright and J. North, eds. *Exploring Forgiveness.*)

PRACTICE *You may have decided to forgive the person who harmed you or your family, but it is not easy. Try to think about him and his needs. Did he have a bad childhood? Has he been attacked or abused? As you think about him, your attention moves from your pain to his need. You become aware of your shared humanity and recognize that we all do bad things. Everyone needs forgiveness. You may like to repeat part of the prayer that Jesus taught his disciples: "Forgive us what we do wrong, as we forgive those who do us wrong."*

An Oasis of Peace in Your Home

When wives and children and their sires are one,
'Tis like the harp and lute in unison.

—FROM THE CONFUCIAN DOCTRINE OF THE MEAN 15.2-3

We avoided giving our children toy guns when they were small, but some friends said fighting is part of human nature. A group of eminent scientists has said this is not true. The Seville Statement on Violence says that "warfare is a peculiarly human phenomenon and does not occur in other animals." Humans are not genetically programmed to fight. "Warfare is a product of culture," which means that it is possible to create a culture of nonviolence. You may not be able to do much about violence at a national level, but you can start to create an oasis of peace in your own home.

PRACTICE *Is your home a peaceful place? Do you have loud music blaring night and day? Do you shout a lot at other members of the family? What about your language? Do you often swear? Do you watch war films or horror movies on television? How could you make the home more peaceful? Some colors are more restful than others, although a big bill for redecoration may make your blood boil! What games do you play with the children? Have you checked what your children are using on the computer? Many video games are quite violent. Consider ways in which you can bring more peace to your home.*

day 154
God's Mercy Is for All

God's mercy is to all creatures. He does not regard caste.
To him, high and low are the same. All castes can be saved.

—EKNATH (c. 1535–1599), MARATHI HINDU SCHOLAR AND POET

Some people are afraid of touching those with leprosy or HIV. In sixteenth century India, the high-caste Brahmins avoided the so-called untouchables. They would not eat with them nor have any physical contact. The scholar and poet Eknath, however, ignored these rules if anyone needed help. Once an untouchable beggar came to his home for food. Eknath had nothing to eat in the house so he gave the beggar food that had been offered to the gods. Another untouchable man was so ill that he could not walk, so Eknath lifted him up and carried him to get help.

PRACTICE *How great is your sense of freedom? If you are a religious person, is your religion a matter of rules? Do you picture God as a judge or as an understanding parent? Are you rigid in your dealings with your children? Consider whether this is because of the way you were brought up or because you are afraid of pressure from your relations. Does it reflect your own insecurity? Eknath was aware of his failings and weakness but was confident that God loved him. Perhaps you could echo his words:*

Great sinner though I be,
I am still your darling child,
So take good care of me.

—FROM *THE SAINTS AND SAGES OF INDIA*

Illness

Man is born broken, he lives by mending; the grace of God is glue.

—EUGENE O'NEILL (1888–1953), AMERICAN PLAYWRIGHT

Illness in the home is always difficult, but that's where most people would like to be cared for. The serious illness of a child is distressing for the entire family. Other children in the family may feel neglected. Parents may recognize these feelings in their other children but they are compelled to care for their sick child and may need to be with them if the child has to go to hospital. At Helen House in Oxford, England, there are apartments where a whole family can stay and be with a sick child.

PRACTICE *When a child is very ill, parents are likely to ask, "Why did God let this happen?" There is no easy answer. Often the best help friends can offer is to be alongside parents in their distress. The more deeply you have entered into yourself and discovered a peaceful heart at the core of your being, the more you will be able to convey that peace to the child and his or her parents. There are many stories of those in the midst of great distress who have sensed divine peace and reassurance. The conviction that love is the meaning of all things, despite the suffering in the world, is based on the experience of that love.*

day
156 A Year-round Gift

There are places in man's heart which do not yet exist, and into them enters suffering, so that they may have existence.

—Léon Bloy (1846–1917), French novelist and spiritual writer, quoted in Mary Craig, *Blessings*

Many disabled children show a remarkable happiness and open affection. "It is astonishing," wrote Father John Harriott, "how often they draw out from others, especially their parents, hidden reserves of patience and affection." In a Christmas reflection, Father Harriott continued, "How we treat them seems to be in some ways our own and society's acid test. In them, as in the Child of Bethlehem, we see, uncamouflaged, the native value of humanity itself, helpless, vulnerable, possessing nothing. . . . They are fearless: they have no enemies. They are trusting. They are loving. . . . They are a year-round Christmas gift, however crumpled the wrapping." (*The Tablet*, December 18–25, 1976.)

PRACTICE *It is very hard to watch a child who is in pain. Mary Craig, whose child Nicky inspired Father Harriott, wrote, "In the teeth of the evidence, I do not believe that any suffering is ultimately absurd or pointless." Many people have found that caring for those who are suffering has helped them discover a strength beyond their own and taught them a universal sympathy. "Caring is the greatest thing," wrote the philosopher Baron von Hügel. "Caring matters most." (Mary Craig,* Blessings.*) As you reflect on your own experiences of suffering or on the pain in the world, are you moved to a deeper compassion? Can you discover ways to express your concern?*

Every Child Is Embraced by God

God is Love: and God enfoldeth
All the world in one embrace;
With unfailing grasp God holdeth
Every child of every race.
And when human hearts are breaking
Under sorrow's iron rod,
Then they find the selfsame aching
Deep within the heart of God.

—TIMOTHY REES (1874–1939), HYMN WRITER

Children everywhere need the basic resources to develop their full potential. "One of the greatest of all human aspirations is now within reach," wrote James P. Grant, Executive Director of UNICEF, in 1993. "Within a decade, it should be possible to bring to an end the age-old evils of child malnutrition, preventable disease, and widespread illiteracy." (*State of the World's Children* report.) The cost, he reckoned, would be about $25 billion a year—less than Americans spend each year on beer or Europeans on wine. Some 10 years later, the hope has not been realized.

PRACTICE *The poverty of millions of children in Africa and elsewhere is preventable. The world has the resources, but it lacks the will to apply them to those most in need. There are many problems, including the endemic violence in parts of Africa, but the basic question is one of priorities. It is a moral issue. Is it possible to have a peaceful heart until these issues are addressed? If you sense the divine compassion for every child, your heart will be troubled and you will share the pain of God.*

day

158 I Am the Refugee and the Pirate

I am the twelve-year-old girl, refugee on a small boat, who throws herself into the ocean after being raped by a sea pirate, and I am the pirate, my heart not yet capable of seeing and loving.

—THICH NHAT HANH, VIETNAMESE ZEN MASTER AND POET, *BEING PEACE*

When pictures of Vietnamese boat people were in the news, the Asian theologian Choan-Seng Song said God's face could be seen in the suffering of the Indo-Chinese people. "In the disfigured bodies of the children fallen victim to hunger and bullets, someone must have seen God disfigured with horror." (Choan-Seng Song, *The Compassionate God*.) Through their pain, God pleaded with the conscience of humanity. In his poem, the Buddhist monk Thich Nhat Hanh identifies with a young refugee and with the pirate who raped her. If we have self-knowledge, we recognize that we share in oppressive structures that cause much suffering. If we have a heart full of compassion, we identify with the victims. In seeking to help, we are channels of God's mercy.

PRACTICE *In your meditation, ponder the poem of Thich Nhat Hahn or look carefully at a picture of a refugee child in Africa. Imagine the child as your child. Feel for the distant child. Feel for his or her parents. Feel their pain. Only as you feel in your heart your oneness with all who suffer will you be moved to act and to help. Then if you commit yourself to loving concern for others, you heart will be at peace because as Choan-Seng Song suggests it will be at one with the heart of God.*

The World as One Big Family

Make me a channel of your peace.
Where there is hatred, let me bring your love;
Where there is injury, your pardon, Lord;
And where there's doubt, true faith in you.

—Sebastian Temple, based on "The Prayer of St. Francis"

"Will you protect our future?" was the question that 17-year-old Susannah Begg of Australia put to an international meeting of governmental representatives to protect the environment. (*A Source Book for the Earth's Community of Religions,* ed. Joel Beversluis.) Our actions help to determine whether children will grow up in a peaceful home and a peaceful world. As Ryan Phillips, a prison officer in Barbados put it, "If each individual family unit plays its part in loving, caring and enriching personalities, then the world can some day work as one big family." (The Brahma Kumaris, ed. *Visions of a Better World.*)

PRACTICE *Reflect on your own responsibilities. If you are a parent, is your home a peaceful one? Do you provide a loving and peaceful environment for your children? You can do this only if you have a peaceful heart. Whether or not you have children to care for, ask yourself how concerned you are about ensuring that every child grows up in a loving and peaceful home. You can help by supporting parents and educators, by giving money to appropriate charities, by exercising your influence as a voter, and by praying, through which you identify with all in need and become a channel of peace.*

part four

PEACE IN THE COMMUNITY

Like most people, you desire your community to be a peaceful one. Spiritual teachers of many faiths have taught that to bring about peace in the world you must first find peace within yourself. All people share a common humanity and, as some religions teach, each person reflects the divine image. The contribution of young and old, men and women, people with disabilities, and people of a different color and culture should be welcomed, and all should give and receive mutual respect. The individual who seeks the transformation of society requires sensitivity—an ability to apologize and to forgive. The qualities of courage, honesty, and hope flow from nourishing your inner life and nurturing a peaceful heart.

A Carpet of Many Stitches

Broad indeed is the carpet God has spread and beautiful the colors he has given it.

—SUFI SCRIPTURES, FROM SID HEDGES, *WITH ONE VOICE*

Have you watched a craftsman making a Persian or Turkish carpet or seen a skilled worker laying a mosaic? The most precious Indian carpets may have more than 2,000 knots to a square inch. Their intricate detail and variety join together to form an overall pattern. In a similar way, all the human diversity in a large urban area needs to be woven into a unity where each finds enrichment. 'Abdu'l-Baha (1844–1921), who was head of the Baha'i faith from 1892 to 1921, compared a multicultural and multiethnic society to a string of gleaming pearls. This, he believed, was God's purpose for humanity.

PRACTICE *People of different traditions who enter deeply into the life of the Spirit discover a fellowship that transcends community boundaries. If you get to know members of another community, you may find a real meeting at the level of the Spirit. If you do so, then you will see the varieties of human expression as an enrichment of our common life. 'Abdu'l-Baha said that "Religious, racial, political, and patriotic prejudices are the destroyers of human society." If they are to be removed, each person has to look into his or her heart. Each soul is precious to God. If you are confident that your life is valuable, you will give value to others.*

day 161 Recognize Your Brother and Sister

O humankind, behold we have created you all out of a male and female, and have made you into nations and tribes, so that you might come to know one another.

—QUR'AN: 49.13

Do you treat other people as if they matter? A rabbi asked his disciples, "How do you know that night has ended and the day is on its way back?" One disciple answered, "Is it when you see an animal in the distance and can tell whether it is a sheep or a dog?" "No," the rabbi replied. "Is it," suggested a second disciple, "when you look at a tree in the distance and can tell whether it is a fig or an olive tree?" "No," replied the rabbi. "It is when you look on the face of any man or woman and see that he or she is your brother or sister," he said. "If you cannot do this, no matter what the time, it is still night."

PRACTICE *Do you have time for a joke with colleagues at work? Do you really care about victims of a flood or an air crash that you see on TV? If not, ask yourself whether something in your life is lacking. Do you appear self-important or are you self-absorbed? In your time of quiet, think about someone you are going to meet today or someone you have read about in the papers. What could you do to show you really care? John Wesley (1703–1791), the founder of Methodism, said "Love constrains a person to do all possible good, of every possible kind, to all people." How well do you measure up to that?*

Who Is Our Neighbor?

No man is an Island, entire of itself; every man is a piece of the Continent, a part of the main. . . . Any man's death diminishes me. . . . Therefore never send to know for whom the bell tolls; it tolls for thee.

—JOHN DONNE (1572–1631), POET AND PRIEST,
DEVOTIONS UPON EMERGENT OCCASIONS, MEDITATION XVII

How much time do you spend thinking about the needs of other people? If you only think and talk about your own worries, you may end up being lonely. People tire of listening to the same complaints. Even so, many people are limited in their concerns. In the story of the Good Samaritan, who helped an unknown man who had been attacked by robbers, Jesus taught us that our neighbor is not just a member of our family or community, but anyone who is in need of our help.

PRACTICE *It is easy to become self-absorbed. This is why using the imagination is valuable when you hold others in your thoughts. Pictures may be helpful—of family members who live far away or of people in other countries who are victims of violence or hunger. Remembering and praying for unknown people in countries where there is violence or poverty helps us recognize that they are also our neighbors, who deserve our compassion and help. Listen to this prayer from Africa:*

Busy normal people: the world is here.
Can you hear it wailing, crying, whispering?
Listen: the world is here.
Don't you hear it
Praying and sighing and groaning for wholeness.

—FROM *AN AFRICAN CALL TO LIFE* IN *1,000 WORLD PRAYERS*

day 163 In God's Image

God said, "A favorite and chosen slave of mine fell sick. I am he. Consider well, his sickness is my sickness."

—Jal al-Din Rumi

Do you have a family tree? Many people like to trace their ancestors. As vicar of an English village, I get enquiries from people living in Australia or the United States who want to know if their great-grandparents were married in the parish church. Some rabbis think that the most important verse in the Bible is the one that says that everyone is descended from Adam and Eve. All people, therefore, are equal, and no one can claim superior birth because everyone is of the same family.

PRACTICE *As you sit quietly, ask yourself if you treat others as equals or if you go along with society's class distinctions. Do you think people who have a lot of money or high-powered jobs are more important? Do you blame poor people in other countries for their misfortune? If someone in your own family fell on hard times, would you try to help? Spiritual teachers insist that all people are part of one human family. Look at a picture of a starving refugee child and think what you would do if he or she were your own child. Decide how you can help. Remember: When you help the sick and hungry, you help God.*

Rejoice in Our Differences

A man came to his teacher and said, "The king says that I must kill a certain man, or he will put me to death. Shall I put him to death to save my own life?" "No," said Rava, his teacher, "For how do you know that your blood is redder than his?"

—BABYLONIAN TALMUD, PESACHIM

Would you kill someone else to save your own life? You probably cannot answer for certain, because you do not know how you would behave in such extreme circumstances. The conviction that all people are made in the image of God speaks of the sanctity, dignity, and equality of all human life. Jewish teachers point out that when a king stamps his image on coins, all the coins are identical. God, however, makes each person different, although every human being bears his image. Differences should not be a cause of hostility, let alone ethnic cleansing. We should value the rich diversity of human cultures, languages, and religions.

PRACTICE *Reflect honestly on whether you find it easy to get along with people who are different. Do you try to speak to them or do you avoid them? If you avoid them, ask yourself why. If you are too self-conscious or uncomfortable, have you really accepted God's love for you as a unique and special individual? Quietly recollect God's love for you. Then remember that God has the same love for every other person. You might ponder these words in Monica Furlong's poem:*

I am glad you made my Neighbor different from me;
. . . She knows all the things I don't know.

—FROM *LAUGHTER, SILENCE AND SHOUTING*, ED. KATHY KEAY

day

165 Can We Live Together?

Love is not concerned
With caste or creed or race.
Wash yourself of such distinctions

—BABA FARID (1169–1266), EARLY INDIAN SUFI

Can people of different races and cultures live peacefully together? This is a problem not just between nations but within many countries. Governments hope tough measures to stop immigrants and bogus asylum seekers will win popular support. Remember that this can cause much suffering to genuine refugees. Take the story of Pierre, whose father was assassinated at the family home in Brazzaville in the Congo. Pierre and his family were found by the militia. For 2 days Pierre was beaten and tortured with electric shocks, before escaping to a refugee camp in Gabon. Pierre sought asylum in England because, he said, "It is a country of human rights." However, on arrival at Dover, he was sent for 5 months detention in Lindholm prison—although he was eventually given exceptional permission to remain in the United Kingdom until 2007. (From *The Times*, November 8, 2002.)

PRACTICE *Peace in the community requires learning to value people of different cultural and ethnic backgrounds. Long-established inhabitants of a town may resent newcomers if they speak a different language or belong to a different religion. Problems are made worse if jobs or housing are in short supply. If you are to promote harmony in your community, each group needs to see the situation from the other person's point of view. Imagine the hopes and fears of refugees. Try to understand the feeling of a long established resident who finds a "stranger" has moved in next door.*

Flowers of Many Colors

We know there's a difference in the colors of our skin;
So be proud of your heritage and learn from the lesson they give.

—MARVIN WINANS ET AL, QUOTED IN *IN ALL GOOD FAITH*,
EDS. J. POTTER AND M. BRAYBROOKE

What is your model of a multiracial society? There's an old saying, "When in Rome, do as the Romans do," which suggests that newcomers should fit in to the existing patterns of behavior—but what about language? Should everyone be expected to speak English or should the local authorities provide translators and leaflets in the minority languages? For many Asians in the West, language is a way of preserving cultural and family ties, so parents want their children to be at home both in English and the family's mother tongue. Cultural diversity can enrich a community just as Indian, Chinese, Mexican, and many other restaurants have added to the variety and enjoyment of eating out.

PRACTICE *If all the flowers in your garden were the same, it would be very dull. The infinite variety of customs and cultures in most large cities is a great enrichment. In a time of quiet reflection, consider the special gifts different people in your community have to share with each other. How do others enrich your appreciation of the world? The song quoted above concludes:*

If we can learn to love with our hearts and not our eyes—
Love for all brothers, all kinds and all colors—
What a world this would be—for you and me.

Do You Speak My Language?

I saw the hoop of my people and it was holy. Then I saw it was one hoop of many hoops, all of which were holy.

—BLACK ELK, NATIVE AMERICAN SPIRITUAL LEADER

How well do you know your neighbors? Diversity can be enriching, but can also be divisive. In some multicultural societies, people share geographic space but little else. In parts of Northern Ireland, Catholic, and Protestant communities have their own schools and social life. Despite being neighbors, young people grow up in ignorance of each other.

PRACTICE *The ideal is "a community of communities"—a society in which people have a strong sense of belonging to their own community but also to the larger society. There are values that all people share, and a harmonious and peaceful town or city is based on mutual respect. How much does your town or city do to encourage community feeling? Do you take part? Some Palestinian women are learning Hebrew and some Israeli women are learning Arabic so that they can communicate with each other and help break down the hostility between their communities. What could you do to promote harmony and peaceful relations where you live?*

Face Your Prejudices

Pray that two enemies will shake hands.
That makes four hands at peace with each other

—MODERN PRAYER FROM SARAJEVO, *BRIDGE OF STARS*,
ED. MARCUS BRAYBROOKE

Stereotyping whole groups of people is dangerous and divisive. Lady Mountbatten, who was severely injured by the bomb that killed her father, said, "I believe that people can learn from any experience, and they can learn from suffering." She said that her understanding of other people's suffering became much keener. She insisted that, although members of the Irish Republican Army planted the bomb, it was Irish doctors and nurses who saved her life. (Alf McCreary, *Tried by Fire.*)

PRACTICE *As you sit quietly, honestly recognize those groups of people to whom you feel an antipathy—perhaps people of a different color, race, or sexual orientation. Have you had a bad experience at the hands of someone from that group? If so, can you think of others from that group about whom you have positive feelings? Have you picked up your attitudes from your family and never questioned them? Rather than being afraid of those who are different, can you learn anything from them? Make a point of meeting and talking with members of the group you dislike. You will be breaking down barriers and sowing seeds of peace.*

day

169 Discover the Joy of Profound Unity

Lord, you come through thick stone walls, armed guards and bars. . . . Even my cellar blooms with stars and peace.

—VIKTORAS PETKUS OF LITHUANIA

Are there parts of your city where you are afraid to go? Fear of terrorist attacks has added to feelings of insecurity, but urban violence in many countries is also on the increase. Drug-related crimes terrorize many areas. Women are afraid of attack. Violence breeds violence. A 6-year study in King County, Washington, found that if a gun is kept in a home, there is an 18-to-1 chance it would eventually be used in the death of a family member. Yet, even in the darkest places, love can penetrate the hardest hearts. (Charlene Spretnak, *States of Grace.*)

PRACTICE *These problems can be tackled at various levels, by new laws or better law-enforcement, but the crisis is essentially a spiritual one. It is a challenge to reject a selfish and divisive view of life that puts "me" first. Listen to the appeal of Charlene Spretnak: "Find a way that dissolves the deeply ingrained patterns of negative, distrustful behavior caused by past cruelty and disappointment. Find a way that grounds your deeds in wisdom, equanimity, compassion, and loving kindness. Find a way that reveals to you the joy of our profound unity, the subtle inter-relatedness of you and every being." Let the Lord penetrate the cellar of your heart and transform it with his light. (From* States of Grace.*)*

Proud to Be a Woman

O African woman, shed the yoke you have been bearing . . . put on again the dignity by which God created you in the divine image and stand proud—proud to be a woman.

—FROM A PRAYER BY RACHEL JAMES MOUKOKO OF THE IONA COMMUNITY, *LAUGHTER, SILENCE AND SHOUTING*

Men have been dominant in the great majority of societies throughout history. A harmonious and peaceful community today should be one in which women and men share responsibilities. In many countries, there is now legislation against discrimination based on sex, but the particular contribution women have made to community building and peace work is not always appreciated. Elise Boulding, a former Secretary General of the International Peace Research Association, writes, "Women's work of feeding, rearing and healing humans—building and rebuilding communities under conditions of constant change, including war—has produced resources and skills within women's cultures that have been critical not only to human survival but to human development." (Elise Boulding, *Cultures of Peace: The Hidden Side of History.*)

PRACTICE *Does your religion or your community encourage the contributions of both women and men? If you are a woman, you may wish to consider whether you feel treated and accepted as an equal. If you are a man, reflect on recent research that suggests that many men are limited in the healthy expression of their feelings. These thwarted feelings can lead to violent outcomes. The best way of helping men overcome feelings of hurt and frustration is through male support groups, where men can discuss their feelings, and through sharing with women in parenting.*

Small Beginnings

Do all the good you can
By all the means you can . . .
In all the places you can
At all times you can.

—JOHN WESLEY (1703–1791), FOUNDER OF METHODISM

Marjorie Sykes is a woman who made a major contribution to peace. She saw the importance of small local groups in effecting change. Born in a Yorkshire coal-mining village, she settled at Gandhi's ashram at Sevagram, where she was trained in nonviolent action. In 1957, Vinoba Bhave (1895–1982), a Hindu reformer, revived Gandhi's dream of a nonviolent peace army and asked Marjorie to help. She found the program unsatisfactory for training a large number of people. Instead, she set up an alternative model of small village training centers, where eight or nine people came for a month's intensive training. The model was adopted by Peace Brigades International.

PRACTICE *Small beginnings can have a wide influence. Many of the people who make a major contribution to community life never become well known. The influence of small peace-building initiatives cannot be overestimated. Do not worry if you cannot think of some grand scheme. As you sit quietly, consider if there is something you could do today that would make a difference to at least one person. If you do that each day, you do not know how much difference you will make. These words of a Native American prayer remind us to act today:*

Creator, open our hearts
to end exclusion, violence and fear among all
this day and every day.

—FROM *1,000 WORLD PRAYERS*, ED. MARCUS BRAYBROOKE

Children Are Part of the Community

Children have their own thoughts. You may house their bodies but not their souls, for their souls dwell in the house of tomorrow, which you cannot visit, not even in your dreams. You may strive to be like them, but seek not to make them like you. For life goes not backward nor tarries with yesterday.

—FROM *THE PROPHET* BY KAHLIL GIBRAN

The twentieth century was supposed to be the "Century of the Child." The entertainment and commercial world is well aware of children as a potential market, but teenagers, let alone children, are seldom consulted about developments in the community to which they belong.

PRACTICE *If you are older than 30, do you find it easy to engage in conversation with young people? If you are younger than 20, how many people older than 50 do you know well enough to have a serious conversation with? In villages there may be more inter-generational activity, but in many urban areas people are segregated by age as well as by ethnicity. Are there ways in which you could help to bridge the generation gap? It can contribute to a more peaceful society.*

day 173 The Umbrella Man

A poor man from the favelas of Rio de Janeiro climbed up to the colossal statue of Christ of Corcovado and said, "I have climbed up from the filthy, confined quarters down there. . . . Come with me into the favelas and live with us there.

—A PRAYER FROM RIO DE JANEIRO, BRAZIL, JOHN CARDEN, *ANOTHER DAY*

Street children are a problem in many cities. Harry Eva, an orphan, ended up sleeping in the street in Boston. After a week, with no money left, Harry made God a promise. If he found work, he would give money to help other homeless children. On the ground he saw a cent—enough to buy a newspaper. From the advertisements section, he found work at a café, although he was 29th in the line. He started saving. Eventually, he got a job selling umbrellas and later the use of a warehouse for the street children. Over 50 years, the umbrella man provided a home and a start in life for more than 50,000 boys. (Cyril Davey, *50 Lives for God.*)

PRACTICE *When 40 street children met with members of the government of Brazil, they said they wanted education and work. If you are homeless, it is not only the cold and the hunger that gets you down but also the sense that nobody cares—no one will notice if you live or die. Are there ways you could help or support children who have problems so they do not end up destitute? Many voluntary agencies need support, but it is also important to change public attitudes. Are you helping to create a society based on the "survival of the fittest" or one that cares?*

Peace Child

Children are not partial human beings, humans-in-progress. They are full citizens and members of the Human Race.

—SECTION 4 OF THE INTERNATIONAL KEEPING THE PROMISE DOCUMENT

In our village, the annual pantomime brings all ages together. One of the most successful international all-age ventures has been *The Peace Child*. This is a theatrical production that has been taken around the world. Hundreds of versions of *The Peace Child* have been performed on every continent. The productions make both children and adults more aware of peace issues and give greater visibility to the participation of children in public life.

PRACTICE *Do you have artistic, dramatic or musical talents that you could enjoy with children and young people? Sport can also bridge the generation gap. Think back to your own childhood and adolescence. Of the adults in your life, whom did you relate to best? Why? Are you prepared to listen to young people or do you tell them how to behave or what they should think? Consider how much you could learn from the young, as this poem,* To My Students *by Therese Becker suggests:*

You showed me how well you hear
the earth's music,
the music in yourselves
and each other.

—FROM *A SOURCE BOOK FOR THE EARTH'S COMMUNITY OF RELIGIONS*

day 175 No Strangers Here

O Lord give me strength that the whole world look to me with the eyes of a friend. Let us ever examine each other with the eyes of a friend.

—Hindu Scripture: Yajurveda

Can you remember when you first started at school how desperately you wanted to have a friend? We have a plaque by our doorway with the words, "There are no strangers here, only friends we have not met." However, many people are afraid to open their door to strangers. Governments try to keep out refugees because voters fear that aliens take away their jobs.

PRACTICE *In many traditions, the gods often disguise themselves as strangers. Instead of seeing aliens as a problem, put yourself in their position. Remember that first day at school when you wanted a friend. What does it feel like to arrive in a strange country where you may not know the language and do not understand the customs? Imagine how fearful they must be. As you imagine what it is like to be a refugee, the foreignness begins to fade and their common humanity shines through. Reflect on these words:*

Grandfather: Look at our brokenness.
We know that in all creation
Only the human family
Has strayed from the Sacred Way

—Native American Objibway Prayer

Gay or Straight Does Not Matter

We are taught as Hindus that everyone is God's child.
Whether the child is gay or straight doesn't matter.

—MA JAYA SATI BHAGAVATI, FOUNDER OF THE KASHI ASHRAM IN FLORIDA

If you are working with sick people or caring for a loved one in pain, does it sometimes seem overwhelming? Sympathy naturally goes to the sick and the needs of caregivers may be ignored. Ma Jaya Sati Bhagavati, a Hindu swami with a Brooklyn-accent, has devoted herself to looking after people with AIDS and combating the prejudice they have faced. To avoid becoming burned out, every night she says, "At the feet of Lord Shiva, I offer my life, my day, and the hideous, foul things, all that I see. Without this great power of relieving myself of all that I pick up during the day, I would not be able to be."(From Kashi Ashram newsletter.)

PRACTICE *How do you cope with the pressures of your daily life, especially if you live in pain or work with ill or distressed people? You will collapse if you try to take the sorrows of the world on yourself. Meditation is a way to regain your balance, to rediscover your inner self. Believers in a personal God recognize that God bears the suffering of the world. They are only agents of divine mercy. At the end of the day, they place their burden at the feet of the Lord and in the morning ask for strength for the tasks ahead.*

day 177 Break Down Walls

I want to break down walls, Lord
Between your friends and foes, Lord

—From a poem by Father Roger Lesser,
a Roman Catholic priest in India, *Breath of God*

To know Divine Love and acceptance can change your attitude to other people. In prison, none of the other prisoners speak to sex offenders. David "Packie" Hamilton, a member of a Protestant paramilitary organization was in the Maze Prison in Northern Ireland for armed robbery. One night he started reading a Christian tract and by the morning he had given his life to Jesus Christ. He started talking to Catholic prisoners. At teatime, he sat at the table where the sex offenders were by themselves. "When you become a Christian," he said, "you cannot retaliate and you know that God loves everybody, whatever they have done." (Alf McCreary, *Tried by Fire.*)

PRACTICE *Are there "no-go" areas in your life—people you avoid and would not speak to? If so, ask yourself why. Is it someone who has hurt you or a member of your family and you still bear a grudge? Do you disapprove of their behavior? Are you worried about what other people may think? Are you afraid that they will scorn you? Is it because you doubt yourself and want other people's approval? Rest in the assurance of Divine Love to which you and all people are precious. Say to yourself, "I want to break down walls, Lord."*

When Friends Quarrel

Who is the mightiest of the mighty?
One who controls his passions and makes his enemy his friend.

—YALKUT SHIMONI, HUKKAT 764

If two of your friends quarrel, what do you do? Moses' brother Aaron would go to one of the men who had quarreled and say, "See how your friend beats his breasts and tears his hair out, saying, 'How can I face my friend! I would be too embarrassed because I am the one who acted offensively towards him.'" Aaron would sit with the man until he had had removed all anger from his heart. Then, Aaron would go to the other man and say the same thing. Later when the two men met, they would hug each other and kiss.

PRACTICE *Have you ever acted as a go-between? It can be time-consuming and difficult. Both parties will expect you to take their side. You may have to make yourself vulnerable and absorb some of their anger. You will need to do a lot of listening. Avoid giving advice or telling either person what they should do. You are there to represent each person's views to the other and to help each change his or her attitude. It is those in dispute who have to reach agreement.*

day 179

Together to the Finish Line

O God, I place before you my weakness, my helplessness and the little esteem people have of me. . . . There is no power or strength except through you.

—THE PROPHET MUHAMMAD, FROM THE *HADITH*

Those with disabilities can teach the able-bodied the need for co-operation. At the Seattle Special Olympics, there were nine competitors for the 100-yard dash. All of them were physically or mentally disabled. At the sound of a gun, they all started, but one little boy did not get far. He stumbled and fell over and started to cry. The other children heard him crying, and one by one, they turned round and came to help. A little girl with Downs syndrome bent over and kissed the boy saying, "This will make it better." The boy got up. Then they all linked arms and walked happily together to the finish line, to the cheers of the crowd. (B. Martin Pedersen, ed., *Prayers for Peace.*)

PRACTICE *The emphasis on competition in Western society may make you blind to the needs of others. The example of children, as well as those with disabilities, can help you get your priorities right. This is a poem about a 5-year-old refugee "mother":*

At this station another girl I saw, about five years old;
she fed her younger brother and he cried,
the little one, he was sick;
into a diluted bit of jam she dipped tiny crusts of bread,
and skillfully inserted them into his mouth. . . .
This my eyes were privileged to see!

—FROM *LITURGIES OF THE HOLOCAUST,* ED. MARCIA SACHS

Do Not Look Away from Suffering

God—let me be aware!
Stab my soul fiercely with other's pain.

—Miriam Teichner, quoted in *Laughter, Silence and Shouting*

Visiting a geriatric ward or an old people's nursing home can be depressing. Sue Silvermarie worked on an Alzheimer's unit. During her lunch break, she made notes and from these wrote poems expressing her feelings about her work. She used her poems to "counter the tendency only to see the residents as bodies occupying beds." She learned to listen differently to those thought to have lost the skill of communication and found the patients were her spiritual teachers.

Mattie May and Eydie were two patients who always walked hand in hand and were always cheerful.

By their smiles they defy the institution everyday. . . .
Their smiles enchant us out of our despair.

Sue realized that the patients "live immediately and completely in the present." Sue also learned to look the patients in the eye:

Suffering
In the eyes
My job not to look away.

—Sue Silvermarie, *Tales from my Teachers on the Alzheimer's Unit*

PRACTICE *Too easily we look away from those who do not fit in. Perhaps they can teach us a deeper understanding of life. When Sue asked Lupe, another patient, what happens next, she answered, "Rest, Divine Rest."*

day
181

Getting Older

Your old men will have dreams
And your young men will see visions.

—BIBLE: JOEL 2.28

Are you anxious about getting older? It is not only a matter of looks. Many older people feel that their opinions no longer count and they are baffled by a fast-moving society. A peaceful community is one where everyone is valued regardless of age and each person is encouraged to make a special contribution.

PRACTICE *If your hairs are turning gray, are you willing to accept that you are getting older or do you dream of perpetual youth? If you are young, do you get impatient if an older person is fumbling for change? Some people choose to live in retirement communities, but a healthy society should have room for people of all ages. Youth's energy and enthusiasm needs the experience of older people. Reflect on relationships in your own family and community. Is there more that you could do to make older people feel valued or, if you are a "senior citizen," should you be more tolerant of the concerns and needs of young people?*

Do You Know What Causes Me Pain?

To whom can anyone say, "Behold my wounds,
my secret grief . . . my pain."

—SENECA (4 BCE–65 CE), ROMAN PHILOSOPHER

As a child, do you remember doing something naughty just to get your parents' attention? Sometimes people resort to violence because they feel no one is listening to their grievances. There is an old Hasidic Jewish story about two peasants. One said, "Ivan, do you love me?"
"Of course, I do," Ivan replied. "So, Ivan, do you know what causes me pain?" "How could I know what causes you pain?" Ivan replied. "Then you do not truly love me," replied the other. Lack of empathy is one reason why conflicts drag on so long. Failure to understand what causes another's pain easily prolongs misunderstanding.

PRACTICE *Are there people at work whom you seem to rub the wrong way? Have you stopped to wonder why this is? Do you know what causes them pain? In a time of quiet reflection, try to see the situation from their point of view. Could you ask them why you touch a raw nerve? It may be because of some past experience that you know nothing about. Even husbands and wives sometimes show little understanding of what hurts the other. Through contemplation and action, try to develop the kind of empathy that will bring peace to these situations.*

day
183 Remember the Bereaved

Pure religion . . . is this: to visit the fatherless and widows in their affliction.

—BIBLE: JAMES 1.27

Suffering can make you more sympathetic to the pains and problems that other people face. Lady Mountbatten spent long months in hospital recovering from the injuries caused by the bomb that killed her father. She said how greatly she was encouraged by messages from all over the world. Now, when she hears of anyone in distress, she does not make excuses but writes to say she is thinking of them. The kind words of another can bring a message of hope. Hope is essential to keep you from losing heart. It helps you realize that, however devastated you are by misfortune or the death of a loved one, you still have responsibilities toward others. (Alf McCreary, *Tried by Fire*.)

PRACTICE *Spend a few minutes thinking of someone you know who has been bereaved. Have you time to go and see them? People make a lot of fuss of the bereaved immediately after a loved one's death, but the emptiness can go on for many months. It is good to remember their special anniversaries. The bereaved often want to talk about their loved one, but many people are embarrassed and avoid mentioning the loved one's name. Give them an opportunity to express their feelings. If you cannot visit, perhaps you can write or phone. You may be the angel to bring them the message of reassurance and peace for which they long.*

Wisdom as Well as Compassion

Peace is achieved when we control our minds at every step.

—Maha Ghosananda, senior Cambodian Buddhist monk

"Compassion without wisdom can cause great suffering," warns the senior Cambodian Buddhist monk Maha Ghosananda. After 13 years meditating in a monastery in Thailand, Maha Ghosananda returned to his homeland just before the Khmer Rouge were driven into the forests by an invasion from Vietnam. It was a time of chaos and immense suffering. Although he tried to apply the Buddhist principle of the Middle Way, which he interpreted as compassion and wisdom, bringing the right kind of help sometimes takes great discernment. He told the story of the peasant who found a dying poisonous snake that he took home and put in his bed to cure. When the snake was better, it bit the peasant, who died of the venom.

PRACTICE *If you want to help others, you need a clear head as well as a kind heart. Unless you are practical in your help, your assistance may be mere sentimentality, which makes you feel good but does little to benefit those who suffer. For example, if you give money to a tramp whom you can see is an alcoholic, you may merely make him worse. Think about this prayer by the American theologian Reinhold Niebuhr (1892–1971):*

God give us the grace to accept with serenity
the things that cannot be changed,
courage to change the things that should be changed,
and the wisdom to distinguish the one from the other.

day 185 A King Who Would Not Save Himself

Hatred does not cease by hatred at any time: hatred ceases by love, this is an unchanging Law.

—THE BUDDHA

"It would be better to surrender without a fight," King Longevity told his ministers, when the king of Kasi invaded his country. "Then no one on either side will be killed." His ministers rejected his advice, so King Longevity hid in the mountains so that no one would die protecting him. Eventually, King Longevity was betrayed to the king of Kasi, who was still determined to kill him. As he burned to death, King Longevity called out, "If anyone tries to avenge my death, he will soil its purity. Vengeance only leads to revenge and the chain of hatred is not broken. But if one party forgives the other, then the desire for vengeance disappears."

PRACTICE *Forgiveness is the only way to break the cycle of revenge. Some police forces are experimenting with what is called "restorative justice," which involves getting the criminal to meet his victim in the hope this will make him sorry for what he has done and do something to try to make up for his bad actions. However, restorative justice also depends on the victim's willingness to meet the criminal. Would you be prepared to meet someone who had robbed or attacked you or would you want him locked up to pay for his crime?*

Apologizing

In a world full of hatred, let us be loving.
In a world full of conflict, let us be peaceful.

—THE BUDDHA'S LAST WORDS,
SUTTA PITAKA: MAHAPARINABBANA SUTTA AND DHAMMAPADA

King Longevity's son witnessed his father's death, but ignored his father's words. By disguising himself, he eventually became the enemy king's bodyguard. Once when hunting, the king was overcome by tiredness. "Now," thought Longevity's son, "here is my chance for revenge." However, as he lifted his sword, the lad remembered his father's dying words. The king awoke, saying he had dreamed that King Longevity's son tried to kill him. This happened three times. Then the bodyguard admitted he was King Longevity's son and had sought revenge, but had remembered his father's dying words. The king of Kasi confessed his wrongdoing. As the two men clasped hands, the Buddhist story says, "Dawn broke and the morning sun beamed into the forest."

PRACTICE *Reconciling with an enemy takes more courage than exacting revenge, although our macho culture thinks apologizing is for wimps. After an accident you are advised by insurers not to admit when it's your fault and, if you want to sue, not to accept apologies. However, everyone makes mistakes. How do you act if a member of your family damages your car or forgets to record your favorite television program? Apologizing is as difficult in the urban jungle as it was in the ancient forests of India. Accepting the apology takes just as much strength.*

Lifting Up the World

There is no such thing as insignificant work.
Do everything with your heart's love and your life's respect.

—SRI CHINMOY (b. 1916), INDIAN TEACHER OF MEDITATION

As you get older, you may be reluctant to try new activities. An 80-year-old friend attended a talk about yoga. When he told the swami he was too old to try, the swami replied, "It's never too late to bend!" Another spiritual teacher, Sri Chinmoy, has said, "When age is in the heart and not in the mind, nothing remains unattainable." Sri Chinmoy, who is older than 70, has demonstrated this with his "Lifting Up the World with a Oneness-Heart" program. People who have made a special contribution to peace climb onto a platform, which Sri Chinmoy then physically lifts up with one arm to hold them up as an example to others.

PRACTICE *How often do you take time to encourage others or to thank them for what they are doing? Most people welcome some appreciation. Think of the many people who make your life possible—those who enable you to get to work or to get the children to school; those who produce and supply your food; those who provide medical care when you are ill; those who ensure security when you fly—even if you get impatient standing in line for the x-rays. If you consider all those on whom you rely, you will sense the "Oneness-Heart" that Sri Chinmoy teaches.*

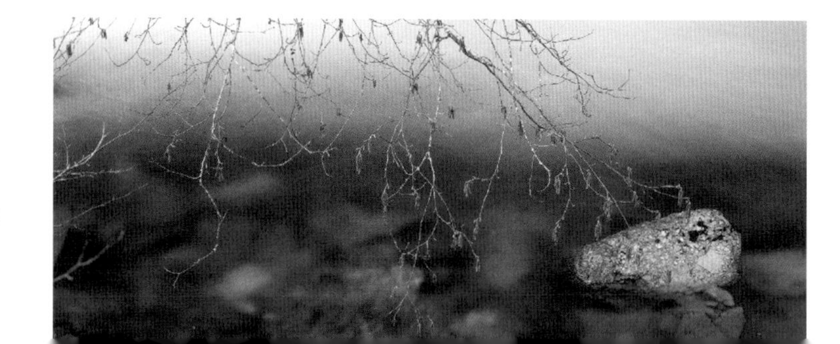

Compassion

Other people do not study the welfare of those who mean them well
As much as you study that of those who seek to harm you.
To an enemy intent on ill, you are a good friend intent on good.

—FROM THE MAHAYANA BUDDHIST SATAPANCASATKA
OF MATRCETA, (C. SECOND CENTURY CE)

Do you think of yourself as a compassionate person? It would be difficult to measure up to the Dalai Lama's standard for compassion. True compassion, he points out, is free from attachment. It is easy to have sympathy for someone we like, but the Dalai Lama says, "Genuine compassion springs from a clear recognition of the other's suffering and that every person is worthy of compassion and affection." Real compassion extends even toward people who are hostile to you. Tibetan Buddhism teaches that compassion is not something to switch on and off depending on your feelings. It is the attitude you should show to all living beings without exception. (Edwin A. Burtt, *Teachings of the Compassionate Buddha*.)

PRACTICE *One way to develop compassion, as suggested by Tibetan Buddhism, is to reflect on the kindness of all sentient beings. It is easy enough to recognize the kindness of those you love, but consider your physical survival. How long could you survive without electricity? It is not just the food in the freezer but also your heating and lighting. How long could the sewage plants operate without electricity? Yet you are unlikely to know those who produce electricity or ensure it reaches your home. Our lives are interdependent and the Dalai Lama teaches that it is compassion that binds us together. As he points out, you cannot even be famous without other people to applaud you!*

day 189

The Surprise of Being Loved

No revolution will come in time to alter this man's life
except the one surprise of being loved.

—SIDNEY CARTER (b. 1915), HYMN WRITER

Soon after becoming a priest, I held a service at a nursing home. The matron asked me to pray with a dying woman. "She won't understand anything," the matron said, "but she's still a child of God." Sheila Cassidy became medical director of a hospice after making the headlines for treating a wounded revolutionary in Chile. "Care for the handicapped and dying," she wrote, "is an expression of *our* need to serve . . . but also an unspoken message to the world that this 'dead loss to society' is infinitely precious." Sheila Cassidy's calling is "to wash the feet that will not walk tomorrow." She added that giving an hour of her clinic time to a woman with only weeks to live was a "statement of her worth." (Sheila Cassidy, *Sharing the Darkness*.)

PRACTICE *How well do you cope with those who do not fit in? Are you tempted to avert your eyes from those who are disabled or dying? They may make demands that you cannot cope with. Their presence is disturbing, and even doctors are uncomfortable with those whom they are powerless to help. Can you cope with their anger or their pain? It is good to recognize your limitations as well as your special strengths and to pray for others who do work you could not face.*

Withstanding Opposition

A peace above all dignities,
A still and quiet conscience

—WILLIAM SHAKESPEARE, *HENRY VIII*, (1613), ACT 3, SCENE 2, L. 380

How would you react if you faced severe questioning or even persecution for your beliefs? One reaction is to respond with counter-accusation and abuse. Another is to doubt your own beliefs. Most great spiritual teachers have endured persecution and self-questioning. The prophet Muhammad suffered physical as well as verbal abuse. One day when prostrate in prayer in the courtyard of the Ka'aba, someone placed the entrails of a camel over his shoulders, but the prophet continued his devotions and a daughter removed the mess. When there was a scuffle, Muhammad restrained his followers. As the Qur'an says (73.10), "Bear with patience what they say and part from them with a courteous farewell."

PRACTICE *Witnessing to the truth is no guarantee of popularity. When you persist in the face of opposition, it is hard to know whether you are being pigheaded or faithful to your beliefs. Give yourself time to reflect. It is easy to confuse your opinions with the voice of God. Self-questioning and humility are appropriate. It is helpful to talk to someone whose honesty and wisdom you respect. You may also need to wait until your mind is clear or, some would say, your prayers are answered. In the end, you will be at peace with yourself only if you observe the voice of conscience.*

day 191

A Prisoner Who Shared

Give to everyone who asks you.... Give it and it will be given to you; good measure, pressed down, running over, will be put in your lap.

—BIBLE: LUKE 6.30–38

Even life in a torture cell can be transformed by people's attitude to each other. Leonard Wilson, who was a Japanese prisoner of war, said that greed is almost overwhelming when you are desperately hungry. However, a young Roman Catholic in his cell, who was a privileged prisoner, was allowed food from outside. He could have eaten it all, but he always shared some of it with other prisoners. The extra food was very welcome, but says Leonard Wilson, "His action raised the whole tone of our life. Others followed his example and learned to share with others."

PRACTICE *Are you good at sharing? Do you point out to your children how much everything costs? Do you try to avoid paying when it is your turn? If you find sharing difficult, reflect on why this may be so. Do you have financial worries? Are they genuine or imaginary? Are you too anxious about the future? Is your reluctance to share because you felt deprived in childhood? Are you jealous of how much young people today have and take for granted? If you recognize your feelings, you may be able to adjust your attitudes.*

Facing the Past

History, despite its wrenching pain,
Cannot be unlived, but if faced
With courage, need not be lived again.

—MAYA ANGELOU, AMERICAN AUTHOR, *ON THE PULSE OF THE MORNING*

How do you regard the past? Public commemorations of past wars besides comforting the bereaved should purge the memory of past guilt and bitterness lest it poisons the present. When the Channel Islands celebrated the fiftieth anniversary of their liberation, Robert Runcie, former Archbishop of Canterbury, warned that failure to heal past memories could perpetuate suspicion into the future. Genuine public apology can be very helpful. President F. W. de Klerk of South Africa apologized for apartheid, saying that the government's change of policy was not the result of sanctions, but of "deep self-analysis on our knees before God." (Nicholas Frayling, *Pardon and Peace*.)

PRACTICE *Healing past memories is important. Spend time identifying memories that trouble you. Sometimes they come when you lie awake at night. There may be memories of something you said or did of which you are ashamed. Be honest and acknowledge it was wrong—even if it is too late to apologize to the person whom you hurt. Some act of penance, such as a gift to a charity, is a sign that you are sincerely sorry. Other memories may be of hurts inflicted on you. Even if there has been no apology, let go the bitterness, both for your own good and for the healing of the world.*

day 193

Whom Do You Call Friend?

A friend loves at all times.

—BIBLE: PROVERBS 17.17

For Jews, the Day of Atonement is the most holy day of the year. On that day, some Nazis took a pious Jew into the yard and whipped him. Then they said to him, "Jew, on this Day of Atonement, preach to us about the Jewish religion." He replied to his tormentors, "My friends, the fundamental principle of the Jewish religion, as of all the other great religions of the world, is: Love thy neighbor as thyself."

PRACTICE *Think about the word "friend." I had an e-mail returned, which I had started "Dear Friend," because the person's program to block junk e-mails assumed that "Dear Friend" must be a commercial advertisement! The word has become cheapened, but the pious Jew used it to his tormentors on the Day of Atonement. A dictionary defines the word "friend" as a person one likes and trusts. Could you say the word "friend" of those who anger or hurt you?*

Forgiveness Frees Us

The only hope for the future lay in an all-embracing attitude of forgiveness of the peoples who had been our enemies. Otherwise one became a member of a chain gang of mere cause and effect from which life has labored so long and painfully to escape.

—LAURENS VAN DER POST (b. 1906), WRITER, EXPLORER, AND CONSERVATIONIST, *THE NIGHT OF THE NEW MOON*

Is Jesus' teaching about forgiveness an impossible ideal? During the Second World War, Ernest Gordon attended a Good Friday service with other prisoners held by the Japanese. Jesus' words from the cross, "Father, forgive them, for they know not what they do," challenged him. "He was innocent," he wrote, "Whereas I was not. Humbly, I had to ask 'Forgive me *and* my enemies, for we know not what we do.'" Slowly, the spirit of Jesus changed the prisoners' attitude to their captors. When the liberating allied soldiers found the condition of the prisoners, they wanted to shoot their Japanese guards, but the exhausted prisoners called out, "Let mercy take the place of bloodshed." (Ernest Gordon, *The Miracles of the River Kwai.*)

PRACTICE *In many conflicts, there comes a time when both sides are weary of the killing. They are exhausted and can see that neither side will gain a complete victory. The same sense of stalemate may help to end a long-running industrial dispute. If only those involved could have seen this at the beginning. In any negotiation, it is sensible to leave room for the other side to maneuver and to avoid deadlines and ultimatums. Even with children, threats should be avoided. Do you carry them out and provoke a scene or do you backtrack and undermine your credibility? In the Jewish tradition, it is said that God prays, "May my mercy suppress my anger." (Marcus Braybrooke,* Time to Meet.*) Humans could well use the same prayer!*

Does Nonviolence Work?

He who is devoid of the power to forgive is devoid of the power to love

—MARTIN LUTHER KING, FROM *THE WORDS OF MARTIN LUTHER KING*

Do you believe that nonviolent protest can really achieve change? Some people think it depends on circumstances and say that Gandhi's tactics were only effective in India because British rule was weakened by an exhausting world war. Some black leaders criticized Martin Luther King for rejecting violence and advocated "black power." Martin Luther King insisted, "Love of our enemies is the only force capable of transforming an enemy into a friend. . . . We get rid of an enemy by getting rid of enmity. By its very nature, hate destroys and tears down; by its very nature, love creates and builds up. Love transforms with redemptive power." (Martin Luther King, *Strength to Love*.)

PRACTICE *How far do you practice nonviolence in day-to-day relations? If you are caught up in a legal dispute, do you encourage your lawyer to seek an agreed settlement or do you go for victory and maximum compensation? When a child is being particularly fractious, do you switch to an authoritarian mode, shouting at the child to do what you say? If you do, you may convey the message that, in the end, it is the person who is strongest who gets his way.*

Are You Honest in Business?

Let justice roll on like a river, righteousness like a never-failing stream.

—BIBLE: AMOS 5.23

Like most people, your main contribution to the good of the community is probably through your work. Rava, a fourth-century Talmudic teacher, said when you enter the next life, the first question you will be asked is "Did you deal honestly in business?" Another rabbi, Ishmael (second century CE), taught that if you conduct yourself with integrity in your economic affairs, it is as if you had fulfilled all the requirements of the religious life. "Morality," writes British Chief Rabbi Jonathan Sacks, "belongs no less in the boardroom than in the bedroom, in the market-place as much as in the house of prayer." (Jonathan Sacks, *The Dignity of Difference.*)

PRACTICE *As you spend time in quiet reflection, ask yourself about your own standards at work. Do people know that they can trust you? Are you honest? Do you do what you say you will do? Would you question instructions from your boss that you thought were unfair or unethical? What about the company for which you work? Does it treat its employees well? Is it concerned about the environment? You may want to use this Jewish prayer:*

Be with us, O God, during the coming week. . . .
Help us to overcome our failings, our forgetfulness of you, our indifference
to the needs of others, our heedlessness of the claims of our souls.

—*FORMS OF PRAYER FOR JEWISH WORSHIP*

day 197 God's Trustees

Our records speak about you with truth. . . . Those who believed and did righteous deeds, their Lord will admit them to his Mercy.

—QUR'AN: 45.29–30

Do you see yourself as God's representative when you are at work? The Qur'an says God created human beings with his spirit to be his trustees on earth (33.72–73). Islam does not make the distinction, common in the West, between the secular and the sacred. According to al-Ghazali (d. 1111), who is considered the greatest religious authority after Muhammad, the whole of life is subject to the law of God or *Shari'ah*. The Law aims to provide for the well-being of all people by safeguarding their human dignity, their families, and their prosperity.

PRACTICE *What do you see as the main reason for your work? Islam sees the primary value of work in its contribution to the life of the community. Voluntary and unpaid work may be as important as that for which people earn large sums of money. No useful work is degrading. Women are permitted to work, provided this does not harm family life. They are allowed to keep any money they earn. They may use it for the family if they wish. All work should be done as well as possible. The Prophet Muhammad said, "God loves it when whatever you do, you do it in the best way." (Hadith: Abu Dawud 6370.)*

Daily Work Is Their Prayer

One who makes his mind up to study Torah (God's Law) and not to work but to live on charity, profanes the name of God and brings the Torah into contempt and extinguishes the light of religion.

—Moses Maimonides (1135–1204), Jewish philosopher and codifier

The prophet Muhammad was told about a man who spent all his time in the mosque praying. "Who feeds him?" asked Muhammad. "His brother," was the reply. "Then his brother is better than he," said Muhammad. In Islam, piety is no substitute for hard work. The great teacher al-Ghazali also held that the ordinary person's devotion was as important as that of the religious elite. "Trust the religion of the old women," he said toward the end of his life. In the Bible, there is a verse that speaks of craftsmen—"Their daily work is their prayer."

PRACTICE *Do you take other people's work for granted? Do you have time for a word with the woman at the supermarket checkout? Are you polite to the worker who repairs your telephone? Our lives are interdependent. The Bible recognized that life in the city depends on the skill of its craftsmen. Manual and semiskilled workers, it says, may not sit in congress or on the judicial bench nor be found "frequenting with philosophers," but "they sustain the structure of the world." Class divides many societies, whether it is based on birth or wealth, but in God's sight each person is valuable and all worthwhile work contributes to the common good. (Ecclesiasticus 38.31–34.)*

day 199

Reflecting on Inner Peace

It is a great mistake to suppose that God is interested only, or even primarily, in religion.

—William Temple (1861–1944), Archbishop of Canterbury

The peaceful person reflects his or her inner peace in all the dealings of daily life. "I do not serve God only when I am praying," writes the doctor Paul Tournier, "but quite as much when I am giving a patient an injection or lancing an abscess or writing a prescription. I serve him when I am laughing at a joke or soldering an electric wire. . . . God has created everything and has put me in creation so that I can participate in it fully." (Paul Tournier, *Adventure of Living*.)

PRACTICE *To those with faith in a God who is the creator of everything, the whole of life is lived in God's presence. The division, common in the modern world, between the sacred and secular makes no sense to the believer. Belief in God's presence should be reflected in all your actions. You will find yourself less impatient in a line, less anxious if the flight or train is delayed, more courteous in your dealings with others. Charles Wesley in a well-known hymn asked the following:*

In all my works your presence find
And prove your good and perfect will.

In your time of reflection, think how you can share your inner peace with those whom you will meet today.

Work without Attachment

No work that is done in God's name and dedicated to God is small. A scavenger who works in God's service shares equal distinction with a king who uses his gifts in God's name.

—MAHATMA GANDHI, *YOUNG INDIA* (1926)

India's caste system has been a cause of much injustice. To overcome that, Gandhi pointed to the interdependence of all people in a community. "It is a law of spiritual economics," he said. "It has nothing to do with superiority and inferiority." The Rigveda, a very early Hindu scripture, compares the different groupings in society to the limbs of the body. The feet are as essential as the head.

PRACTICE *Sri Chinmoy, a Hindu spiritual guide, says, "There are two kinds of work. In the ordinary kind of work, you do something and then you look for the result. In the second kind of work, you do not care about the result. Only by having the right attitude will you become a happy person. If you do the work with a divine attitude, then it will not be the result that gives you joy, but the very act." Reflect on this poem by Sri Chinmoy:*

There is no such thing
As insignificant work.
Therefore,
We must need do everything
With our heart's love
And our life's respect.

—BHAGAVAD GITA: 2.38

day 201 Do Not Let Rules Get in the Way

The Sabbath was made for man, not man for the Sabbath.

—BIBLE: MARK 2.27

Religious rules should not get in the way of genuine human need. Buddhist monks are supposed to avoid contact with women. Once two monks were journeying to another monastery on a stormy day. They came to a ford swollen with rain. A woman was standing there wondering if it was safe to cross. The stronger and taller monk realized her problem and carried her safely to the other side. Afterward, the tall monk noticed that his companion was silent and rather surly. As they approached the monastery, his companion said, "Our rules say a monk should not touch a woman." "Yes," the tall monk replied, "I put her down at the ford, but you are still carrying her."

PRACTICE *It is easy to adopt a rigid attitude in your behavior to others, but your rigid adherence to rules may show a wish to be in control or mask an antipathy to human need. In your time of quiet, reflect on whether you have hidden behind the rules to shut out the needs of another. The peaceful person, in the Taoist phrase, "goes with the flow." He or she does not have to be in control, but is in tune with the movement of life. Picture a river flowing on its way to the sea. Try to let go control, and feel yourself being carried along with the current.*

Speak the Truth

One should not speak the truth in an unpleasant manner
nor should one speak untruth because it is pleasing.

—The Hindu Laws of Manu, 4.138

Do you grow tired of politicians hurling personal abuse rather than addressing the issues? Political debate often becomes a matter of digging up the dirt about opponents. The follower of nonviolence puts up with personal abuse but does not compromise the truth. When the Buddha was attacked and injured by Devadatta, he endured it patiently; however, when Devadatta began to pervert his message, the Buddha strongly denounced this. He insisted that false teaching should be rebuked, although the teacher should not be attacked. "Incorrect things should be corrected," he said. If the authorities heap abuse on you for proclaiming unpopular truths, do not respond in kind. Deal with issues not personalities.

PRACTICE *When you know something is wrong, do you remain silent because you want a quiet life? If you speak up, does it become a slanging match? Before a confrontation, try to have a time of quiet so that you see the issues clearly. Recognize your own fears. Recognize also that you have a responsibility to those affected by dishonesty. Then think about the people you have to speak to so that you avoid personal abuse. Your aim is to help the wrongdoer to admit his error and to change his behavior.*

day 203

Think of Justice First

Think not of life and children first and of justice afterwards, but of justice first . . . Now you depart in innocence . . . a victim, not of the laws, but of men.

—SOCRATES (470–399 BCE), ATHENIAN PHILOSOPHER, FROM *CRITO*

How should you react to laws that you consider unjust? The Athenian philosopher Socrates was condemned to death on trumped-up charges of "corrupting the youth." Political expediency demanded that Socrates drink the poisonous hemlock. His friends urged Socrates to bribe his way out of prison, but he refused. Socrates saw justice as an eternal principle. Disobedience to the law would be disobedience to his parents, to the city that had provided for and educated him, and to the mutual agreement of a citizen to observe the city's laws. Socrates died to uphold the law, even if his opponents had unjustly manipulated it.

PRACTICE *Do you always uphold the law when you are driving? It is tempting to break the speed limit if the roads are not busy. Should you obey a law that is unjust? Undermining respect for the law sets a bad example and may lead to anarchy. Socrates lived in a democracy where change to the law was possible, but in a dictatorship, civil disobedience may be the only form of protest. This is why those committed to a peaceful and harmonious society should seek by nonviolent means for just laws and an impartial judicial system.*

Justice Is Next to Piety

O believers, be steadfast witnesses for God with justice. . . .
Be just, for justice is next to piety.

—QUR'AN: 5.8

If the alarm goes off next door, do you go to investigate or are you worried about getting involved or even of getting injured? There may be a time when you want others to stand up for you. Furthermore, if those who are responsible for criminal behavior are checked, they may have the opportunity to reform their way of life. The Qur'an underlines the importance of everyone upholding the law and helping to protect the victims of crime and exploitation. British Prime Minister Benjamin Disraeli (1804–1881) said, "Justice is truth in action." (From *Hansard*, February 11, 1861.) Others have said that justice is love applied to the community.

PRACTICE *If you are tempted to turn a blind eye to wrongdoing, ask yourself why. Are you afraid of getting hurt or of getting into trouble? Do you feel you will waste a lot of time at the police station? But then think what would happen if everyone did the same? The Irish-born politician Edmund Burke (1729–1797) said, "It is necessary only for the good man to do nothing for evil to triumph." Peace does not come from the easy option of keeping quiet, but from an active struggle for a more just and peaceful world.*

Close to the Gallows

Help us to bear difficulty, pain, disappointment and sorrows, knowing that in your perfect working and design you can use such bitter experiences to mould our characters and make us more like our Lord.

—St. Ignatius of Antioch (c. 35–107), Christian martyr

Anyone in public office should be prepared for sudden swings of fortune. M. F. Jamali, a former Prime Minister of Iraq was condemned to death after the 1958 revolution. Although he was eventually released, while in prison he wrote a series of letters to his son expressing his feelings "while close to the gallows for a year and a half." Despite a natural fear, he felt "comfort and inner peace" because of his deep faith in Allah and confidence that God's will would prevail. He also had a clear conscience, and the sympathy of many friends reassured him that his sentence was a result of revolutionary politics and not because of any wrong behavior. (M.F. Jamali, *Letters on Islam*.)

PRACTICE *Belief that God is in control can free you from anxiety about the future. It gives you a certain detachment even if you have great responsibilities in government or at work. If you act to the best of your ability and in an ethical way, you will have a clear conscience, even if you are not successful. Those who are too worried about success or popularity may be tempted to do what they know in their heart of hearts is wrong, just to stay in power. Try, like Pope John XXIII, to say to yourself, "I do my best and leave the rest to God."*

The Greatest Englishman

Some people think that God gives the faithful one who hopes in Him the shadow of His holy shoulders . . . then what weapon of the devil can give us any deadly wound while that impenetrable shield of the shoulder of God stands always between?

—SIR THOMAS MORE (1478–1535), CHANCELLOR OF ENGLAND, MARTYR

Some people think that Sir Thomas More, who was the author of *Utopia* and Chancellor of England, was the greatest Englishman. More fell out of favor with Henry VIII when he opposed the king's marriage to Anne Boleyn and rejection of papal authority. More was imprisoned in the Tower of London, where he wrote *A Dialogue of Comfort Against Tribulation*. As he walked to the scaffold, he declared, "I am dying in the faith and for the faith of the Catholic Church." Before his death, he wrote a beautiful prayer expressing his longing to be with God.

PRACTICE *Although condemned to execution on a false charge, Thomas More prayed that he would die "without grudge of death." He prayed too for "a full faith and a firm hope" in God's unfailing love. Such confidence helps you to face the trials of life with greater equanimity. St. Paul said he was convinced that "neither death nor life, neither the present nor the future, nor anything in all creation will be able to separate us from the love of God that is in Christ Jesus our Lord." (Romans 8.38–39.) Look into your heart in your time of quiet. Do you have a similar confidence in the love of God?*

day
207 Change is Possible

All my hope on God is founded;
He doth still my trust renew.
Me through change and chance he guideth,
Only good and only true.

—A HYMN WRITTEN BY THE POET ROBERT BRIDGES (1844–1930)
BASED ON ONE BY JOACHIM NEANDER (1650–1680)

Did your parents smoke? Now in some places smokers have to slink outside if they want a cigarette. Many people still "light up," but the public has become aware of the health risks of smoking. In recent years, more people have become aware of the threat to the environment. Real attempts have also been made to break down racial and sexual discrimination. These are examples that change is possible. Change is always slower and less complete than its advocates hope, but alterations in global consciousness do occur.

PRACTICE *Although you can see evidence that change is possible, the real basis for hope is that this is a moral universe, sustained by the power of love. Judaism and Christianity both have a firm hope in the coming of God's kingdom of righteousness. This creates the confidence that redemption is possible. This is why those who seek a better world have to be optimists even though the outlook may seem bleak. On a cellar wall in Cologne, Germany, where Jews hid from the Nazis, these words were found:*

I believe in the sun when it is not shining.
I believe in love even when feeling it not.
I believe in God even when God is silent.

Small Fears Can Seem So Big

I think over again my small adventures,
My fears,
Those small ones that seemed so big,
For all the vital things
I had to get and to reach.
And yet there is only one great thing,
The only thing,
To live to see the great day that dawns
And the light that fills the world.

—A PRAYER OF THE INUIT PEOPLE OF THE ARCTIC REGION

Conflict should not be confused with violence. Violence is the intentional harming of other people for one's own ends. Some societies have been good at educating children to resolve conflict without violence. The Inuit people, who live in the circumpolar North, survive the harsh and unforgiving winter through cooperation and social warmth. Violence and aggression are under strong social prohibition. Social values center on *isuma*—impulse control and calmly thinking through the consequences of actions—and *nallik*, which is love, protectiveness, and a concern for the welfare of others.

PRACTICE *Did you mind being teased as a child? There is a lot of teasing of Inuit children, which teaches them to laugh at their fears and equips them to cope with a hostile environment. It takes place in the context of great affection. There is much fondling of infants, food sharing, communal eating, laughter, and playfulness. Conflicts are handled through song duels rather than fighting. There is no sense of "we-they" or "in-out" dichotomy. Is there anything you could do to break down the anonymity of city life? Your efforts might help to reduce violence and make for a more peaceful environment.*

day

209 Greet One Another

PEACE IN THE COMMUNITY

So long as we enjoy the light of day
may we greet one another with love.
So long as we enjoy the light of day
may we pray for one another

—A PRAYER OF THE NATIVE AMERICAN ZUNI PEOPLE

The Zuni people, who live in the arid mountain canyon country of western New Mexico, are known for their peaceful way of life, their antipathy to overt violence, and their arts and crafts. They practice rituals for sharing, healing, and conflict resolution. Their love of harmony is based on a sense of oneness with nature and a sense of place. The Zuni people's traditional agriculture and irrigation practices are remarkably well adapted to their dry environment. The culture devalues authority, leadership, and individual success. No one wants to stand out.

PRACTICE *It is easy to give an idealized picture of traditional societies, one cannot put the clock back. However, there may be values from which you could learn. You could also reflect on the emphasis given to competition and coming top in our society. Does this undermine a sense of community and of mutual responsibility? How do you cope with conflict resolution at home and at work? The lack of shared rituals adds to the anonymity of modern urban life. Do you greet those who live nearby with love? Do you pray for them?*

Prayer Works

To seek peace is to attain peace.

—GIASUDDIN AHMED (b. 1952), HAGEN BERNDT, *NONVIOLENCE IN THE WORLD RELIGIONS*

Perhaps you think that "doing something" is the only way to make positive changes in the world. When Bangladesh fought for its independence from Pakistan, Giasuddin Ahmed was horrified by the brutality of war and worked as a volunteer with refugees in West Bengal. When he returned home, he concentrated on deepening his life of prayer. He recognized that becoming a true representative of Allah by practicing goodness, forgiveness, and justice is the only way to act effectively against violence. The most important study, he said, is to strive for wisdom. "I must know myself. I must know my Creator and my fellow human beings." By praying, Ahmed gained inner strength and discovered that "prayer in fact works."

PRACTICE *How much time do you spend in prayer? Perhaps you are unsure that prayer makes any difference. However, time spent in quiet reflection helps clarify your aims. You speak with greater confidence and are more likely to inspire others and win their support. When you commit your plans to God, you have less anxiety that everything depends on you. Like a farmer who has to wait for the sun and rain to do their part once the seed has been sown, wait patiently for the results. Muslims, recognizing that success or failure is in God's hands, are told to spend 7 days seeking God's guidance. However, if a quick decision is essential, you might repeat their simple prayer: "O Allah, guide me and make me do the right thing."*

I Have a Dream

I have a dream that one day this nation will rise up, live out the true meaning of its creed: We hold these truths to be self-evident, that all men are created equal.

—MARTIN LUTHER KING (1929–1968)

I have never forgotten hearing Martin Luther King speak. Even if you never heard him, you will probably know of his "I have a dream" speech, delivered on the steps of the Lincoln Memorial in Washington, D.C., in 1964. A carved inscription was later unveiled on the step where he stood, but as David Rennie wrote on that occasion, "It's clear how far away is the table of brotherhood." Washington has the highest percentage of postgraduates of any city—mostly white. However, more than one-third of its population is functionally illiterate—mostly blacks. Racial divisions not only are unjust but also threaten the harmony of any community.

PRACTICE *Are you a dreamer? It is easy to point to difficulties and then do nothing. Congressman Lewis, the only surviving speaker from the Lincoln Memorial Rally, says, "America is a different place. I shall never forget blacks and whites standing in such an orderly, peaceful, non-violent fashion. The march helped to transform the American psyche." Because change is never complete, it is easy to write off what has been achieved. This can then become an excuse for not addressing injustice. The hope that change is possible is essential for those who seek a more peaceful world. As Martin Luther King said, "I say to you today even though we face the difficulties of today and tomorrow, I still have a dream." (Coretta Scott King,* My Life with Martin Luther King.*)*

The Holy City

For I dipped into the future, far as human eye could see,
Saw the vision of the world, and all the wonders that would be . . .
Till the war-drum throbbed no longer and the battle-flags were furled
In the Parliament of man, the Federation of the world

—"LOCKSLEY HALL," ALFRED, LORD TENNYSON (1809–1892), ENGLISH POET

Like Martin Luther King, John the Divine had a vision of the Holy City coming down from heaven. It was as beautiful as a bride ready for her wedding. There was abundant fresh water. The gates of the city were never locked because there was no one to fear. There was no crying there because God had wiped away every tear. There was also no place of worship because God was present in the city. The vision, in the last book of the Bible, was written when Christians were suffering fierce persecution. The problems of urban life may seem insurmountable, but the hope that God promises a happier future is an inspiration to work for peace in the community.

PRACTICE *If you work for change in society, you need times of quiet to renew your vision. Otherwise you may lose hope that change is possible. It is tempting to compromise and settle for second best, but dreams, even if not fulfilled, continue to inspire others to seek a more just, harmonious, and peaceful society. When Chief Albert Luthuli, an early leader in the struggle against apartheid, was imprisoned he commented, "My cell became a sanctuary . . . the opportunity to rededicate myself . . . to be quiet in God's presence." (Cyril Davey,* 50 Lives for God.*)*

part five

PEACE BETWEEN FAITHS

People of faith long for peace and justice, the relief of suffering, and the protection of the environment. However, growing religious extremism has brought violent conflict to many places. To foster the aims of peace, people of many faiths feel the need to dispel past prejudice, to promote dialogue, to forge friendships, and to work together for the good of all. Only as individual people of faith discover an inner unity with the Spirit and become peaceful at heart will they find a unity with each other and all life, which is the true basis for peace between religions and in the world.

Hold Hands

Do not be satisfied until each one with whom you are concerned is to you like a member of your family. Regard each one either as a father, a brother, or as a sister, or as a mother, or as a child.

—'ABDU'L-BAHA (1844–1921), A BAHA'I LEADER

On September 11, 2001, a young Muslim from Pakistan was evacuated from the World Trade Center, where he worked. He saw a dark cloud coming toward him. Trying to escape, he fell. A Hasidic Jew held out his hand, saying, "Brother, there's a cloud of glass coming at us, grab my hand, let's get the heck out of here." People of all faiths have condemned that act of terrorism and held hands to support and comfort each other as they joined together in prayer. As the young Muslim said afterward, "We need to continue to hold hands as we shape a more just and peaceful society."

PRACTICE *Consider how you use your hands. Do you use them to push people away or to welcome them? People use their hands in greeting: to shake hands, to hug, and to embrace. In India, it is customary to join hands and raise them level to the face, greeting people with the word, "Namaste," which may be translated as, "I greet the divine in you." The media often gives to others an enemy image, the person of peace sees in all people a reflection of God. John Wesley (1703–1791), the founder of Methodism, said that like God's love, human love should "embrace neighbors and strangers, friends and enemies; [and] . . . every person of whatever place or nation."*

day 214

What Is True Religion?

I have given each person a separate and unique way of seeing and knowing and saying. The ocean diver does not need snowshoes. The Love-Religion has no code or doctrine, only God.

—JAL AL-DIN RUMI (1207–1273), FOUNDER OF THE SUFI MAWLAWIYYA ORDER

In pondering the question of faith, do you ask, "What is true religion?" or, "Which religion is true?" In every religion there is a struggle between extremists, whose views add to the divisions in the world and those who see a message of unity and peace in every religion. At one level, religion is a matter of cultural identity. What you wear, what you eat, or what festivals you keep unites you with fellow believers—but it can also isolate you from others of different cultural identities.

PRACTICE *Do you picture the world divided between "good guys" and "bad guys," between the "holy people of God" and "infidels or heathen"? This is how many religious people have been taught to see the world. The zealot sees it as his duty to rid the world of evil, which he sees personified in his opponents. The saints in every religion tell you to look within. Recognize the evil in your own heart, and purify your own life. Then instead of condemning others, you will recognize that it is up to you to realize your own spiritual potential. However, to achieve that goal, you need other people's support and compassion as much as they need yours.*

God Is Love

The good news, which the World Redeemer brings and which so many have been glad to hear, zealous to preach, but reluctant apparently to demonstrate, is that God is love, that he can be, and is to be, loved, and that all without exception are his children.

—JOSEPH CAMPBELL, MYTHOLOGY SCHOLAR, *THE SOUL'S ALMANAC*, ED. AARON ZERAH

Religion functions at many levels. At its deepest level, it is the union with the Divine, or the Absolute. It is a personal relationship with the One Spirit that pervades all life. Although the aim of ceremonies and teachings is to help you discover that experience, rituals and doctrines often become important in themselves. When taken to extremes, they lead to division. The Bible itself is often critical of such extremism. Zealots have a fierce loyalty to their particular understanding of God's will, but they see those who believe or act differently as enemies of God. Mystics recognize that God relates in a special way to each individual.

PRACTICE *What is your own attitude to religion? Were you put off as a child by a religion of stern injunctions, rather than the assurance that you are loved by God? Are you an active member of a faith community? Do you recognize that God's love is for all people and not just for fellow believers? You may be "a devout skeptic," seeking spiritual reality, but you may be put off by organized religion. You may have found the divine treasure in your religion, but you may be uneasy with all the trappings. Try to see beyond the "packaging" to discover an authentic spiritual way that is right for you.*

day

216 True or False

All the people of the world are equally brothers and sisters. There is no one who is an utter stranger. The souls of all people are equal, whether they live on the high mountains or at the bottoms of the valleys.

—OFUDESAKI, TENRIKYO SACRED TEXT

In the West, we are conditioned to thinking in terms of right or wrong, guilty or not guilty. This same thinking applies to religion. Only one religion—my religion—can be true, other religions are false. However, each of us is different. We must go beyond that limited thinking to recognize that each person has to make his or her own inward journey. This is because spiritual truth is a personal discovery. Faith helps you find an authentic way to live in harmony with the Universe. As the Dalai Lama says, "I always believe that it is much better to have a variety of religions, rather than a single religion because of the different mental dispositions of each human being." (Dalai Lama, *Ancient Wisdom: Modern World*.)

PRACTICE *Do you feel your beliefs are threatened if someone takes a different point of view? If you do, see if you are protecting a hidden insecurity. See if this fear is leading you to respond with argument or even violence. Those who persecute others think they are defending what is sacred. In reality they are betraying their own lack of conviction. If you are really confident in your beliefs, then you will trust that eventually they will be shown to be true. This is the confidence of the martyrs of every religion. They are prepared to die for their faith, but are not prepared to kill others in its defense.*

Avoid Argument

When a man said to the pious Hasan al-Basri (d. 728) "Let's have debate about religion." Hasan replied, "I know my religion. If you've lost yours, go and look for it."

—WORDS OF HASAN, QUOTED BY MICHAEL COOK IN *THE KORAN, A VERY SHORT INTRODUCTION*

Arguments about religion seldom do much good. According to one of Aesop's fables, the Greek god Hercules was walking along a narrow road when he saw an object that looked like an apple lying on the ground. He trod on it and it doubled in size. Then he hit it with his club and the object swelled until it filled the road. Athena then appeared and said, "Leave that thing alone, dear brother! It is the spirit of argument and discord. If you don't touch it, it does no harm, but if you try to fight with it, it grows as you have seen."

PRACTICE *Differences of opinion cannot be avoided, but it is more productive to listen patiently to each person's point of view, rather than to interrupt and argue. Otherwise you run the risk of escalating the situation. In religious discussion, it is often better to understand the experience or conviction that underlies a religious teaching. Rather than disagree, you could ask, "Why is this teaching so important to you? Does it make a difference in how you live?" You may discover you have a similar view, but express it in a different way. Religious teachings are often communicated through story, myth, and parable. Because of this, there is often room for various interpretations of a Mystery no one fully understands.*

day
218 Pointless Discussion

Let us be united; Let us speak in harmony;
Let our minds apprehend alike. Common be our prayer;
Alike be our feelings; Perfect be our unity.

—HINDU SCRIPTURES: THE RIG VEDA

The needs of the suffering can make arguments about religion irrelevant and offensive. The Buddha said such debates are like a man "who had been wounded by an arrow thickly smeared with poison," telling his relations, who wanted to send for a doctor, "I will not have the arrow taken out until I know what caste the man belonged to." Such debates are also like a man who refused help until he learned whether the person who injured him was "black or dusky or of a yellow skin." The man would die, the Buddha said, "without having learned the answer."

PRACTICE *Do you find yourself engaged in arguments that lead you away from what you originally set out to do? It is important to concentrate on the main objective. Religious groups can become concerned about status rather than their stated aims. I remember an instance when the patrons of one organization argued about the order in which their names were printed on the stationery. The Buddha said that putting an end to suffering is more important than arguments about who was to blame for causing it. If you are to be effective in working for peace between religions, you need to purify your heart and be free from attachment to winning an argument or proving your point. Avoid wasting time trying to assign blame for the world's problems. Instead, concentrate on healing the world.*

Discovering What You Share

Let all listen and be willing to listen to the doctrines professed by others.

—EMPEROR ASOKA (THIRD CENTURY BCE),
INDIAN RULER WHO CONVERTED TO BUDDHISM

If you meet someone of a different religion or political party, do you emphasize your differences or do you try to find some common ground? Abbé Paul Couturier (1881–1953) was a French Catholic priest who worked in Lyons. In the 1920s, he met some Russian refugees, who were Orthodox Christians. This led him to start the Week of Prayer for Christian Unity. During the Second World War, he was imprisoned by the gestapo and found himself sharing a cell with a young communist. After about a week, the young man was taken away and shot. Abbé Paul sent a letter to the young man's parents, saying, "Although we were separated in many things, we shared a passion for justice."

PRACTICE *How good are you at listening? If you want to get beyond disagreements, you need to hear and understand what the other is saying. We are often too quick to interrupt. In his prison cell, Abbé Paul had time to listen to the deep concerns of the young communist. Do you have friends who belong to another religion or who are skeptical of all religion? Have you had time to talk with them in depth? Do you welcome the exchange of ideas and concerns or are you closed to the views of others? As you grow in inner assurance and peace, you become more open and receptive to others. It has been said, "We are really only ready for Heaven when we are completely open." (Wayne Teasdale,* The Mystic Heart.*)*

God Sees No Difference

Make mercy your mosque and faith your prayer mat.

—GURU NANAK: VAR MAJI 7.1

Have you sometimes thought that religion does more harm than good? Although many conflicts are embittered by religious differences, spiritual teachers insist that there is only one God, who is lover of all people. Guru Nanak (b. 1469), the founder of the Sikh religion, had a profound experience of God. He declared, "God is neither a Hindu nor a Muslim." Rejecting religious differences that divide people from each other, Nanak insisted that there is One God, the Creator of all people. When he visited the Muslim holy city of Mecca, he fell asleep with his feet toward the holy Kaaba. When someone complained, he replied, "Kindly turn my feet in some direction where God is not."

PRACTICE *It is right to celebrate your own faith, but there is no need to denigrate the faith of others. Although rituals and special clothing may strengthen some people's religious commitment, they should not become a cause for division. Indeed, the more you value your religion, the more respect you should develop for the religious practices of other people. The ways of worship may be different, but all religions teach love, respect, and care toward other people. Do you have a tendency to look for commonality or differences? Have you tried to make friends with people of other religions or prayed for them?*

What Is Your Religion?

Don't ask my caste or creed
These only cause division.

—KABIR (b. 1518), INDIAN SAINT AND POET

Although he grew up at a time of fierce rivalry between Hindus and Muslims in India, the Indian saint and poet Kabir insisted that their respective names for God, Rama, and Allah are only different ways of addressing the same Divine Reality. Stressing God's love for all, Kabir rejected divisions based on caste, class, or religion. At his death, it is said that Hindus wanted to cremate him, whereas the Muslims insisted on burying him. When the cloth covering his body was pulled aside, they found nothing but flowers.

PRACTICE *Do you believe God has a special link with your own faith community or do you agree with Kabir that there are different names for the one God? Religious differences can still cause divisions, even in a modern family. How would you feel if your son or daughter started going out with a member of another religion? Some traditional faith communities strongly discourage this. Would you welcome your child's friend into your home or would you try to persuade your child to change his or her mind? Spend some time analyzing your reactions.*

A Parliament of Religions

When the religious faiths of the world recognize each other as children of one Father . . . then, and not till then, will the nations of the earth yield to the Spirit of concord and learn war no more.

—CHARLES BONNEY, PRESIDENT OF THE WORLD'S PARLIAMENT OF RELIGIONS, 1893

The celebration of the 400th anniversary of the "discovery" of America by Christopher Columbus was marked by a World Fair in Chicago. Charles Bonney, a prominent lawyer from Illinois, suggested that the "crowning glory" of the fair should be a series of academic congresses. Chief among these was a meeting of the representatives of the world's religions. That meeting was the genesis of the modern interfaith movement. Since that time, a number of spiritual leaders have been exploring the values religions share and the ways people of different faiths can work together for a more peaceful world.

PRACTICE *Do you think that dialogue between faiths can bridge differences and help promote peace? Over the last 100 years, interfaith groups have grown up in many parts of the world. Some are large international organizations. Others are small groups of people meeting in someone's home. Regardless of their size, the friendships made in these meetings have transformed the relations between the world's religions. Find out if there is a local interfaith group in your area. By speaking with those of other faiths, you might find that you have deepened your own as well as promoting the cause of peace.*

Vivekananda

We believe not only in universal toleration, but we accept all religions as true.

—SWAMI VIVEKANANDA (1863–1902),
LEADER OF THE RAMAKRISHNA MOVEMENT

Swami Vivekananda, the most colorful character at the 1893 World's Parliament of Religions, nearly did not get there. He happened to see in India a notice about the meeting and made his way to Chicago, where he arrived late in the evening and spent the first night sleeping in a box at the station. He had arrived in July, but the Parliament was not until September. The next day Vivekananda walked to the center of the city and sat down, waiting to see what would happen. A friend of one of the organizers saw him in his bright robes and took him to her house. At the Parliament, his message that "all religions are attempts of the human soul to realize the Infinite" received a great welcome.

PRACTICE *Have there been "accidents" in your life that led you to the right place? When you look back, do you find that some of the turning points in your life have been unexpected? Some people derive confidence from these events that their life is guided by God or shaped by destiny. Does the recognition of a pattern in your life encourage you to think about the future and what you should be doing in the years ahead? Does it make you want to put your life to good use? Could you be doing something in your community to promote friendship between people of different outlooks on life?*

A Friend in Need

In five ways a person should minister to his friends and companions: by generosity; by courtesy, by benevolence; by equality, treating them as he treats himself; and by being true to his word.

—BUDDHIST SCRIPTURES: DIGHA-NIKAYA.

My wife and I traveled to India for the centenary of the 1893 World's Parliament of Religions. We began our visit at Vivekananda's rock at the southern most tip of India. We were not acclimatized to the heat, and Mary felt rather faint. A Baha'i arranged for us to reboard the ferry, and a Hindu drove us back to the hostel. After a while there was a knock on the door. It was a Zoroastrian lady who handed us an envelope, which we had dropped, containing our passports, tickets, and some traveler's checks. Each person helped in our journey.

PRACTICE *In times of need, racial and religious differences cease to matter. Can you think of a time when someone of another country or religion came to your aid? Perhaps there was an occasion when you helped someone from abroad. When you get to know someone as a person, differences fade. You discover that you have the same feelings and needs. When there is a natural disaster, people from many countries come together to help. By building up friendship with people of other religions or cultures, you break down the divisions in society and help to create a more peaceful world.*

Unite Our Hearts

O God, Make good that which is between us, unite our hearts and guide us to the paths of peace.

—MUSLIM PRAYER, FROM *THE GIFT OF PRAYER*. ED. JARED T. KIELING

Would you hesitate to help the victim of an accident because they belonged to another religion? Francis Younghusband, who founded the World Congress of Faiths, was run over by a car in Belgium in 1915. "A crowd with agonized expressions collected round me," he said, "They showed the utmost concern for me, and did all they could to help me." "No one," he continued, "enquired whether I was Belgian, French German or English or whether I was a Hindu, Muslim or Christian. . . . I was a human like themselves. What hurt me hurt them." (Marcus Braybrooke, *A Wider Vision*.)

PRACTICE *As you meet people of another faith, you discover a common human bond. As you look more deeply into yourself in meditation, you will sense a oneness with the Spirit in which you also feel a deep peace and sympathy toward other people. Younghusband spoke of his experience, "That in the Heart of Things and in the heart of every single person, a Power is working not merely for good but for unbelievable joy." In the stillness, be aware that you are part of a Whole, in which every other person has a place.*

If You Prick Us, Do We Not Bleed?

Hath not a Jew eyes? . . . senses, affections, passions? If you prick us do we not bleed? If you tickle us, do we not laugh? If you poison us, do we not die?

—Shylock in Shakespeare's *The Merchant of Venice*, Act 3, Scene 1

Sadly, people of all nations have used religious differences as reason to kill each other. Christians and Muslims killed each other during the Crusades. Muslims and Hindus slaughtered each other when India was partitioned. Christian prejudice and persecution of the Jews has caused untold suffering. Even today suicide bombers, who kill innocent victims, claim to do so in the name of religion. The danger is that people can put loyalty to a religion in the place of God. The one God is Creator and Savior of all. True religion repudiates the cruelty done in its name.

PRACTICE *Do you allow your beliefs to separate you from other people? The peaceful person respects the beliefs and behavior of another person, provided they do no harm to others. If you follow a moral way of life, do you find yourself looking down on others who are not so disciplined? Once you cut yourself off from others, you may find yourself believing malicious information about others. Are you open to others or are there certain groups of people whom you avoid?*

Grow in the Light

The great prophets of all religions have wanted peace—peace within ourselves and within our world. Each of us is called to grow in the light so that this peace is achieved, at least a little more, right now right here.

—KAMILAH, A MUSLIM MEMBER OF MULTIFAITH EXPLORATION AND EXCHANGE, DALLAS, TEXAS

Learning about other spiritual traditions not only is personally enriching but also enables you to contribute to a more peaceful world, as Kamilah, a devout Muslim in Dallas discovered. Islam, she says, helped her discover her inner self. "As we travel life's road," she said, "we sometimes live only from the outer trappings of ourselves. We have to discover and control the inner core of ourselves or we will never be able to control our outer world." Thanks to the Multifaith Exploration and Exchange, Kamilah has worked with people of other religions. This, she says, "has reinforced and enhanced my own beliefs. It has shown me that Allah's light is for everyone, that it is a light that must be carried into the twenty-first century." (E. Espersen, *Meeting in Faith.*)

PRACTICE *Do you have friends who belong to other religions? A new relationship between religions depends on individual members discarding old prejudices and meeting and getting to know members of other faiths. Increasingly, members of different religions are working together for peace and justice, for the relief of suffering, and for the protection of the environment. This is done through both local and international organizations. If you get involved you will discover that despite the wonderful variety of teachings and ceremonies, we are members of one human family and share the divine nature at the deepest level of the Spirit.*

day 228

You Can Be a Bridge Builder

You are one and the same God, pleased and displeased by the same things for ever.

—FROM THE ZOROASTRIAN SCRIPTURES

Local interfaith groups work together for the good of the community. Zoroastrianism is an ancient religion, but now has very few followers. Charlotte grew up in Pakistan, where her family were practioners of that faith, but it was not until she was a teenager that she discovered the ancient wisdom of Zoroaster, the great teacher of her family's religion. She moved to the United States when she was 24. She wanted her new community to make a positive contribution to America. One of Charlotte's hopes is that she can help the Zoroastrian community feel secure in its identity. She says that by joining in Dallas' Multifaith Exploration and Exchange program, the Zoroastrian community has gained in self-esteem. Sharing in the local interfaith program this way has brought Dallas' Zoroastrians themselves closer together. (E. Espersen, *Meeting in Faith*.)

PRACTICE *Do you stick to your own community or do you make an effort to build bridges? You can help newer communities feel they have a place in society by getting to know them. Charlotte was glad to find other Americans were interested in the Zoroastrian community. I recently asked a Muslim woman at the supermarket checkout line where she was from and how she liked living in England. "Not much," she said, "No one ever speaks to me." It is the small local bridges that really count.*

Long Hair

You, Lord, are my father, you are my mother,
You are my Savior everywhere,
So why and from whom shall I be afraid?

—FROM THE SIKH SCRIPTURES, THE GURU GRANTH SAHIB

"How do you cope at school?" members of an interfaith group asked Kulbirm, a teenage Sikh. "Did other students laugh at your long hair and turban?" "My parents always believed in me and encouraged me to explain to others what seemed different," Kulbirm answered. "Whenever I could, I told them why Sikhs do not cut their hair and wear turbans. Gradually, other students realized I would not waiver in my convictions and they came to respect me." Honest explanations can help undo prejudice. A harmonious community is not one where everyone is the same, but where everyone is respected. (E. Espersen, *Meeting in Faith.*)

PRACTICE *How sensitive are you to the needs of minorities? Have you ever been treated as a minority? If so, you may understand the difficulties of minorities. In fact, most of us belong to several minorities. A peaceful society depends on each group respecting the other. Take time to imagine what it is like to belong to a minority. Does it help you to see how you can help bridge the divide between your groups?*

day 230

God of Many Names

Religions meet, where religions take their source in God.

—Evelyn Underhill (1875–1941), English writer on Mysticism

"If you make friends of people of another faith, you will make enemies in your own religion." This half-serious comment has an element of truth. Dadu Dayala (c. 1543–1603) was born into a Muslim family, but his spiritual poems were written in Hindi. He taught people constantly to repeat the name of God, saying, "In remembrance of God is peace. . . . Delight in God through constant remembrance, so shall you find happiness." He knew both the Hindu and Muslim scriptures, but insisted "I am neither a Hindu nor a Muslim. I love the all merciful God." As a consequence, he met with opposition from members of both religions. (Roger Lesser, *Saints and Sages of India.*)

PRACTICE *How often during the day do you say the name of God? In the West, God's name is often used only as a swear word. Eastern traditions stress the value of repeating the name of God, much as a lover repeats the name of his or her beloved. Repetition of God's name is a good focus for stilling the mind in meditation. Choose the name for God that is most familiar to you or use a more universal word, such as "Beauty" or "Love." As you slowly repeat it, your mind will be uplifted and you will be at peace. In the presence of the Divine, you realize that names do not matter provided they lead you to the reality.*

Interfaith Football

It is when you give of yourself that you truly give. . . .
Through the hands of such as these God speaks,
And from behind their eyes, God smiles upon the earth.

—KAHLIL GIBRAN, *THE PROPHET*

Getting to know people of another religion can be great fun. It does not have to be serious discussion poring over learned commentaries. More than 150 children, aged 9–12, from 16 different Jewish, Muslim, and nondenominational schools took part in the Interfaith Football Program 2003. Arranged by the Maimonides Foundation, it was held at the Arsenal Football Club in London. The children played in mixed Jewish and Muslim groups according to their age. The Muslim children were from several countries, including Pakistan, India, Bangladesh, Morocco, Egypt, and several African countries. The Jewish children came from Orthodox, Reform, Masorti [Conservative], and Liberal congregations. (From the local community newsletter.)

PRACTICE *Sport is not the only interfaith activity. Several interfaith groups arrange pilgrimages to sacred places. As you travel together, you get to know each other and you see the holy place through the eyes of those who worship there. I had visited the Western Wall at Jerusalem several times as a tourist, but late one evening I went with a Jewish friend whose father was very ill. As she approached the wall to put a scroll with a prayer for his recovery into it, I sensed the sacredness of this holy site. As you enter into the spiritual yearnings of members of other religions, you become aware that at heart humanity is one.*

day 232

Music and Food

When you speak of your faith, do not be defensive. . . . Be like the birds in the skies: they sing and fly and do not defend their music or their beauty.

—Ramon Panikkar (b. 1918), global scholar of religion

Music can be another way to bring people together. In Delhi, at a time of high communal tension and violence in India, I attended a children's concert in which choirs from 11 religions took part. Although the music was varied, there was a pervading harmony. Most people also enjoy sharing meals together. In many religions, special foods are associated with religious festivals. Sometimes at interfaith gatherings, each religious group shares its unique delicacies. If you visit a place of worship you will usually be offered some refreshments. Sharing food is a good way to establish friendship and build bridges over religious bigotry to a more peaceful world. Music also has universal appeal, but if you arrange an interfaith concert, be careful to consult with all participants so that everyone is happy with the program.

PRACTICE *Have you entertained members of another religion at a meal? Ancient Greeks were urged to entertain a guest as if they had invited a god to dine with them. Many other traditions place great importance on honoring their guests. Preparing food for members of another religion requires thoughtfulness and care. Most Hindus and Jains are vegetarian. Jews and Muslims do not eat pork. Hindus and Muslims do not drink alcohol. When an interfaith group in Dallas visited a mosque, members were invited to enjoy a light lunch. This was in the middle of Ramadan, the month of fasting. The Muslim women could not themselves partake of the meal, but they wanted to honor their guests by offering them a meal.*

Reading the Scriptures Together

When a company meets together in a house of God to pore over the scriptures and to study them together, the holy presence of God comes down to them and mercy overshadows them and angels surround them.

—THE PROPHET MUHAMMAD

Do you find religious texts puzzling when you first read them? I once heard a preacher read out a knitting pattern in the middle of a sermon. His point was that almost every activity has its own technical language. Most people need some guidance. This is why it is helpful to read passages of scripture with a member of the relevant religion. There are parallels to some Biblical stories in the Qur'an, so when Jews, Christians, and Muslims read texts together, everyone gains fresh insights. Some of the Dalai Lama's comments on the Sermon on the Mount have helped Buddhists and Christians see what they share, even if they come from different starting points.

PRACTICE *If you are interested in reading scriptures of traditions other than your own, it is helpful to begin with an anthology. Sharing in study with members of other religions is even better. Each religion has its own way of approaching the Divine. Their scriptures are like so many guidebooks to the same journey. Each one has its special information and point of view. You may prefer your chosen book, but if you keep an open mind, you will be enriched by learning from others. Chances are, you will learn more about your own tradition by enquiring into the views of others.*

day 234

Let Your Studies Melt in the Mind

The fish trap exists because of the fish; once you've gotten the fish, you can forget the trap. . . . Words exist because of meaning; once you've gotten the meaning, you can forget the words.

—CHUANG-TZU, CLASSICAL TAOIST TEACHER

A young Tibetan monk returned to his monastery after being away for a long time studying. A senior monk said to him, "Your mind must be full of Dharma [or religious teaching] after all your study." "Venerable sir," the young monk replied, "I have learned much Dharma, but I do not know how to practice what I have been taught. Are there instructions which will help me?" The senior monk gave him an initiation which transferred spiritual power, saying to him:

Just as the particles of precious metal
become well-fused by the smith,
so the various things you have studied
must melt together in your mind.

—*THE SOUL'S ALMANAC*, ED. AARON ZERAH

PRACTICE *If a philosophical or religious teaching is to transform your life, you must make it your own. In the past, religious teachers often relied on authority. The faithful were required to believe fixed doctrines and to behave in certain ways because this is what their religion demanded. Teachings and practices need to become part of you, through your own contemplation and experience, if your faith is to be authentic. Spend time reflecting on your basic beliefs. It may help to write them down as a sort of personal creed. Do they rest on a firm foundation of understanding or are you simply repeating what you have been told? Reflect on the truth of what you understand. Then what you have learned at different stages of your life will melt together in your mind and provide an integrity and wholeness to your outlook and behavior.*

Humility

The person who looks down on others because of his own wisdom has never won people's hearts. The person who in spite of his own wisdom is humble to others has never failed to win people's hearts

—BOOK OF LIEH-TZU, CLASSICAL TAOIST TEXT

Status is unimportant to the truly religious person. But some teachers rely on their position for authority. A traditional Jewish story tells that the rabbi of Chelm and one of his students stayed overnight at an inn. The student asked a servant to wake him before dawn so he could catch an early train. Not wanting to wake the rabbi, the student groped for his clothes in the dark, but mistakenly dressed himself in the rabbi's garments. He hurried to the station and was amazed when he glanced in the compartment mirror. "What an idiot the servant is," he cried angrily, "I asked him to wake me, but he woke the rabbi instead." (Aaron Zerah, ed. *The Soul's Almanac.*)

PRACTICE *The zealot assumes that his teaching has the authority of God. One may believe that a scripture is literally the word of God, but the true teacher knows that his interpretation may not be perfect. You can be convinced your religion is true, without claiming that your understanding of it is complete. True spiritual authority is not a matter of special clothes or titles, but of the humility that comes from true wisdom. A Sufi master reproved a follower, saying, "By fixing your eyes only on me, you learn nothing from the holy souls we meet on our journeys." Without this humility, you cannot approach members of other religions and help to heal the religious divisions in the world.*

day 236

Finding a Guru

Let us worship our guru as we worship God, but let us not obey him blindly. Let us think for ourselves.

—SWAMI VIVEKANANDA, QUOTED IN *RELIGIOUS LEADERS*, ED. JACQUES BROSSE

It isn't always easy to find a spiritual teacher. Appearances can be deceptive. Once two Brahmins went to see Dadu Dayala, a North Indian saint. On their way, the Brahmins met a bald man, which was a bad omen. They knocked on the man's head and demanded, "Where is the teacher's house?" When they arrived there, they were told the teacher had just gone out. When Dadu returned, they were horrified and ashamed to see he was the same bald man. Dadu said, "When a customer buys an earthen pot, he taps it to see it is not broken. You should also test a Master before you follow him."

PRACTICE *There are many paths to inner peace, but it is best to find one that suits you and then to follow it. Otherwise, you are like someone with a map who keeps changing his route to a city and never gets there. Some people like to have a soul-friend with whom they can share the deepest confidences. Others follow a guru or spiritual guide. Sometimes the most helpful teacher is not the most famous. Spiritual teaching should be free, although devotees like to offer gifts. The true guru respects the follower's freedom and avoids pressure. As Dadu said, make sure the teacher is right for* you, *even if a spouse or best friend is an admirer.*

The True Teacher

Work out your own salvation with diligence.

—The Buddha

How do you find the right religious teacher for you? Advertisements for religious groups are almost as plentiful as cereal boxes at a supermarket. Jacques Brosse, in his book *Religious Leaders*, provides criteria by which a true spiritual teacher can be recognized. First, he or she does not derive material benefit from teaching. Secondly, a true leader is not concerned with his or her status and is totally indifferent to people's opinions. The religious leader is a guide along the spiritual path. The teacher should be able to lead based on his or her own experience. The teacher should lead by example, never by imposing truths that he or she has discovered, because each disciple has to discover the truth for himself or herself. Most teachers, although true to their own religion, respect other paths and stress the link between inner peace and service in the world.

PRACTICE *Is your faith community meeting your spiritual needs? If not, is that your fault? Should you make suggestions to the leaders about how they could be more helpful? Should you move on? If you do not belong to a faith community, do you think joining one would be supportive and strengthen your commitment? If you are looking for a spiritual teacher, consider the guidelines outlined by Jacques Brosse.*

day

238 How Does the Rabbi Tie His Shoes?

Write it on your heart that every day is the best day in the year. He is rich who owns the day, and no one owns the day who allows it to be invaded with fret and anxiety.

—RALPH WALDO EMERSON (1803–1882), TEACHER OF TRANSCENDENTALISM

How considerate and peaceful are you in daily life? Holiness is not just a matter of regular religious observances but of the quality of your daily life. A Hasidic Jewish story tells of Reb Lieb, who met a friend while he was on the way to visit his great teacher, Mezritcher Maggid. "Are you going to learn about the scriptures from your rebbe (teacher)?" the friend asked. "No," said Reb Lieb, "I'm going to see the way he ties his shoes." What Reb Lieb meant was that those with a peaceful heart reflect their inner tranquillity in every detail of life. They are aware that each moment is precious and that each action is an act of worship to the Most High.

PRACTICE *Spend time stilling your body and your mind. Take stock of your spiritual progress. What areas of your life do you need to work on? Has your heart become more peaceful? Studies suggest that those who are happy are more healthy. Do you feel more relaxed and at ease with yourself? Are you more considerate to others? Does your day-to-day behavior reflect a peaceful heart? The writer Maya Angelou said in an interview, "I never whine." People, she said, get impatient in line for a bus or a plane. They should remember that millions of people never have a chance to travel at all.*

Blindfolded but Not Silent

Only by directly confronting our deepest differences can we come to know one another fully.

—EUGENE BORROWITZ, AMERICAN RABBI

Can conversation really break down barriers? Ibrahim Issa, a peace activist, was taken from his home in Bethlehem by Israeli soldiers. Handcuffed and blindfolded, he was taken for questioning. The soldier who was guarding him asked Ibrahim, "What is your religion?" "Interfaith," Ibrahim said. He explained that he believed all religions are given by God and that people of different religions should live in peace. As they talked, Ibrahim felt the soldier's initial hostility gradually disappearing. When he was released, Ibrahim was more convinced than ever that Palestinians and Israelis could solve their problems if they at least listened to each other. (From the International Interfaith Center Newsletter.)

PRACTICE *Are you willing to talk about your beliefs? How would you answer the question, "What is your religion?" Would you refuse to answer? Do you feel it's nobody's business? Would you "preach" at the other person, trying to convince him or her that your beliefs were correct? Dialogue with people of other faiths requires confidence in your own beliefs and a willingness to listen to other people's convictions. Spend some time thinking what you would say if a person of another religion asked you, "What do you believe?" An honest answer builds bridges across the divisions that can separate religions.*

day 240

God's Peace Be on All Believers

May all believers, through the protection of their prophets and saints, experience the beneficence and kindness of God. May God's peace be on all. There is no power nor strength but in God, the Exalted, the Mighty.

—SHARAFUDDIN MANERI (1290–1381), A MUSLIM MYSTIC FROM BIHAR, INDIA

Those whose religious path has led them to God's presence respect others who follow different paths to God. People who fight about religion are those who make their religion more important than the One God. The fourteenth-century Indian mystic Sharafuddin Maneri was a devout Muslim who recognized that God gave sustenance to Zoroastrians, Christians, and Jews. He wrote in a letter to a disciple, "If you go to the churches you will see everyone searching for God with joy and if you go to the synagogues you will find all in eagerness for God's beauty." (Roger Lesser, *Saints and Sages of India.*)

PRACTICE *Have you ever visited another religion's place of worship? It is a great way to appreciate other faiths and strengthen peaceful relationships. Be prepared to observe traditional customs, such as removing your shoes before entering a mosque or a temple or covering your head before going into a synagogue or Sikh gurdwara. If you feel shy going by yourself, there may be a local interfaith group listed in the phone book or at a library. Such groups arrange visits to synagogues, mosques, churches, and temples, particularly for special festivals. These are usually followed by lavish refreshments and the chance to talk with those who worship there regularly.*

Open to All People

The more a tree is laden with fruit, the more its branches touch the ground. . . . The Temple should be the lowest building of all.

—GURU ARJAN DEV (1563–1606), FIFTH SIKH GURU

Great religious edifices sometimes reflect the competitiveness of devotees. When the Sikh Guru Arjan Dev was building the Golden Temple at Amritsar, his advisers said it should be higher than all the buildings in the neighborhood so that everyone would be impressed. The Guru refused. Recognizing the spiritual importance of humility, he said the temple should be at ground level, with steps for people to go down to enter it. He instructed that the temple should also have four doors to show that it is open to all people, whatever their caste or religion.

PRACTICE *Do you feel that religious buildings serve to glorify the adherents rather than God? Religious or charitable institutions can become self-seeking. If you are a member of a faith community or peace group, ask yourself if your activity is really disinterested. Do you mind if someone else in the choir sings the solo? Are you offended if you are not elected to the governing board? Every member, especially officers and trustees, has a responsibility to see that such bodies serve the purpose for which they were established. When Jesus expelled the traders from the Temple in Jerusalem, he said, "God's house is a place of prayer for all people." (Mark 11.17.)*

day

242 Can People of Faith Make Peace?

In that which we share let us see the common prayer of humanity, in that in which we differ, let us wonder at the freedom of men and women.

—FORMS OF PRAYER FOR JEWISH WORSHIP

Have you ever thought that religion brings conflict rather than peace? To counter this possibility, the Dalai Lama has called for close contact between believers at various levels. Scholars should identify the differences and similarities between religions. Monks and nuns should share their deep spiritual experiences. The Dalai Lama, who has met with the Pope and other leaders on several occasions, also says such meetings are important in the eyes of the public as a sign of the desire for common understanding. He also stresses the value of going on pilgrimage to one another's holy places. (Dalai Lama, *The Good Heart.*)

PRACTICE *It is not necessary to travel to distant lands to develop an appreciation for another's faith, although I certainly learned more about Sikhism by visiting Amritsar's Golden Temple than from any number of books. Have you visited another faith's place of worship in your own community? The Three Faiths Forum suggested that every place of worship should have an annual open day to welcome neighbors of other religions or of no religion. Perhaps you could begin by suggesting that your own group invite others to share a service with you.*

Welcoming the Guest

All hearts are God's, also all places.

—Guru Arjan Dev (1536–1606), Fifth Sikh Guru

David Brown, a former Bishop of Guildford in England, had a deep knowledge of Islam. He once spent a day in Khartoum in the Sudan talking with Muslim friends. However, when the time of prayer came, his request to stand with them was refused. He did not belong to their community of faith. Many religions have similar rules that set boundaries that keep the faithful apart. It is important to follow your own path, but there are times when guests of other faiths should be welcome and when you may wish to join friends of another tradition in prayer. You do not entertain a friend on the porch or in the lobby. You invite them into the best room in the house. When it comes to the most meaningful and sacred times of your faith, a friend of another faith may hesitate to join you unless you specifically invite them.

PRACTICE *Have you shared sacred moments with friends of another faith? A Jewish friend was gravely ill and I visited him regularly in hospital. On many occasions, I read a psalm with him. At times, his pain was so intense that words were no help. We sat together silently and both sensed the presence of the Holy One. Prayer and meditation is a private activity, and you do not want to make a show of them, but you will find your experiences deepened if you are able to share them with someone you trust, regardless of their faith.*

day 244 Thanksgiving

O my Father, Great Elder, I have no words to thank you,
But with your deep wisdom, I am sure you can see
How I value your glorious gifts.

—A PRAYER OF THE KIKUYU PEOPLE OF KENYA

How often do you say "thank you"—not just to other people, but for the beauty of the world and the richness of life? Thanksgiving has proved a good way of bringing people from different backgrounds together. Sharing moments of personal gratitude with others creates a strong sense of fellowship. Meals where people of different faiths testify to their sense of gratitude have united people of many cultures and countries. This approach has been promoted by the Center for World Thanksgiving in Dallas, Texas. The beautiful Chapel of Thanksgiving set amid towering skyscrapers is a reminder of the importance of the Spirit at the center of life.

PRACTICE *Is thanksgiving a regular part of your spiritual practice? Do you say grace before your meals? Giving thanks can remind you of the blessings and richness of life. It counters self-pity and deepens your compassion for those who suffer. It can also be a way to bond with other people on a spiritual level. Saying grace before meals used to be a tradition in many homes, but today it might seem embarrassing. Perhaps you could devise a simple ritual in which family and guests share something for which they are thankful as you come together for a meal. You will find you have also come together in a spiritual fellowship.*

Love Knows No Barriers

Let there be spaces in your togetherness. . . .
Give your hearts but not into each other's keeping
For only the hand of Life can contain your hearts.

—Kahlil Gibran, twentieth-century Lebanese spiritual writer

How do you feel about interfaith marriages? Members of the Unification Church believe that cross-cultural marriage will help the unity of nations and make the world more peaceful. On several occasions I have been asked to officiate at a marriage in which one person is Christian and the other Jewish or Muslim. The ceremony needs to be worked out with care so that the members of both families are happy with it. Each time, the ceremony has been deeply moving because the couple was assured of their family's support as well as God's blessing.

PRACTICE *Have you been to a marriage in which bride and groom belong to different religions? Would you see it as a problem? Mixed-faith marriages are becoming more common in the West. Some couples evade the religious differences, but others celebrate the festivals of both traditions and encourage their children to appreciate both religions. True marriage means allowing the other his or her beliefs. It means finding mutual enrichment by respecting each other's individuality.*

day 246 A Declaration Toward a Global Ethic

We affirm that a common set of core values is found in the teachings of the religions and that these form the basis of a global ethic.

—FROM THE *DECLARATION TOWARD A GLOBAL ETHIC*

Some 100 years after the historic 1893 World's Parliament of Religions, spiritual leaders of many religions met again in Chicago and committed themselves to a "culture of nonviolence, respect, justice, and peace." They recognized that many in the world are suffering. "Peace eludes us . . . the planet is being destroyed . . . neighbors live in fear . . . women and men are estranged from each other . . . children die." The situation could be transformed only "if the consciousness of individuals is changed first." The leaders committed themselves "to increase our awareness by disciplining our minds, by meditation, by prayer or by positive thinking."

PRACTICE *Did you notice something unusual about this declaration? Unlike many statements by religious or political leaders, it was not telling other people what they should do. It was a personal commitment of those who signed what is called "A Declaration Toward A Global Ethic" to seek inner transformation. They suggested that a peaceful world depends on a peaceful heart and that outer change results from an inner change of consciousness in every individual. They ended with an appeal: "We invite all people whether religious or not to do the same." How do you respond to that appeal?*

The Golden Rule

Hurt not others in ways that you yourself would find hurtful.

—BUDDHISM: UDANA-VARGA 5.18

Did you know that "the Golden Rule" is common to all the world's major religions? The best-known version is probably found in the words of Jesus: "All things whatsoever you would that people should do to you, do you also to them." Confucianism has this version: "Do not do unto others what you would not have them do unto you." Although the Golden Rule underlies the world's religions, it is far from being universally practiced. Imagine how different the world would be if everyone actually lived by this principle. There would be no discrimination based on race, sex, or color and no exploitation of the powerless.

PRACTICE *Do you live up to the standard of the Golden Rule? Do you really treat others as you would want to be treated yourself? It's a demanding standard. Think about how you behave toward members of your family or toward colleagues at work. Do you put your own interests first or do you give equal weight to their concerns? A change of attitude will not come about just by making a good resolution. You need a change of inner consciousness. This comes from the sense that you are at one with all people and with Life itself. This is the discovery of the inner journey of meditation and prayer. Your regular time of quiet reflection will lead you toward a change in your attitude and behavior to other people. It will make you more peace loving.*

day
248 A Culture of Nonviolence

Do not create enmity with anyone, as God is within everyone.

—GURU ARJAN DEV (1503-1606), FIFTH SIKH GURU

One of the four guidelines for behavior or "irrevocable directives" in The Global Ethic is a "commitment to a culture of nonviolence and respect for life." Some members of the 1993 Parliament of Religions nearly came to blows when they debated nonviolence! This was at the time of the conflicts in the former Yugoslavia. Some people at the Parliament held the view that brutal dictatorships and genocidal killers had to be stopped by force. Others held that there is no justification for violence. In the end, there was general agreement that if force is unavoidable, it should be exercised by international authorities such as the United Nations. Gandhi himself preferred the use of force to cowardice in the face of evil.

PRACTICE *Are there ways in which you could help to spread a culture of nonviolence? Do you tend to shout at home if you do not get your own way? Do you bang the table at board meetings or walk out if your suggestions are ignored? Are you subject to road rage? Some normally polite people become aggressive when they are behind a driving wheel. Try to see where this rage comes from. Aggressive behavior often reflects inner anxiety or frustration. A peaceful heart is reflected in peaceful behavior.*

Beware of Greed

In happiness and suffering, in joy and grief, we should regard all creatures as we regard our own self.

—MAHAVIRA (599–527 BCE), THE LAST JAIN TIRTHANKARA

If your flight is canceled and an announcement says there are 10 seats on an alternative flight, do you rush to get to the front of the line? When resources are scarce, people inevitably compete and may grow violent. Poverty and economic injustice in the world cause social unrest, which is aggravated by widespread corruption. The high salaries paid to film stars, professional athletes, and corporate leaders generate jealousy and discontent. As the *Declaration Toward a Global Ethic* says: "In greed, humans lose their 'souls,' their freedom, their composure, their inner peace, and thus that which makes them human."

PRACTICE *Is money a frequent source of argument in your household? Do you wish you had a higher income? Ask yourself whether this is because you need more money or because you want others to view you as important and successful. Most religions recognize that people need enough for a satisfying life, but they also encourage simplicity and detachment from worldly pursuits. Luxury and extravagance distract you from the search for life's meaning. The quest for riches leads away from inner peace. Possessions become a cause of anxiety. In protecting them, we become unsympathetic to those in need. Jesus said, "You cannot serve God and Money." (Matthew 6.24.)*

day
250 Speak and Act Truthfully

Truthfulness is the foundation of all human virtues. Without truthfulness, progress and success in all the worlds of God are impossible for any soul. When this holy attribute is established in men and women, all the divine qualities will be acquired.

—FROM THE BAHA'I SACRED WRITINGS

"If it's true, there's nothing we can do about it." This was Pope John Paul XXIII's reply when a Vatican official asked how they should handle allegations that Pope Pius XII accommodated the Nazis. All the great religions emphasize the vital importance of truth. Trust is the basis of community, which is why integrity is so important. As the *Declaration Toward a Global Ethic* says, "Let no one be deceived: there is no global justice without truthfulness and humaneness." Truthfulness is also essential for deeper understanding of the universe, which is why religions should never fear scientific discoveries and new knowledge.

PRACTICE *Is your word your bond? Do you keep your promises—especially to children? If someone asks your advice, do you speak your mind or do you say what you think they want to hear? A good teacher should encourage his or her students, but it does not help them to gloss over their mistakes or to be overgenerous in marking. Are you honest in your judgment of yourself? Do you exaggerate your achievements or do you exhibit false humility while actually seeking praise? It is difficult to admit mistakes or to apologize when you are wrong, but both are signs of integrity. You can make your contribution to a new culture of truthfulness by acting and speaking honestly.*

At Ease with Your Sexuality

Whenever two are linked in this way, there comes another from the Unseen world. . . . The intense qualities born of such joining appear in the spiritual world.

—RUMI, SUFI MYSTIC AND POET, FROM *THE SOUL'S ALMANAC,* ED. AARON ZERAH

Sexuality relates human beings to both creative and destructive forces in the Universe. The right use of sexuality is vital for a more peaceful society. As the *Declaration Toward a Global Ethic* says, "Only what has already been experienced in personal and familial relationships can be practiced on the level of nations and religions." The great religions all say, "Respect and love one another." No one should be treated as a sex object or held in sexual dependency. Although religions themselves have sometimes discriminated against women, a new sense of partnership between the sexes is vital for a more peaceful world.

PRACTICE *Do you feel at ease with your sexuality? Many people have a sense of inadequacy or frustration. If you are not at peace with this part of your personality, it will disturb other aspects of your life. If you are seriously disturbed, you should seek expert advice. The quality of your relationships with the person who is closest to you will be reflected in your relationships with other members of the family, and with your colleagues at work. The* Global Ethic *says, "Sexuality as a life-affirming shaper of community can only be effective when partners accept the responsibilities of caring for one another's happiness."*

Learn from Difficulties

God gives himself to those who seek him—
The poor, the low, the least.

—NANDA THE PARIAH, ELEVENTH-CENTURY HINDU SAINT

Have you had a bad experience while visiting a religious site? Perhaps you were turned away because you did not belong. If so, do not let it stop your search for the Divine. Nanda, a South Indian slave who lived in the eleventh century, longed to visit the holy temple of Chidambaram. Eventually, his master allowed him to make the journey, but when he arrived, he found only high-caste Hindus were allowed inside the temple. In a dream, the priests were told that Nanda would be purified in a "fire bath." Because of his deep devotion to God, Nanda submitted to this. To the priests' surprise, Nanda emerged unscathed, entered the temple, and was united with Nataraja, the dancing embodiment of the god Shiva.

PRACTICE *Difficulties on the path to realization of inner peace may test how serious you are. It is easy to use obstacles as an excuse for failure. It is a question of enthusiasm and motivation. If you really want to see a film or a concert, you would probably line up for hours. Nanda at first resented the obstacles placed in his way, but he came to recognize that "God knows what is best for me . . . until I practice cheerful resignation, how can I obtain God's grace?" Reflect whether there is any message for you in the difficulties you encounter.*

Serving the Needs of the World

The humble, meek, merciful, and devout souls are everywhere of one religion. When death takes off the mask, they will know one another, though diverse liveries they wear here make them strangers

—William Penn (1644–1718), English Quaker who founded Pennsylvania

Have you found you often get to know people best when you do something together? As a student in India, I used to help at a leprosy clinic. I would make the long trek to the clinic in the company of a Muslim student and a Christian from Sri Lanka. The clinic's doctor was a devotee of the Hindu god Shiva. The fact that we were from different countries and worshipped God by different names did not matter at all. We were linked by a common wish to help the people who not only had a severe illness but also were shut out from society by centuries of prejudice.

PRACTICE *Do you meet with people of other religions at work or in voluntary activity? Do you ever talk about your beliefs? The daughter of a friend of mine was ill, and she happened to mention it at work. During the weekend, a Hindu colleague phoned to ask how the girl was. He told her, "We've been praying for you." My friend told me this made her consider whether the Hindu colleague was praying to a different god or is there only one God whom we call by different names.*

day
254 Kidney Donation

Through love of fellow beings, through search for Truth,
And the yearnings and prayers of my heart;
Renew, Oh Ahura Mazda (Wise Lord), the strength to serve.

—ZOROASTRIAN PRAYER: YASNA 34.15

If you died in a car crash, would you want your organs to be donated to help another person? If so, have you made your wishes clear? Would you be happy for the organ to be donated to a person of another country or religion? Normally, organs are given to the person most in need. In the same way, Christian Aid, a relief and development agency, had as its motto "need not creed." Help is offered to anyone who requires it. Consider the truth that at moments of need, we recognize our common humanity. Ask yourself why we find it so difficult to do this at other times.

PRACTICE *Caregiving can bridge racial and religious boundaries. If you have been a hospital patient, you have probably been cared for by people from different countries and religions. At the Hadassah hospital in Jerusalem, Israeli, Palestinian, Jewish, Muslim, and Christian doctors and nurses work together to care for patients without regard for their racial or religious background. There are also stories of the organs of a person killed as a result of political upheaval being given to a member of the other community. "Such organ donation," one parent said, "is not only a gift of life to the individual but an act toward the healing of two divided communities."*

Peace: A Symbol All Can Share

Peace appears to be the symbol for our times.
No other symbol has the power and universality of peace

—RAIMON PANIKKAR, INTERFAITH SCHOLAR,
QUOTED BY PAUL KNITTER, *ONE EARTH, MANY RELIGIONS*

People of faith, who may disagree about doctrine and ritual, are joining together in many parts of the world to work for peace and justice. Their longing for peace is perhaps as close as we get to a universal symbol in this generation. Their efforts involve much more than ending armed conflict. They include relieving the poverty that causes violence, protecting the environment, and advocating for the victims of human rights violations. Long-term peace also requires patient efforts at peace-building after a conflict and reconciliation of the warring parties. It is an enormous agenda, but religion's special contribution is helping individuals find the inner resources this task demands.

PRACTICE *Try to visualize a world at peace. Write down the key features of what it would be like. Then try to turn your words into a poem or a prayer. Perhaps this vision of the Indian writer and film director Ramanand Sagar will stimulate your own thoughts. "My vision is that of a world bathed in the celestial light of the spirit, wherein one will see God in every other person and worship him or her as one would worship God. That is the way of Indian saints, whereby color, caste, creed, religion, poverty, superiority, inferiority—everything vanishes. What remains is the* LIGHT OF LOVE*—radiant and celestial." (Brahma Kumaris,* Visions of a Better World.*)*

day 256

Worship in a Prison Cell

Where the mind is without fear and the head is held high, where knowledge is free and the world has not been broken up by narrow walls . . . into that heaven of freedom my Father, let me awake.

—RABINDRANATH TAGORE (1861–1941), FROM *GITANJALI*

In South Africa, members of different faiths first prayed together in a prison cell. Christians, Muslims, Hindus, and Jews had joined together in a peaceful protest against one of the apartheid laws. The group, which included an imam and a rabbi, was arrested and put in prison. In the cell, someone suggested that they take turns reciting from their holy scriptures. Time passed quickly, and they discovered how much they had in common. When the Parliament of the new South Africa was opened, prayers from all the South African religions were said at the inauguration.

PRACTICE *Would you be happy joining in prayer with a person of another faith? Some people would feel this is disloyal to their own tradition. However, people of all religions oppose racism and injustice in the quest for peace. Joining in prayer shows that God is not "owned" by any one religion and that all people are children of one God. The Qur'an says that the steep and difficult path of virtue is "freeing the slave, giving food in the day of hunger to the orphan . . . or to some needy soul in distress." For that work we all need the blessing of God.*

For Whom Did We Pray?

When you speak ill of others
You have already exposed
Your own inner weakness
To the outer world

—SRI CHINMOY (b. 1916), CONTEMPORARY POET AND ARTIST OF PEACE

Young people from Catholic and Protestant communities in Northern Ireland are regularly invited to spend a week together at the Corrymeela Community. Many of those involved have lost loved ones in the troubles. At the end of the week, participants meet in the chapel and pray for anyone they wish. One girl requested prayers "for a person who is very troubled tonight." Afterward the leader asked her if she wanted to tell him who the person was. "Yes. He's the man who murdered my father. He gets his sentence tomorrow. He and his family are very worried." The girl had been able to see beyond her own grief to sense the fear of the killer and to pray for him.

PRACTICE *In your time of quiet—as you relax the body and still the mind—think of those you view as enemies. Recall the pain they caused you, and then try to pray for them. Put yourself in their situation. Slowly, your hostility will fade and you will begin to empathize with them and feel more peaceful. Sri Chinmoy says, "Strangely enough, the deeper we plunge, the clearer it becomes that the imperfections of others are our own imperfections, but in different bodies and minds."*

day 258

The Same Goal?

Your Light is in all forms, Your Love in all beings
Allow us to recognize You in all Your holy names and forms.

—HAZRAT PIR-O-MURSHID INAYAT KHAN (1882–1927),
FIRST GREAT SUFI MASTER WHO TAUGHT IN THE WEST

Do you believe there is only one true religion or are the various religions only different paths up the same mountain? Sri Ramakrishna (1836-1886), Swami Vivekananda's spiritual guide, claimed his own experience showed that all religions lead to the realization of God's presence. Sri Ramakrishna, at age 19, became the priest of Kali, the Divine Mother, at Dakshineswar, near Calcutta. After months of intense devotion, he realized her presence. Then focusing his devotion on Rama, he had a vision of the child Rama and Sita, Rama's consort. Following other spiritual disciplines (*sadhana*) he had visions of Krishna as a friend and then of Jesus and of the Prophet Muhammad. His claim, although it has been disputed, suggests an underlying unity of mystical experience.

PRACTICE *Have you had a mystical experience? Have you ever had an intense sense of unity? It may be a sense of the most intimate communion with God, or of being a part of Nature or of being absorbed into the Spirit of Life. Rather than wasting energy comparing your experience with others, be thankful for it and express that unity in your life. The contemporary Christian mystic Wayne Teasdale recognizes that there are different types of mystical experience, but rejects arguments that one is superior to the other. "Although the ultimate goals are not identical, they are complementary. The religions need one another precisely because they complete one another! Together, they enlarge our understanding of the Ultimate." (Wayne Teasdale,* The Mystic Heart.*)*

Be the Best You Can

By routes diverse folk may the mountain climb,
Each path presenting different views, sublime—
But when to the proud summit they do rise,
The self-same smiling moon doth greet all eyes.

—A Shinto prayer, from *The Lotus Prayer Book*

"The Hindu should be a better Hindu, the Muslim a better Muslim, the Christian a better Christian," was the aim of Mahatma Gandhi. He opposed attempts to convert people from one religion to another, although individuals may change religion if this helps their spiritual progress. Recognizing truth in other religions should not dilute your conviction or devotion. If you are a Buddhist or a Jew, be the best Buddhist or Jew you can be. Many people have found that learning about other religions has helped them in their own spiritual pilgrimage and deepened their appreciation of their own religious path.

PRACTICE *Are you afraid that finding out about other religions will confuse your own beliefs? There's no need to be anxious. Religions should not be in competition. The truth is that people everywhere have similar hopes and fears. When you travel to another country, you may find some local customs you wish to imitate and some things you think are done better at home. If you see a beautiful garden, it may encourage you to make your own even lovelier. The example of others should be a spur to your own spiritual development. They are ways to help you grow in truth and love.*

God in All the Great Ones

Let us find God not only in Jesus of Nazareth but in all the Great Ones that have preceded him and all that are yet to come.

—SWAMI VIVEKANANDA, *CHRIST THE MESSENGER*

Are the great souls confined to one religion or do they have a truly universal message? Sri Ramakrishna, who followed various devotional paths, had some acquaintance with Christianity. He claimed to have had a vision of Jesus. *The Gospel of Ramakrishna* says of Ramakrishna, "Breaking through the barriers of creed and religion, he entered a new realm of ecstasy. Christ possessed his soul. As the two faced each other, a voice sang out in the depths of Sri Ramakrishna's soul: 'Behold the Christ, who shed his heart's blood for the redemption of the world, who suffered a sea of anguish for love of men. . . . It is he, the master Yogi, who is in eternal union with God. It is Jesus, Love Incarnate.'"

PRACTICE *Many Christians are puzzled by Sri Ramakrishna's claim. But as the people of the world come together, they will learn from each other's religions. The Dalai Lama recommends that people be loyal to the religion to which they belong, but recognize that different religions suit different people. How much do you know about religions other than your own? Sometimes people know about the history or teaching of another religion, but little about its spiritual experience. Others have found their own faith renewed by spiritual insights from other traditions.*

The Jesus Place

I worship you in every religion that teaches your laws and praises your glory. I worship you in every person who follows your way of righteousness.

—ZOROASTER (C. 660–583 BCE OR EARLIER), ALSO KNOWN AS ZARATHUSTRA

When I first visited a Sikh interfaith community called Gobind Sadan on the outskirts of New Delhi, the receptionist told me she prayed every day that she would have a vision of Jesus. When I went back some years later, she told me of her recent vision of Jesus as a luminous figure standing beside her, who assured her of his love and blessing. The woman remains a devout Sikh. The founder of the ashram, H.H. Baba Virsa Singh, had a vision of Jesus some years ago and created a beautiful garden, known as the Jesus Place, which contains a statue of Jesus.

PRACTICE *Choose a religious figure about whom you know very little. It could be the Buddha, Muhammad, Jesus, or Guru Nanak. Find out a little about his life and teaching, but try also to read some devotional material from the relevant faith. This will help you to see how followers of a religion view their teacher. You will begin to appreciate the religion from the inside. Does the teacher have anything to say to you? Perhaps the Buddha encourages you to be calm and detached. Muhammad exhorts you to live your whole life in obedience to God. Jesus asks you to love others more fully, and Guru Nanak helps you to recognize the unity of all humanity.*

day 262 A Prophet for Every Nation

We assuredly sent amongst every People a Messenger,
(With the Command), "Serve Allah, and eschew Evil."

—QUR'AN: 16.36

The Qur'an says that "For every nation there is a messenger." Muslims believe that God sent messengers to every people to teach the one true religion. The Qur'an mentions Noah, Abraham, Moses, Jesus, and other prophets (6.84-86). The Buddha and the Hindu avatars are not necessarily excluded, as only some prophets are named in the Qur'an (40.78). When I visited the great Jama Masjid in Old Delhi, the guide included Krishna, Rama, and Zoroaster among the prophets.

PRACTICE *Muhammad said members of different religions should strive like runners in a race to excel in virtue (5.48). You do not have to become a member of another religion to benefit from its teaching and example. As you learn about another religion, you reflect more deeply on your own beliefs. Religious teachings are not something to be repeated mechanically, but to be tested through your own experience. You are on a spiritual journey. When mountaineers meet, they tell each other their adventures. In the same way, religious explorers should share and learn from each other. Wesley Ariarajah, a Methodist from Sri Lanka, wrote, "If my Hindu, Buddhist, or Muslim neighbor is as much a child of God as I am, then we are indeed brothers and sisters. . . . We have much to learn from each other."* (All in Good Faith, *eds. J. Potter and M. Braybrooke.)*

Isa

Christ reflects in his every act God's mercy in all its fullness; in other words Christ is the embodiment of that tender aspect of God which the Qur'an calls divine mercy.

—PROFESSOR VAHIDUDDIN, AN INDIAN MUSLIM SCHOLAR, QUOTED IN MARCUS BRAYBROOK, *WHAT CAN WE LEARN FROM ISLAM?*

Did you know that Jesus, Isa, is mentioned in the Qur'an in 93 verses? The Qur'an gives Jesus more honorable titles than any other figure of the past. He is called a "sign," a "mercy," a "witness," and an "example." Muslims may address prayers to Abraham and Jesus as prophets of Islam. Muslims do not believe that Jesus is the Son of God nor that God allowed his servant to be crucified, but Muslims always regard Jesus with reverence and add, "May God bless him," whenever they mention his name. The Prophet himself allowed a delegation of 60 Orthodox Christians to pray in a Mosque, which they did facing East.

PRACTICE *A Hindu friend who spoke at a Christian missionary conference surprised people by beginning, "I speak to you as a fellow lover of Jesus." Many people who are not Christians have a reverence for Jesus, just as some Christians have a deep reverence for Muhammad or the Buddha. The Sufi mystic Ibn al-Arabi (1165–1240) wrote, "Within my heart, all forms may find a place, the cloisters of the monk . . . the tables of the Jewish law, the Word of God revealed to his Prophet true. Love is the faith I hold and whereso'er his camels turn, the one true faith is there." Is your heart as open to truth and love wherever it is to be found?*

day 264

The Prophet Muhammad

No one can estimate the power of Islam as a religion who does not take into account the love at the heart of it for this figure. It is the strongest binding force in a religion which has so marked a binding power

—CONSTANCE PADWICK, *MUSLIM DEVOTIONS*

Muslims respect Jesus. Christians should also recognize Muhammad as a genuine prophet of God. Many Christians scarcely know anything about Muhammad. The Western media often gives an unflattering picture of Muhammad. In the past, some Christian leaders made offensive remarks about him. As a Christian, I see him as a true prophet, akin to the great Biblical prophets Isaiah and Jeremiah, although not as the final prophet. Keith Ward, who was Regius Professor of Theology at Oxford, has written, "Christians can see Muhammad as truly inspired by God, as called to proclaim a strict monotheistic faith, and as chosen by God for that purpose."

PRACTICE *You may like to contemplate this prayer by Muhammad.*

O Lord, grant us to love You;
Grant that we may love those that love You;
Grant that we may do deeds that win Your love.
Make the love of You to be dearer to us than ourselves,
Than our families, than wealth, and even than cool water.

Muhammad's wife A'ishah said, "Truly the character of the Prophet was that of the Qur'an." One way you may begin to appreciate your Muslim neighbors is to learn more about the influence and example of Muhammad. It can help you bridge the divisions in the world and contribute to peace.

Too Great for Words

What name shall we call You, You who are beyond all name?

—Gregory of Nyssa

Many religious arguments are based on words, but spiritual teachers of various traditions suggest that the Divine Reality is beyond our full comprehension. Even the people we are closest to remain in part a mystery to us. We do not fully know what another person thinks or feels. Indeed, we are not altogether conscious of our own motivation. How then can we claim to know all there is to know about God? We can learn from other people's experience of the Divine, even if they express it in different language.

PRACTICE *Look back at how your beliefs have changed. Can you recall times when your understanding of the mystery of Life was altered or enlarged? You can have a sense of the presence of God, even without fully comprehending God's nature. The Bible says, "God is greater than our hearts." (I John 3.20.) Many mystics suggest that God is more wonderful than our images can portray. When you are ready, God will reveal new insights to you. If you read a book for a second or third time you will realize things you did not see the first time. In the same way, enlightenment is not a state but a process. Day by day, try to open yourself more fully to the Spirit of Truth.*

part six

PEACE IN THE WORLD

Those who discover inner peace through meditation will be restless until all people are in harmony. Peace in the world requires prayer and action. Peacemakers need the renewing energy of a peaceful heart to sustain their efforts. Their examples will encourage you to discover your particular calling, but the land mines in the world will not be removed until you remove the land mines of hatred, greed, and deception in your heart. As you become more loving and nonviolent, the world is healed and the seeds of peace are sown.

Seeing the World as God Sees It

The contemplative person unmasks the illusion and falsehood of the world and sees the world as God wants it to be.

—Thomas Merton (1915–1968), Trappist monk and social activist

You might be surprised to find how many spiritual teachers have been in trouble with the authorities. Sir Thomas More was beheaded by Henry VIII, and the Sufi al-Hallaj (d. 922) was executed in Baghdad. More recently, Mahatma Gandhi and Martin Luther King spent time in jail. Those who come close to God in prayer begin to see the divine purpose for the world. They become more aware of injustice and suffering. They are typically the most fearless critics of tyranny and dictatorship.

PRACTICE *Prayer is not just about peaceful feelings. God requires integrity and holiness. As you enter more deeply into yourself in meditation you will become aware of unresolved conflicts and shabby compromises. You will not be at peace until you heal the breach with your brother or sister or correct some petty dishonesty at work. You may also find that your conscience prompts you to give more money to the hungry or to give time to help at the local hospice. Peace is God's gift to those who do God's will.*

Where There Is Hope, There Is Peace

O peoples of the world, the Sun of Truth has risen to illumine the whole earth. . . . Let human beings see no one as their enemy, but think of all humankind as their friends.

—'ABDU'L-BAHA (1844–1921), SUCCESSOR OF BAHA'U'LLAH AS HEAD OF THE BAHA'I FAITH

One of the greatest threats to peace is apathy. Your commitment to work for peace will not survive for long without a boundless supply of hope. The French novelist Victor Hugo (1802–1885) spent many years in exile because of his lifelong support for republican ideals. He said, "Where there is hope, there is peace." David Krieger, founder of the Nuclear Age Peace Foundation, writes that choosing hope is a conscious decision he made, "because I feel a deep responsibility . . . to pass the world on to a better place that when I came into it. It is what gives meaning to life. To fight for a better world is a form of living life to its fullest and richest." (D. Krieger and D. Ikeda, *Choose Hope.*)

PRACTICE *As you sit quietly, ask yourself, "What do I hope for?" What are your hopes for your family, for your work, for the world society? What are the implications for how you live and how you spend your time and your money? Nelson Mandela, on his release from long years in prison, committed himself to building a society where all could live in equality. "It is an ideal which I hope to live for and to achieve. But if needs be, it is an ideal for which I am prepared to die." How much are you prepared to sacrifice for your ideals?*

Prayer and Action

In this laborious world of thine, tumultuous with toil and struggle, among hurrying crowds shall I stand before thee face to face?

—Rabindranath Tagore (1861–1941), Indian poet

Have people told you that you would be better spending your time praying than marching for peace? If you pray, have other people said you would be of more help doing something practical? In fact, the two belong together. Prayer makes you a peace activist and activists burn out without prayer. Gandhi said that all human endeavors should be guided by the ultimate goal of the vision of God, but he insisted that the way to reach that goal was by the immediate service of all human beings (*sarvodaya*). "If I could find God in a Himalayan cave, I would proceed there immediately. I know I cannot find God apart from humanity." (Mahatma Gandhi, *Harijan* journal, August 29, 1936.)

PRACTICE *Are you more interested in discovering inner peace or trying to solve the problems of the world? Imagine you are quietly reflecting in your garden or a quiet part of the park. Suddenly, you hear the squeal of brakes, the sirens of emergency vehicles, screams and shouting. You are likely to go and see what is happening. Perhaps you are a nurse or an off-duty fireman. You have to help the people trapped or injured by the accident. Because you are part of humanity, you cannot isolate yourself from suffering, but you cannot help unless your inner resources are constantly renewed.*

Where Is God to be Found?

I left off all rites and ceremonies. The person who is kind and who practices righteousness and who considers all creatures on earth as his own self . . . He attains the Immortal Being, the true God is ever with him.

—KABIR (b. 1518), INDIAN POET OF PERSONAL DEVOTION TO GOD

Rabindranath Tagore (1861–1941) was probably India's greatest modern poet. He encouraged traditional Indian industries and arts. He was a close friend of Gandhi and supported India's struggle for independence. He insisted that unless spirituality resulted in practical concern for the poor, it was self-indulgent. In one of his poems he wrote:

Leave this chanting and singing and telling of beads!
Open thine eyes and see thy God is not before thee!
He is where the tiller is tilling the hard ground
and where the path maker is breaking stones . . .
Put off thy holy mantle and even like him come down on the dusty soil!
Meet him and stand by him in toil and in the sweat of thy brow.

—RABINDRANATH TAGORE, *GITANJALI*

PRACTICE *Where have you felt closest to God? I was asked to contribute to an anthology called* Glimpses of God *(Dan Cohn-Sherboked, ed.). I started writing at Father Bede Griffith's Satcitananda ashram in south India. Why, I asked myself, had I come? Was it in the hope of a deeper experience of the Divine? Yes, but had I not experienced God in the welcome of an old friend who had waited in the heat to greet me at Madras airport—or in the affectionate farewells of my family? Should I have experienced God in the cripple on the station platform, too weary to sit up and beg? If you withdraw to be close to God, it must be to recognize that God is close to you in every activity of life.*

Many Paths to Peace

Persons of all religious traditions need to do more to conscientize their own constituencies into relating prayer and worship to the agonies and ecstasies of God's children in the world.

—ANGELO FERNANDES, ARCHBISHOP OF DELHI AND FIRST PRESIDENT OF THE WORLD CONFERENCE ON RELIGION AND PEACE

How do you focus your energies to bring about a more peaceful world? Prayer, education, development, human rights, disarmament, and the search for justice all help prevent conflict. Mahatma Gandhi said, "I believe my message to be universal but I can best deliver it through my work in my own country. If I can show visible success in India, the delivery of the message becomes complete." Each person can make a particular contribution to a peaceful world. (Mahatma Gandhi, *Young India*.)

PRACTICE *Take time to reflect on how you can help to make the world more peaceful. Remember to still the body and the mind. You can make little contribution unless you have a peaceful heart. Your way of life, your care for your family, your work, your faith all spread peaceful vibrations. If your work or voluntary activities are specifically directed toward peace, they will be beneficial. No one can do everything. Do not waste energy in being guilty about the causes you do not support, especially if this distracts you from the work you are doing. Although Gandhi concentrated on his work in India, it has had worldwide repercussions.*

Deepening Our Sense of Reality

It is impossible to have peace without prayer, the prayer of all, each one in his own identity and in search for the truth.

—POPE JOHN PAUL XXIII, REFLECTIONS ON ASSISI

"Does prayer make any difference?" a reporter asked Lord Ennals, a former British minister, who was an active supporter of the 1986 One Million Minutes for Peace Appeal. "Can you show it doesn't?" Lord Ennals replied. In 1986, Pope John Paul XXIII invited leaders of all religions to join him at Assisi—the hometown of St. Francis—in prayer for peace. After that day, President Reagan and President Gorbachev met for the first time and the Cold War began to thaw. The outpouring of prayers expressed the deep longing of the peoples of the world. "Prayer," the Pope said, "entails conversion of heart on our part. It means deepening our sense of the ultimate Reality." If that happens, then we see the futility of war. (Pope John Paul XXIII, *Assisi: World Day of Prayer for Peace*.)

PRACTICE *Whether or not you believe there is a God who answers prayer, getting in touch with your deepest inner reality changes your perspective. After stilling the body and the mind, try to focus on your most significant concerns, or your highest values, and on the moral basis of your actions. You may instinctively feel revulsion at the waste of life through poverty, violence, and preventable disease. As your sense of Ultimate Reality deepens, your heart and your priorities are turned around. You will recognize how precious is the gift of life for you and for all people.*

A Nation Under God

Spirit of peace, come to our waiting world,
Throughout the nations may your voice be heard.

—GEOFFREY GARDNER, CONTEMPORARY HYMN WRITER

"Where were you on September 11, 2001?" is a question that most people in the United States and many people elsewhere can answer with chilling detail. The terrible events of that day have changed the perceptions of the world. Writing one year later, Frank Griswold, Presiding Bishop of the Episcopal Church in the United States, reflected on what it meant to be a nation "under God." When the wounds were fresh, he writes, "we had a glimpse of our kinship with a larger world, where acts of terror come in many forms. We entered into solidarity with others based on our common vulnerability." (B. Martin Pedersen, ed. *Prayers for Peace.*)

PRACTICE *Prayer is an important corrective to our partial and prejudiced viewpoint. In prayer, you try to see events in the light of the eternal and universal. Reflect back on your memories of September 11 and the days immediately following. What thoughts were uppermost in your mind? Reflect in the presence of the Eternal. Were your concerns mainly about yourself and your family or about your nation? Did you try to see the events in the context of the needs of all people? Is that how you now view those events and subsequent developments? "Are we unable to understand, even now," asks Bishop Frank Griswold, "that our world is too small and too fragile for a unilateralist stance?"*

day 273

May Peace Prevail on Earth

May we all be in peace, peace and only peace;
and may that peace come unto each of us.

—HINDU SCRIPTURES: YAJURVEDA

A Peace Pole is not what you expect to find on Robben Island, where Nelson Mandela and other opponents of South Africa's policy of apartheid endured long and cruel imprisonment. Planted there at the end of the 1999 Cape Town Parliament of the World's Religions, it is a sign of hope in contrast to the stark prison buildings. Peace poles are one of the projects of the World Peace Prayer Society, which was founded in Japan by Masahisa Goi in 1955. The society seeks to raise peace consciousness by spreading the simple prayer, "May Peace Prevail on Earth." You can even get a T-shirt with these words.

PRACTICE *Masahisa Goi's explanation of the World Peace prayer describes the value of prayer itself. It "elevates the thought waves of oneself and others by wishing for the peace of humanity, which is the same as the thought of Universal Love. If you keep living your life anew from this prayer, your selfish desires will diminish. A deep feeling of humanitarian love will well up from within. Gradually, your character will approach wholeness and your lifestyle will strike a harmonious note—which is the greatest thing an individual can do for world peace." In your time of quiet, use these words to still the mind and to connect with Universal Love and Peace:* May Peace Prevail on Earth.

The Peace Prayer

Lead me from death to Life, from falsehood to Truth
Lead me from despair to Hope, from fear to Trust
Lead me from hate to Love, from war to Peace
Let Peace fill our heart, our world, our universe.

—*PRAYER FOR PEACE*, SATISH KUMAR,
PEACE CAMPAIGNER AND ENVIRONMENTALIST

The "Prayer for Peace" has been said by thousands of people around the world for more than 20 years—often at midday. Notice that the Prayer for Peace starts with you. It begins, "Lead *me*." Only in the third line does it move to a universal aspiration. Inner change is the contribution you can make to the peace of the world. Truth means that you can be trusted. Hope means that you are a source of comfort and encouragement. Trust means that you will not let people down. Love means that even those who have wronged you know that you will show them compassion.

PRACTICE *By simple acts of generosity and sharing you can cross barriers that divide and radiate peace. The prayer was first spoken by Mother Teresa in London in 1981. Once she had taken food to a poor Hindu family in Calcutta. The Hindu mother gratefully received the food. Then she disappeared for a time. When she returned, she said simply, "They are hungry, too." The Hindu mother had taken half the food to a poor Muslim family next door. If rich nations could share their wealth with the poor, hopes for peace would be far brighter.*

day 275 Prayer: An Antidote to Spin

Prayer is vital for the undermining of illusion and falsehood. . . .
The person of prayer takes up a critical attitude towards
the contemporary world and its structures.

—THOMAS MERTON (1915–1968), MONK, PEACE ACTIVIST, AND AUTHOR

"Religion and politics don't mix" is a frequent comment, especially from politicians who do not like moral criticism. Yet, the Trappist monk and writer Thomas Merton claimed that it is people of prayer who see through spin and media hype to the basic moral issues. The violence and unrest of the contemporary world, he said, requires "special searching . . . which is the work of prayer and meditation." In prayer, we listen to neglected voices that proceed from Life's inner depths." Those who find inner peace are, he said, "like trees which exist silently in the dark and by their vital presence purify the air" of a troubled world.

PRACTICE *Sitting quietly, imagine you are in space looking down on the world. What is the world of your dreams? Astronauts comment on the beauty of planet Earth. They also say that they cannot see national barriers. Do you dream of a world where there is no fighting and no hunger? What can you do to make this a reality? Do not give up hope that change is possible. Try to live by your vision and be true to it. You can help filter out sleaze and corruption. As the poet W. H. Auden said, you have a "voice to undo the folded lie." (From "September 1st, 1939," by W. H. Auden, 1940.)*

Smile

Waking up this morning, I smile.

—THICH NHAT HANH, VIETNAMESE BUDDHIST MONK AND PEACE-WORKER, FROM *PRESENT MOMENT, WONDERFUL MOMENT*

Sri Lanka has been the scene of a long and vicious civil war between the Singhalese in the south, who are Buddhists, and the Tamils in the north, who are Hindus. I once met a Singhalese Buddhist monk who wanted to help heal the division. He decided to move to the northern Tamil city of Jaffna. Each day, he walked around in his Buddhist robes, smiling at everyone he saw. After six months, someone smiled back at him. Slowly, others did the same, and he began to make friendships, which bridged the deep chasm of bitterness.

PRACTICE *Smiling is a good way to regain your equanimity. A smile relaxes the muscles in your face and takes away the tension from your nervous system. Smiling helps you to be more peaceful and to feel more kindly toward other people. A smile, it has been said, is "the Ordinary made beautiful." A smile brightens up our face and can cheer another's day. (Peter Shaffer,* Equus, *Act 1, Scene 19.)*

Meditate for Peace

You and I create the world by the vibrations that we offer to the world. If we invoke peace and then offer it to somebody else, we will see how peace expands from one to two persons and in time to the whole world.

—SRI CHINMOY (b. 1916), FOUNDER OF "PEACE CONCERTS" AND "PEACE RUNS"

U.N. Security Council meetings are reported by the world media, but little is known of the meditation meetings, which have been held there for more than 30 years by Sri Chinmoy. Sri Chinmoy, a gifted and prolific poet and artist, who lives in the busy heart of New York City, came to the West in 1964. "Meditation," he says, "speaks in silence. It reveals that matter and spirit are one. . . . We are truly unlimited if we only dare to try and have faith." U.N. Secretary General Kofi Annan told Sri Chinmoy, "In this house dedicated to duty and debate in the service of peace, meditation serves the same cause in silence and stillness."

PRACTICE *You can make a difference to world affairs by your meditation. This is part of Sri Chinmoy's message. Meditation, by making you a more peaceful person, contributes to a culture of peace, which gradually pervades the decision making of international leaders. Do not underestimate your influence. Think how many people you speak to—in person or on the phone—during the course of a week. Like Sri Chinmoy, you can use art and music to spread the message of peace. You can also make your views known by calling in to phone-in programs and by writing to politicians.*

All Are Made in the Image of God

What is hateful to yourself, you should not do to your fellow men.

—BABYLONIAN TALMUD, SHABAT 31A

News of Israelis and Palestinians who work for reconciliation is overshadowed by the tragic events in their lands. Natan Hoshfi, who grew up in Poland, came to Palestine in 1909. When he joined an agricultural cooperative, he encouraged fellow Jews to get to know local Arabs, saying, "There is only one sun that gives light to all of us without differentiation, and the same mother earth supports us all." Natan Hoshfi also stressed the importance of education. "I believe in perfect faith that the days of peace and brotherhood will come only as a result of a new form of education in school and home whose central feature will be 'Man was created in the image of God.'"(Hagen Berndt, ed. *NonViolence in the World Religions*.)

PRACTICE *You may not have any influence on educational policy, but your behavior can be an example to young people, especially as a parent. Does the way you live reflect the belief that every person is made in the image of God? Children easily pick up the attitudes prevalent in the home. Do you speak to children with respect? Will they learn respect for others by your behavior? Reflect on these words:*

If children live with criticism, they learn to condemn.
If children live with hostility, they learn to fight.

—DOROTHY LAW NOLTE

day

279 See Each Person as a Friend

We have returned from the lesser jihad to the greater jihad

—WORDS ATTRIBUTED TO THE PROPHET MUHAMMAD

If you see the word *"Jihad"* in the media, it usually refers to "holy war," but its real meaning is the struggle against wrongdoing in one's own heart. Muslims accept that the use of force may be necessary as a last resort for self-defense or to protect the weak, but the root meaning of the word *Islam* means peace. Muhammad Raceme Boa Muhaiyaddeen, a Sufi from Sri Lanka, wrote that "true holy war is to praise God and to cut away the enemies of truth within our own hearts." He added, that because God is One, we should never see another person as separate from ourselves. (M.R.B. Muhaiyaddeen, *Islam and World Peace.*)

PRACTICE *Do you have friends who belong to a religion or nationality different from your own? If so, do you think of them by their name or as "a Hindu" or "a Russian"? Jesus said that God knows each person by name. In your time of quiet, consider the divisions of the world. It might help you to recall the teaching of some religions that the One God made and loves each individual person. Spend some time quietly considering the ancient Hindu text:*

Let us always look at each other with the eyes of a friend.

Poverty is . . .

If a rich person sees his brother in need, yet closes his heart against him, how can he claim that he loves God?

—BIBLE: I JOHN 3.17

When I first went to India 40 years ago, I was shocked to see children picking through heaps of rubbish in the hope of finding a few grains of rice to eat. President Clinton summarized the situation in a starkly: "A billion people go to bed hungry every night. And a billion and a half people—one quarter of the people on earth—never get a clean glass of water. One woman dies every minute in childbirth." The Kyoto Declaration states: "Development of itself may not bring peace, but there can be no lasting peace without it."

PRACTICE *If you are committed to seeking a more peaceful world, you cannot ignore the problem of world hunger. You need to inform yourself of the basic facts, but also try to enter imaginatively into the experience of those who are poor. Imagine not only the pain and weakness of starvation but also the weariness, humiliation, and loss of human dignity. Ponder this Litany from the streets of Calcutta:*

Poverty is a knee level view from your bit of pavement;
coughing from your steel-banded lungs, alone with your face to the wall;
shrunken breasts and a three-year-old who cannot stand . . .
the prayer withheld
the heart withheld
the hand withheld; yours and mine.

—FROM *1,000 WORLD PRAYERS*, ED. MARCUS BRAYBROOKE

Peace Is an Inner Change

O Lord, baptize our hearts into a sense of the conditions and needs of all people.

—GEORGE FOX (1624–1691), FOUNDER OF THE SOCIETY OF FRIENDS

Peace may mean the cessation of acts of war, but real peace means that everyone has enough material provisions for a life of dignity. As the 30-year civil war in Guatemala came to an end, Abraham García, an indigenous Mayan spiritual guide and healer who had earlier been imprisoned and tortured by the army said, "Peace isn't the simple silencing of the bullets. It must be an inner change toward other people, respect for the way they think and live. . . . For us there is no peace if there are people who walk barefoot, if there is no housing, no land."

PRACTICE *It is easy to leave peace to the politicians, but you can also make a difference. Governments will only provide the resources to rebuild economies shattered by long years of conflict if that is what voters demand. You have a vote and can influence others who vote. There are many ways of helping people in poorer countries. Almost everyone who does this finds they not only help others, but also help themselves, because they gain greater understanding of human life and the values required for peaceful living.*

The Water of Life

We send down water from the sky . . . with it we grow for you gardens of date palms and vines: in them you have abundant fruits and you eat and enjoy them.

—QUR'AN: 23.18-19

How much water do you use each day? You would know the answer if you had to carry it for several miles from a watering hole. Nearly one in six people in the world lack access to clean drinking water. I once visited a remote village in northern India where clean water had just been provided by a drilling operation for which we'd raised money. For the first time, the villagers had clean water, which would improve their health and save them hours of walking. When a village in Mali got a well "it was like coming out of an oven into a cool room. We had such a big party to celebrate," said David Somboro, a well driller. (Christian Aid leaflet.)

PRACTICE *Water in many religions is a symbol of God's love and grace. As you think of those who lack good water, meditate on your own need for spiritual refreshment:*

Living Water, River of Mercy, Source of Life,
From your deep well, quench our thirst and refresh our weariness;
Wash away our dirt, clean our wounds and wipe away our tears.
Be for us a fountain of life;
And for all people be a river of hope to sweep away all injustice
And a constant spring of hope for peace and new life.

—BY MARIE THERESE WINTER,
FROM *THE BOOK OF A THOUSAND PRAYERS*, ED. ANGELA ASHWIN

day

283 No Peace Without Justice

Strengthen us, O God, to hear the groans of the poor . . .
that many be made not poor to make a few rich

—OLIVER CROMWELL (1599–1658), ENGLISH CIVIL WAR LEADER AND LORD PROTECTOR

You have probably seen houses of the wealthy surrounded by high walls, security cameras, and metal gates. It makes you wonder whether riches have brought peace or increased anxiety. It is said that there is no peace without justice. Injustice provides no peace, neither for the wronged nor for those who profit from it. In a village in the Indian state of Orissa, when evening comes, the better-off householders shout out: "Anybody hungry? Anybody hungry?" It is only when everyone in the village has had enough to eat that the wealthy go to sleep in peace.

PRACTICE *Is your conscience troubled by the injustice and inequality in the world? If not, have you been lulled into a false peace? Spend some of your quiet time considering your lifestyle. Is it extravagant and wasteful? Do you contribute to the inequalities of society? How much do you give to charity? Are you engaged in any social service or efforts to help the deprived? Many spiritual writers suggest that those who care for the poor care for the Lord.*

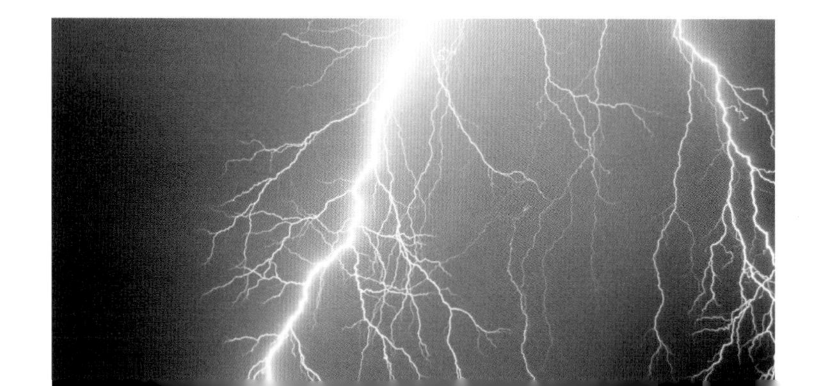

The Sheep and the Goats

Treat all people well,
Perhaps to your surprise
The one whom you are meeting
Is God in some disguise.

—TULSIDAS (1532–1623), HINDU POET WHO RETOLD THE RAMAYANA IN HINDI

Do you know the origin of the saying "to divide the sheep from the goats"? Jesus told a story that on Judgment Day the King will divide the good from the bad, like a shepherd dividing the sheep from the goats. To those on his right hand he will say, "Blessed are you for when I was hungry you gave me food; when I was thirsty you gave me drink; when I was a stranger, you invited me in; when I was naked, you gave me clothes; I was ill and you looked after me; I was in prison and you came to visit me." But the people asked, "Lord when did we do this, when did we see you?" He replied, "Whatever you did for one of the least of my brothers and sisters, you did for me." (Matthew 25.31–40.)

PRACTICE *Teachers of several religions encourage you to see the Lord in the face of the poor. By seeking God, you do not turn away from the world. You see its needs more vividly. Reflect on this prayer written by Mother Teresa (1910–1997).*

Lord, open our eyes,
That we may see you in our brothers and sisters.
Lord, open our ears,
That we may hear the cries of the hungry, the cold,
The frightened and the oppressed.
Lord, open our hearts,
That we may love each other as you love us.
Renew us in your spirit,
Lord, free us and make us one.

day 285

Rainbow

Dear Lord, I expect to pass through this world but once;
and any good thing, therefore, that I can do . . .
let me do it now.

—STEPHEN GRELLET, A CONTEMPORARY WRITER

Yalda Shams is one of the few Afghan girls who received an education while the Taliban governed Afghanistan. She cut off her hair, dressed in boys' clothes, and kept quiet. Now there are 6,000 girls at her school in Herat. During the time when they could not go to school, their only entertainment came from copies of the *Rainbow* magazine, which is brightly colored and full of uplifting stories. It is produced by the Sanayee Development Foundation, which contributes to reconciliation and peace-building in Afghanistan and neighboring Pakistan. Now the magazine is emphasizing practical steps to build a peaceful country.

PRACTICE *Do you find the magnitude of the problem of world poverty daunting? It is easy to feel there is nothing you can do that will make a difference. However, to change the life of one person is worthwhile. It costs about 15 cents to produce each copy of* Rainbow. *At present, the demand is so great that there is only one copy per class. Christian Aid, a British based charity, helped pay the Sanayee Development Foundation to buy a better printing press. There are many agencies that offer relief aid and support development programs. Do you give time or money to any of these?*

Generosity Is the Essence of Peace

All that is there in the universe belongs to God,
Enjoy it, sacrifice all, do not be greedy,
After all whose wealth is it?

—Opening verse of the Isa Upanishad

The gap between rich and poor is growing wider. The situation is like a luxury stretch limousine driving through an urban ghetto. Inside sit the wealthy of the postindustrial world of North America, Japan, Europe, and Australasia. Outside are all the other inhabitants of this planet. Americans spend more on cosmetics and Europeans spend more on ice cream than the cost of providing schooling and sanitation for 2 billion people. Global economics are complex, but Gandhi was right—"There is enough for each person's need, but not for everyone's greed." "In Hinduism God is the Eternal Giver," says the social activist swami Agnivesh. "Generosity, which delights in giving, is the essence of peace or *shanti*. Greed is a symptom of our spiritual underdevelopment." (P. Knitter and C. Muzzaffat, eds., *Subverting Greed*.)

PRACTICE *Live simply so that others may simply live. The high standard of living in the developed world depletes the Earth's resources. Extravagance and luxury in a world where many go hungry is morally unacceptable. Ask yourself whether your lifestyle is too luxurious. Are all the conveniences of modern life really necessary? Gratitude for all God has given should inspire generosity and delight in sharing life's blessing with others. I often use this grace before meals:*

Grant, Lord, to those who are hungry, bread
And to those who have bread, a hunger for justice.

Good Globalization

The people cannot be sustained except by wealth
Wealth cannot be acquired except through development,
Development cannot be attained except through justice.

—BASED ON THE WRITINGS OF IBN KHALDUN (1332–1402),
MUSLIM HISTORIAN AND PHILOSOPHER

Even if you simplify your lifestyle and give more to help development projects in poor countries, it is not enough. A growing number of people of different disciplines and faiths are campaigning for "Good Globalization." It is questionable whether globalization can now be reversed. At present, it is a cause for serious concerns. Some 89 countries are worse off than they were 10 years ago, partly because of debt, unfair trade policies, and the power of global corporations. Professor John Dunning, editor of *Making Globalization Good* calls for Creativity, Cooperation, and Compassion, which includes fairness and concern for the impoverished.

PRACTICE *You may be baffled by the complexities of international economics. Even the experts disagree. However, you can influence political and economic decisions by the way you vote, invest, and spend your money, as well as by campaigning. Shareholders can insist that companies adopt ethical policies, do not exploit workers in poor countries, and do not adopt environmentally unsound policies. You can refuse to buy goods made by child labor. If you are on a company, school, or religious board, you can insist that moral considerations are discussed. Peace requires you to put people's welfare before profit.*

What Did You Learn about Peace?

O God, as Muslims, Jews and Christians, we acknowledge that you have made of one blood all the nations of the earth. You love all of us, as if all were one.

—A PRAYER PREPARED BY A CHRISTIAN, A JEW, AND A MUSLIM, FROM *PRAYERS FOR PEACE*, ED. B. MARTIN PEDERSEN

Were you taught anything about peacemaking at school? History is often presented as a chronicle of wars. By contrast, peace education is neglected. After the Six Day War, Father Bruno Hussar, a Catholic priest who had settled in Israel soon after the state was created, had the vision of a village where Jews, Christians, and Muslims could live together and their children grow up and go to school together. *Neve Shalom/Wahat-as-Salam*, as the community is called, also offers weeklong courses where Israelis and Arabs live and learn together, discovering their shared hopes and fears. (Bruno Hussar, *When the Cloud Lifted*.)

PRACTICE *If you have grown up under the threat of an enemy, it is hard to discover your shared humanity. One Israeli soldier said it was only by going through the possessions of a dead Arab gunman and seeing pictures of his family that he realized the human tragedy of fighting. When you hear the name of a particular group of people, is your instant reaction "enemy" or "terrorist"? Examine why this is so. Have you been conditioned by your upbringing or by the media? Try to see the common humanity you share.*

day 289

Begin with the Children

If we are to attain real peace in this world,
we will have to begin with the children.

—MAHATMA GANDHI

"If you don't become who you are, then what you might have contributed to the world will never have a chance to be." These words inspired Therese Becker to devote herself to encouraging children's self-trust and self-esteem. One of Therese's young teenagers talked to her about the criticisms she had received for "being different." "When I look at my hand," she wrote, "I see nothing but an empty space where my soul used to sit." Therese said, "We must encourage and honor differences if the planet and its various species are going to survive. The bottom line in every school I visit is that children want to love the earth and each other. They yearn to become who they are." (Joel Beversluis, ed. *A Source Book for The Earth's Community of Religions*.)

PRACTICE *Have you tried exploring the wonder of life with young children? Goethe said, "You have to ask children how cherries and strawberries taste." They are tasting them for the first time. Children need adults to share with them the joy of discovery and to keep alive the sense of wonder. Each child also needs to be affirmed in his or her individuality. Pressures to conform may damage a child's self-worth, and the frustration may be expressed through violence. In his poem, the stars said to Robert Jones (seventh grade),*

And you are a true genesis
in your own way, a type of god,
not a big god, but a god

—THERESE BECKER, *WHEN A CHILD SINGS*

Amnesty

He who saves one life is as if he saved the world entire.

—RABBINIC SAYING

A more peaceful world depends on increased respect for human dignity. Amnesty International has become a worldwide voice of the human conscience, challenging torture, capital punishment, and police brutality wherever they happen. In ways we do not understand, victims sense when others are praying or thinking of them. Irina Ratushinskaya, who was a prisoner in the Soviet Union, wrote:

Believe me, it was often thus
In solitary cells, on winter nights
A sudden sense of joy and warmth
And a resounding note of love,
And then, unsleeping, I would know,
A-huddle by an icy wall
Someone is thinking of me now
Petitioning the Lord for me.

—*THE LION PRAYER COLLECTION*, ED. MARY BATCHELOR

PRACTICE *Amnesty International's reputation shows what can be achieved by public opinion, if enough people express their moral outrage. Supporters of Amnesty write to governments on behalf of people wrongly imprisoned or held in degrading circumstances. Your letter could make a difference. Your prayers certainly will. This is a contribution that you can make to a more just and peaceful world even if you are housebound.*

Apology for Slavery

In the face of the oppressed I hear the voice of God
In the face of the brutalized I see the face of Christ.

—FROM A PRAYER BY JOHN JOHANSEN-BERG, FORMER MODERATOR OF THE BRITISH UNITED REFORMED CHURCH, *PRAYERS FOR PILGRIMS*

Young people sometimes see injustice more clearly than their elders. A 12-year-old boy asked if he might speak to some Ghanaian villagers that his father was addressing. He described his visit to a castle at Cape Coast, once a center of the slave trade. The chapel was directly above the dungeon where the slaves were kept. As the boy put it, "This was where my people, the white people, could pretend to worship their God." He apologized for the past and promised to work that such things would not happen again. The headman replied that the last time white men had come, the villagers fled and hid in the bush. The boy's apology made friendship possible. (Brian Frost, *The Politics of Peace.*)

PRACTICE *Loyalty does not mean ignoring what is wrong in a city's or a country's past. An apology may help to heal old wounds. It is important to remember that all human behavior is a mixture of good and evil. Try to build friendships that will ensure the past does not continue to cast its shadow over the present.*

Struggling against Oppression

To see the world for what it is and for what it can be.
To tell truths that show the blue mist rising,
that show the sun shining.

—*Rites for Walter Rodney* by Clifton Joseph,
The Global Dilemma

Nonviolence does not mean indifference in the face of evil. Rastafarians, who take their name from Ras Tafari, who was crowned Ethiopian Emperor Haile Selassie I in 1930, have championed the cause of African people who were enslaved in the Americas and the Caribbean. They rightly say that failure to resist oppression condemns others to a life of exploitation and degradation. Instead of trying to defeat the oppressors, nonviolent protest appeals to their conscience in the hope that they will see the evil of their actions. Its aim is radical change that will help the world become "what it can be."

PRACTICE *A true commitment to nonviolence is not that easy. Mahatma Gandhi spoke about* satyagraha, *or the power of truth to effect change. This requires a radical change in your outlook so that you banish thoughts of victory. Instead of personalizing the conflict and speaking abusively about those you oppose, you need to cultivate compassion for those whose actions you resist. You must appeal to their conscience. This means that you need total integrity and honesty. Ensure that what you say is true and not propaganda. You may like to use this Rastafarian prayer:*

Spirit come within our hearts . . . that the hungry be fed, the aged protected and the infant cared for.

—From *Prayers for Peace*, ed. B. Martin Pedersen

day
293 Open House

Do not forget to entertain strangers, for by so doing some people have entertained angels without knowing it.

—BIBLE: HEBREWS 13.2

Many Israelis and Palestinians have been refugees. Dalia Ashkenazi was only 11 months old when her family came with other Jews from Bulgaria to Israel. They settled in an empty Arab house. In the garden was a lemon tree. Soon after the 1967 war, the bell rang and Dalia, home from university, opened it to find three Palestinians at the gate. Bashir Al-Khayri had been born in the house but fled from the Israeli army when he was six. Later Bashir's father—now blind—visited and asked if the lemon tree was still there. When Dalia finally inherited the house and married Yehezkel Landau, they decided with Bashir to make it an Open House and center of reconciliation for Israelis and Arabs. (Garth Hewitt, *Pilgrims and Peacemakers.*)

PRACTICE *Would you have invited strangers into your own home? Dalia could have easily shut the door, but her conscience held it open. Building bridges for peace involves risk and a willingness to trust people you do not know. Sometimes you are disappointed but without courage, new beginnings are not possible. Are you involved in strained relationships? Is there a new initiative you could take to ease the difficulty? The prophet Zechariah says, "Speak everyone truth to his fellows." (Zechariah 8.16.) Yehezkel Landau comments, "We suffer violence because we do not rectify injustices and those injustices persist as long as we fail to speak truth to one another."*

An Olive Tree

Those who love peace and rejoice in the welfare of creation . . .
do not harm even a mustard seed and are distressed at all damage
and wanton destruction that they see.

—SEFER HAHINUCH, BOOK OF EDUCATION WRITTEN
BY AHARON HA'LEVI (THIRTEENTH CENTURY)

Bashir's father planted a lemon tree. Dalia's father planted a jacaranda tree. In 1995, Yehezkel and Dalia's son planted an olive tree, helped by Arab children from the kindergarten. It was on the Jewish festival of New Year for Trees (*Tu B'Shevat*). The olive tree was a symbol of shared attachment to the land and was dedicated to healing its wounds. Yehezkel said, "We have a common father, Abraham, and a common mother, Jerusalem, and a common parent in heaven and on earth. We can all be siblings in the family of God with different identities. That's what this tree symbolizes for me." (Garth Hewitt, *Pilgrims and Peacemakers.*)

PRACTICE *Scarce natural resources can cause hostility between neighboring peoples. During a conflict, the land itself can become a casualty of war. The Bible warned, "When you are at war and lay siege to a city . . . do not destroy its trees by taking an axe to them, for they provide you with food." (Deuteronomy 20.19.) Modern war deprives civilians of water, sanitation, and electricity, and both sides suffer. Ask yourself how well you get along with your neighbors. You probably have far more in common in caring for where you live than those things that cause friction.*

day

295 Forgiveness—the Key to the Future

I forgive all beings,
I ask forgiveness from all beings,
I make friends with all beings,
I have no enemies.

—From the Jain Pratikraman Sutra,
From *Prayers for Peace*, ed. B. Martin Pedersen

What is the role of forgiveness in both your personal life and the life of your community? Desmond Tutu, former Anglican Archbishop of Cape Town, was a strong opponent of apartheid, but insists that forgiveness was vital in creating a new South Africa. Nelson Mandela, first President of the new South Africa, set the example. When he was released after 27 years of imprisonment on Robben Island, he said, "My mission is to liberate the oppressed and the oppressor, both." A new nation could only be built if past atrocities were acknowledged and pardon was both asked for and granted. (Desmond Tutu, *No Future without Forgiveness*.)

PRACTICE *To overcome hatred and resentment, you need to experience the freedom that forgiveness brings. Jesus taught his disciples to pray, "Forgive us our trespasses as we forgive those who trespass against us." The release from past bitterness also inspires the hope that love can overcome all enmity and hatred. Reflect on these words by Desmond Tutu:*

Goodness is stronger than evil;
Love is stronger than hate;
Light is stronger than darkness;
Victory is ours through Him who loves us.

Pardon the Murderers

Forgive the murderers, return good for evil and out of a hundred wrongdoers ten will be converted, not to your side but to God's side.

—LEO TOLSTOY (1828–1910), RUSSIAN NOVELIST AND SOCIAL REFORMER, FROM *HIROSHIMA PEACE READER*

Is execution and repression the best answer to terrorism? After a terrorist bomb killed the reforming Czar Alexander II, the novelist Leo Tolstoy dreamed that he was Emperor, judging the murderers. On waking, he urged the new czar to pardon the assassin. "If you do not pardon the murderers, you will do away with four individuals, but evil breeds evil and forty terrorists will spring up to replace them. But forgive, return good for evil and of a hundred wrongdoers ten will be converted." Alexander III took no notice, halting constitutional reforms and executing the terrorists. (Henry Troyat, *Tolstoy*.)

PRACTICE *Do you think Tolstoy's suggestion would have worked? How can you best use your influence as an informed citizen? If you are concerned for world peace, it is a question you need to ask. Force may suppress terrorism, but will it destroy it? The danger is that violence breeds more violence. After the horrors of September 11, 2001, the Dalai Lama said two responses were possible. One came from fear, the other from love. Reflect on his words: "If we could love even those who attacked us and seek to understand why they did so . . . we would become spiritual activists." (From the International Interfaith Center Newsletter.)*

day 297

Love Your Opponent

If you do not practice compassion toward your enemy,
then toward whom can you practice it?

—FROM THE BUDDHIST COMPENDIUM OF PRACTICES

When you are faced with injustice, it is difficult not to feel anger. Yet striking out in anger against those responsible does not help. In fact it causes further harm. The Dalai Lama has said that his opposition to the Chinese occupation of Tibet does not mean that he is angry with the Chinese people. I once heard the Dalai Lama being asked to support an economic boycott of China on behalf of the Tibetans. He replied, "I could never do anything that would hurt the people of China." If you cultivate the right attitude, your enemies can become your best spiritual teachers. Those you regard as opponents give you the opportunity to develop tolerance, patience, and understanding. Who else can provide such lessons?

PRACTICE *You probably know many people who give you opportunities to develop patience and compassion. It may be a boss who picks on you unfairly or a bully who gives your child a hard time. As you feel your natural anger rising, take a deep breath and imagine a beautiful sunset or still water. Then, take a moment to try to see the problem from the other person's point of view. You also might wish to repeat the Buddhist mantra "May all beings be happy and at peace"—including the boss and the bully! Next time you encounter someone who annoys you, instead of shouting, you could talk with the person or, even better, just listen.*

Befriending the Enemy

To befriend the one who regards himself as your enemy
is the quintessence of true religion.

—Mahatma Gandhi, *Harijan*, English weekly journal in India

If you have been mugged or swindled, do you want to see the criminal severely punished? Martin Luther King said that the nonviolent approach stirs the enemy's conscience so that reconciliation becomes a reality. During the American Civil War, an enemy officer was brought to President Abraham Lincoln for punishment. After the president and the enemy officer had talked for some time, the man walked free. Some of the troops protested, but Lincoln replied, "The man has seen the error of his ways, so I *have* destroyed an enemy. I have turned him into a friend."

PRACTICE *Love and forgiveness can transform hatred into friendship, but first you need to recognize your feelings of anger and revenge. If you succumb to the enemy, you become as bad as that person. You will fall prey to feelings of violence. Bitter resentment will poison your attitude to others. You need consciously to seek the moral high ground and to live by your principles of nonviolence and peace. This will give you the inner strength to pray for your enemy and the courage to support efforts to rehabilitate him or her. Spend time reflecting on these words of Martin Luther King:*

Love is the only force capable of transforming an enemy into a friend.

People, Not Enemies

The early Christians did not search for the enemy in others but rather in themselves and in this way they transformed the whole world.

—ARCHBISHOP PITRIM

What else besides compassion can break through the hatred and prejudices that divide the world? As a child, the Russian writer Yevgeny Yevtushenko saw hundreds of German war prisoners marched through Moscow in 1941. They were watched by a crowd of women, most of whom had lost a son or husband at the hands of the Germans. However, these German soldiers were now thin, unshaven, and hobbling on crutches. Suddenly, an elderly woman pushed past a policeman, unwrapped a colored handkerchief, and gave a soldier a crust of black bread. Soon other women did the same. "The soldiers," writes Yevtushenko, "were no longer enemies. They were people." (Yevengy Yevtushenko, *A Precocious Autobigraphy.*)

PRACTICE *Have you ever felt enmity against a particular group of people? If you look into yourself, do you find that you have stereotyped them? Do you actually know anyone belonging to this group? Do they fit your stereotypes? Should you try to find out more about these people? Archbishop Pitrim warned that images that reduce the other to an enemy often lead to war. Think about your attitudes and your language. Sri Chinmoy says "If we offer peace to someone else, we will see how peace expands from one to two persons and gradually to the world at large." Is there someone to whom you should offer peace?*

Nonviolence Begins in the Heart

Hatreds never cease through hatred in this world;
through love alone they cease. This is an eternal law.

—FROM THE BUDDHIST DHAMMAPADA, 5

The mushroom cloud from the atomic bomb dropped on Hiroshima is an image of destruction that has hung over the world for 60 years. The Japanese scientist, poet, and mystic, Dr. Takashi Nagai of Nagasaki, recognized that Japanese suffering resulted from his people treating life too cheaply. Through his own suffering and meditation, he realized that "loving our neighbors as we love ourselves" is the only way to peace. Nonviolence has to start in the heart, because that's where killing starts. "Go to the mountains and meditate," Dr. Nagai told enquirers. "In the hurly-burly of the city, you rush around in circles. But the blue mountains are immovable."

PRACTICE *If you are angry or agitated, it can help to go outside and observe the strength and the stillness of nature. Even in the middle of the city, there may be a park nearby. Look at the great trees or the stillness of a lake. Nature contains a depth and strength that is also seen in people with deep spiritual roots. Ask yourself why you are angry. Does it say more about you than about the person who annoyed you? Self-knowledge is essential if you are to root out the potential violence that lies deep in the human heart. Learn to love yourself as a way to loving your neighbor.*

day
301 Forgive, But Do Not Forget

How could a man live at all if he did not give absolution every night to himself and all his brothers?

—JOHANN WOLFGANG GOETHE (1749–1832), GERMAN POET AND PHILOSOPHER

Omagh in Northern Ireland suffered a terrible bombing during the Troubles. When I visited Omagh after the bombing I wondered what help an outsider could offer. The bereaved and injured cannot forget the horrors they witnessed. To do so would be a betrayal of loved ones who were killed. Mufti Camdzic, whose beautiful mosque in Banja Luka was destroyed during the ethnic cleansing of Bosnia said, "We can't forget; but we try to forgive and reconcile, to build again."

PRACTICE *When you read grim news of a massacre or of a devastating earthquake, it is easy to turn the page and to forget the tragedy. However, if you do know anyone connected, it is always worth telling them you are sorry. It helps the person not to feel alone with their grief. If the tragedy is in a distant part of the world, pause and say a short prayer for the victims. Every life is important, and it will help you to remember that we share the one gift of life.*

Strive for Freedom from Fear

Among the fundamental freedoms which people strive for . . .
freedom from fear towers highest, both as a means and an end.

—Aung San Suu Kyi (b. 1945), Burmese Buddhist leader

If you discovered that there were financial irregularities at work or that a colleague was being bullied, would you blow the whistle or keep quiet because you were afraid of the consequences? The democratic leader Aung San Suu Kyi insists that the Burmese people must free themselves from apathy and fear if they are to be rid of dictatorship. Fear, she says, goes with hatred, so the best way to be free from fear is to cultivate the Buddhist virtue of *metta*, or loving kindness, which includes patience, generosity, and wisdom. Through long periods of house arrest and government pressure, Aung San Suu Kyi has cultivated these qualities. By freeing themselves from fear, she hopes the Burmese people will liberate themselves from tyranny.

PRACTICE *How much are you willing to risk for peace? Are you afraid to take part in a protest demonstration? If so, who or what are you afraid of? Do you worry what other people will think? Are you afraid you will get hurt or get into trouble? Sit quietly, relax the body, and quiet the mind. Think of those of whom you are afraid. Then radiate loving thoughts toward them. They, too, may be afraid. Repeat the bodhisattva vow, "As long as living beings remain, may I too abide to dispel the misery of the world." As your mind is filled with compassion, your fears will be soothed.*

day 303

Defending Ourselves with Love

When we defend ourselves with love, we are also seeking the sinners' conversion.

—OSCAR ROMERO (1917–1980), ARCHBISHOP OF SAN SALVADOR, SPEAKING AFTER THE MURDER OF FATHER RUTILIO GRANDE, AT THE INSTALLATION OF A NEW PARISH PRIEST

The day before he was assassinated, Archbishop Oscar Romero warned that many solutions to the country's problems were mere "Band-Aids" and not real solutions. Although opponents argued that "Liberation Theology" was Marxist not Christian, Romero insisted that the first liberation was "from selfishness, violence, cruelty, and hatred." Political and economic reform was important but would only be effective if there was inner reform. Quoting St. Paul's words, "Be free to love," Romero insisted that true liberation is to be freed from selfish greed so as to serve the poor. (James Brockman, ed., *The Violence of Love: The Words of Oscar Romero.*)

PRACTICE *All religions oppose aggression and call for justice for the poor. If you take part in social action or peace protests, it is important to ground all your actions in prayer. Only by regular silent reflection will you be able to ensure your integrity. Your aim is not victory but justice, which is why, like Oscar Romero, you should seek your opponents' change of heart and mind.*

What Sacrifice for Peace?

At all costs I must bear the burden of all beings. I do not follow my own inclinations. I have made a vow to save all beings

—FROM THE VOW OF A BODHISATTVA

How far should one go in protesting against war? Are acts of civil disobedience permissible? Before the second Gulf War, some peace activists planned to act as human shields. As a protest against the Vietnam War, some Buddhist monks burned themselves to death. Unlike suicide bombers, the monks only killed themselves. Buddhists do not encourage suicide, but in the ordination ceremony a would-be monk is expected to burn a small spot to show how seriously he takes his vow. The Vietnamese monk, by burning himself, was saying with all his strength and determination that he wanted to protect his people from the suffering of war.

PRACTICE *There are many ways to work for peace. It is important to see your particular gifts and vocation. One should also avoid judging others who seek peace in different ways, especially if they are from another culture. It is also good to recognize that your contribution to peace may change at different stages of your life. If you have small children, is it fair to them to take them on peace marches? At another stage, you may achieve more by prayer than by too many committee meetings. There are many paths to peace. Take time to consider whether you are on the path that is right for you.*

day 305

Sunflowers Instead of Missiles

If everybody in the world got killed, then there'd be nobody left.

—A 9-YEAR-OLD GIRL INTERVIEWED ON VIDEOTAPE BY ERIC CHIVIAN AND ROBERTA SNOW

After Ukraine gave up its last nuclear warhead, the defense ministers of Ukraine, Russia, and the United States met at a former Ukrainian missile base. They scattered sunflower seeds, which can remove toxins, including nuclear waste, from soil and water. Former U.S. Defense Secretary William Perry said, "Sunflowers instead of missiles in the soil would insure peace for future generations." Although the threat of nuclear war has receded with the ending of the Cold War, there is now the danger that nuclear weapons could fall into the hands of terrorists. It is estimated that 30,000 nuclear warheads still exist—the equivalent of 300,000 bombs of the type dropped on Hiroshima.

PRACTICE *Has the possibility of nuclear destruction scarred your psyche? Is it a legacy you want to pass on to your children? An educator asked, "What have our children learned growing up in a community that calls itself civilized and yet possesses weapons barbarous beyond belief?" Reflect on this verse by Cecil Day Lewis to an unborn child:*

So, child of man,
Remind us of what we have blindly willed—
A slaughter of innocents! You can
Yet make this madness yield
And lift the load of our stock-piling guilt,
O child of man.

—CECIL DAY LEWIS, FROM "AGNUS DEI," *REQUIEM FOR THE LIVING*

Remember Your Humanity

We appeal as human beings to human beings: remember your humanity . . .
If you can do so, the way lies open to a new Paradise; if you cannot,
there lies before you the risk of universal death.

—APPEAL BY ALBERT EINSTEIN (1879–1955), PHYSICIST AND NOBEL LAUREATE AND BERTRAND RUSSELL (1872–1970), PHILOSOPHER

Were you old enough to be active in the protests against nuclear weapons in the seventies and eighties? After the 1995 Non-Proliferation treaty, Abolition 2000 was set up to work for the phased abolition of all nuclear weapons. There are now more than 2,000 Abolition groups. They believe getting rid of all nuclear weapons is the only way to eliminate their threat to all life. Josie Toda (1900–1958), the second president of Soka Gakkai, a postwar Japanese religious and peace movement, says, "This requires an exploration of the inner life of human beings. Only this will guide scientific technology to contribute to the peace of the world." (Josie Toda, *The Collected Works of Josie Toda*.)

PRACTICE *Should nuclear disarmament still be one of your concerns? A child asked her parents about this and got the reply, "It's no good worrying about it. There's nothing we can do. We'll face the problem when we have to." (N. Humphrey and R.J. Lifton, eds.* In a Dark Time.*) By then, it may be too late. You cannot actively campaign on every issue, but your cultivation of inner peace is a small but significant contribution to a more peaceful ethos in society. The youth of Soka Gakkai International-USA have distributed petition cards with a three-part pledge that could be the focus for your meditation:*

1. *I will value my own life.*
2. *I will respect all life.*
3. *I will inspire hope in others.*

day
307 The Killing Goes On

This world was not left to us by our parents, it was lent to us by our children.

—AFRICAN PROVERB

Mines and unexploded cluster bombs kill long after a war has ended. On the day journalist Dominic Nutt visited Amarrah in postwar Iraq, nine children were killed by an unexploded rocket. They were looking for ammunition to earn cash so that their families could buy food. Cambodia is another country littered with landmines and unexploded bombs, which endanger efforts to rebuild village life. Farmers risk plowing up mines. Children step on them on their way to school. It takes several hours work to clear 1 square meter. Kompomg Thom, the worst affected province, is 20 billion square meters in size! (From *Christian Aid News*.)

PRACTICE *Did you join in the campaign against land mines? It gained widespread popular support and a partial ban on their use. Archbishop Desmond Tutu of South Africa wrote a prayer saying that we all are implicated and share responsibility for the life-threatening legacy we have planted for our children.*

> *My heart is filled with a long ache. . . . The arms factory provides a job for my son and my taxes paid for the development of "smart" bombs. I did not protest when the soldiers planted fear into the earth. Lord we are all accomplices in the crime of war. Lord give us back our humanity, our* ubuntu.

The Slaughter of the Innocents

Should we not believe that the immense chorus of the cries of children killed in death camps now hangs over our world as a dark, powerful and accusing cloud?

—HANS JONAS, QUOTED IN MARCUS BRAYBROOKE, *TIME TO MEET*

The death of any child is heartrending, but the slaughter of the innocents in war or as a result of ethnic cleansing is agonizing. There is a sense of waste and a questioning of whether God is in control. But as Rabbi Hugo Gryn, a survivor of the Nazi death camps, said, "Auschwitz is about the death of humanity rather than the death of God." God pleads with the conscience of a cruel world in the cries of the dying children.

PRACTICE *Public indifference allows further atrocities to occur, but moral outrage can persuade governments to take action. You can make your views known to politicians, you can send money to help the victims, and you can pray for them. It is important not to give up hope. As Martin Luther King, in his eulogy for children martyred during the American Civil Rights campaign, said, "God is able to lift you from the fatigue of despair to the buoyancy of hope and transform dark and desolate valleys into sunlit paths of peace." (Coretta Scott King,* My Life with Martin Luther King.*)*

day
309 Rescuers!

Courage is never alone, for it has fear as its ever-present companion. An act deserves to be called courageous, if and only if, it is performed in spite of fear.

—SHOLO BREZNITZ, *HOLOCAUST AND THE CHRISTIAN WORLD*, ED. CAROL RITTNER

In the winter of 1940–1941, a German Jewish refugee asked for help from the wife of the pastor of Le Chambon-sur-Lignon, a village in the south of France. Pastor Trocmé consulted the village's head, who told him to send the woman away because he feared the Nazis. The Trocmés refused and persuaded their congregation to hide Jews, many of whom were later smuggled over the Swiss border to safety. When the Vichy police interrogated the Pastor, he replied, "These people came for help. I am their shepherd. A shepherd does not forsake his flock. . . . I do not know what a Jew is. I know only human beings." Pastor Trocmé was arrested and died in Majdanek concentration camp, but the villagers continued to hide Jews.

PRACTICE *The courage of Pastor Trocmé's congregation stands in stark contrast to the willingness of those who connived with the Nazis in the extermination of the Jews. Studies of the childhood of Nazi leaders show that they were made to feel undeserving and unlovable. Beatings were common. By contrast, the rescuers had no childhood memories of being punished unfairly or physically. At least one of their parents embodied high standards of ethical behavior, which taught their children the value of every human life. When questioned in later years, the rescuers did not think of themselves as doing anything special. One resident of Le Chambon-sur-Lignon said, "It was the most natural thing in the world to help these people." (Charlene Spretnak,* States of Grace.*)*

Hiroshima

Hiroshima. Are we looking at the past or at the future?

—Words of Elie Wiesel, Holocaust survivor and writer

The mushroom cloud over Hiroshima was a symbol of the evil of war to me as I grew up. When I visited the city, I hesitated about what to say to the guide, who was herself a survivor. She recalled her painful childhood memories of August 6, 1945, with honesty yet no hint of bitterness. Her parents were killed, her home was destroyed, and she herself was severely injured. As we came to a place of prayer, I was conscious of Britain's share in the suffering of her people, as she was of Japanese wartime atrocities. In the silence, we—a Buddhist and a Christian—knew that the world's only hope lies in mutual forgiveness and the forgiveness of Heaven.

PRACTICE *Are you reluctant to forgive? Do you hold back from offering an apology? Do you carry a grudge for some past wrong? When you run into someone you have argued with, do you pretend not to see them? It is better at least to make some neutral approach and say hello? Neither of you can hide from the past. Although this may not be the occasion to sort out your differences, you can begin to restore civilized relationships. How can you hope to find future peace if you are unable to mend past quarrels?*

day
311 # Our Common Humanity

This is our cry. This is our prayer. May we build peace in this world.

—WORDS WRITTEN BY A JUNIOR HIGH SCHOOL STUDENT, CARVED ON BLACK GRANITE AT THE CHILDREN'S PEACE MONUMENT AT HIROSHIMA

Why is it we discover our common humanity too late? One Hiroshima survivor, a Methodist minister, often preached about forgiveness, but his daughter, an infant when the bomb was dropped, ignored his message. She was full of bitterness. Her father was invited to America to take part in a television program, and she accompanied him. The pilot of the plane that had dropped the bomb was in the studio. When he met the survivors, he was so choked with emotion that he could hardly speak. At that moment, all the daughter's bitterness drained away. She had discovered our frail common humanity. (Marcus Braybrooke, *Love Without Limit.*)

PRACTICE *Do you avert your eyes from the pain of the world or share the suffering in your meditations? There is still an argument about whether the dropping of two atomic bombs on Japan saved Allied lives. Somewhere between 80,000 and 250,000 died at Hiroshima. Each individual death was a loss to humanity. When you see through statistics and your eyes are opened to the suffering of the victim, you see that the humanity that is shared is more important than the ideologies and politics that divide.*

He Has a Mother, Too

Soldiers killed in two world wars:

—1914-1918: 8,418,000; 1939-1945: 16,933,000

How would you treat an enemy prisoner? Daisaka Ikeda, president of Soka Gakkai International, had four elder brothers who had been drafted into military service by the Japanese during the Second World War. The oldest was killed in action in Burma. "When notification of his death came, I couldn't see my mother's face, but her back conveyed an unforgettable impression of grief. Soon afterwards, an American aviator parachuted to earth near our house. Japanese soldiers beat him with sticks and kicked him before the police took him away. My mother protested, saying the American's mother 'must be so worried about her son.' I have never forgotten her words. I saw the cruelty and futility of war." (David Krieger and Daisaka Ikeda, *Choose Hope*.)

PRACTICE *Have you served in the military? Would you do so again? Do you have memories that you have not faced? What is the effect on those who serve in the armed forces and on their children? When I asked some released prisoners in Northern Ireland how they now felt about their past actions, one replied, "It's what happens in war." Leo Tolstoy, in* War and Peace *was clear. "What are the morals of the military world? The object of warfare is murder—the means employed the ruin of a country and the plunder of its inhabitants." Is it surprising that a country that goes to war becomes a more violent society? In the search for peace, you should ask yourself, what is your role in this?*

Women: Incarnation of Nonviolence

May the God who dances in creation
and embraces us with human love,
who shakes us like thunder,
bless us and drive us out with power
to fill the world with her justice.

—JANET MORLEY (b. 1951), CHRISTIAN WRITER AND EDUCATOR, QUOTED IN MONICA FURLONG, *WOMEN PRAY*

Have you wondered if the world would be more peaceful if it was run by women? Gandhi said, "I learned the lesson of nonviolence from my wife. . . . Her determined resistance to my will on the one hand and her quiet submission to the suffering my stupidity involved . . . ultimately made me ashamed of myself. . . . In the end she became my teacher in nonviolence." He recognized women's competence, firmness, and forgiving spirit and encouraged them to enter politics. He spoke of women as "the incarnation of *ahimsa* [nonviolence]."

PRACTICE *"Are women's voices so different from men's?" asks Monica Furlong in her book* Women Pray. *She says the question is unanswerable because only in recent years have women's voices been regularly heard in public prayer. She states that women are concerned with "roots" and rediscovering female voices from the past. Many women's prayers are about justice, poverty, and ecology. Women pray about childbirth. They are more conscious of the spiritual significance of bodily functions. To picture the Divine in both feminine and masculine terms adds to a sense of the wholeness of life and the oneness of humanity.*

Land Mines

To create peace we must first remove the land mines in our hearts which prevent us from making peace: hatred, greed and deception.

—MAHA GHOSANANDA, SENIOR CAMBODIAN BUDDHIST MONK

Maha Ghosananda returned to Cambodia because, "We must have the courage to leave our own temples and go to temples full of suffering, to the refugee camps, the ghettos and the battlefields." Since 1992, he has led an annual peace march called *dhamma yietra,* or "pilgrimage of justice." When activists came under fire, he insisted that the march must go on. Peace, he said, comes into being "step by step." This was particularly fitting, because the pilgrims were walking through areas infested by land mines, left behind by the long civil war. Each step literally helped to reclaim the land for peace.

PRACTICE *Although Maha Ghosananda has been a leader of the campaign to rid the world of land mines, he sees that the real land mines are the hatred, greed, and deception in the heart. Peace requires meditation, clear understanding, and mindfulness. This is the seventh element of the Noble Eightfold Path, which the Buddha taught as the way to overcome suffering. Mindfulness is the recognition of the motives underlying actions. Its aim is to show the same loving concern to others that you show to yourself. "If we control the spirit," Maha Ghosananda says, "we are free from all suffering." Inner and outer peace both come "step by step."*

Liberation

The liberation that Christianity preaches is a liberation from something that enslaves, for something that ennobles.

—OSCAR ROMERO (1917–1980), ARCHBISHOP OF SAN SALVADOR, *VIOLENCE OF LOVE: THE WORDS OF OSCAR ROMERO*, ED. JAMES BROCKMAN

Violence is not just a matter of individual aggression or military action. For three years, Oscar Romero, Archbishop of San Salvador, warned of "structural violence," or what he called "the violence that lies at the root of all violence." Following the murder of a priest in his diocese, Romero denounced social injustice and the repression under which the poor of El Salvador were being tortured and murdered. Accused of being too political, Romero told a journalist that the inspiration for his work and preaching came from his times of prayer. "In prayer," he said, "I try to keep united with God. Otherwise I would only be a clanging bell."

PRACTICE *Peace is never just a matter of political action for a person of faith. As Archbishop Romero insisted, "structural violence" also has to be tackled. Economic and political justice are necessary for lasting peace. A growing number of stockholders are applying moral principles to their investments. If you own shares, do you know if the companies you invest in ensure adequate working conditions for their employees? Do the companies adopt environmentally friendly policies? Ethical investment and the application of moral values to the business world help to create a climate of peace. Oscar Romero warned the rich not to hold onto their wealth at the expense of others dying of hunger.*

God Is Most Merciful

If they cease (from fighting), God is Oft-Forgiving, Most Merciful.

—QUR'AN: 2.192

The word *"Islam"* derives from the Semitic word for "peace." But the recent actions of extremists have created a false picture of the religion. When the prophet Muhammad returned victorious to his birthplace Mecca, from which he had been driven out, he sent for those who had opposed him. He asked them how he should treat them. They admitted that they deserved punishment but hoped he would treat them as a generous brother. Reminding them of the Bible story of Joseph, who forgave his brothers for selling him into slavery, Muhammad said, "This day let no reproach be (cast) on you. God will forgive you and He is the Most Merciful of those who show mercy." (Qur'an 12.93.)

PRACTICE *When you get the better of your opponents, are you tempted to gloat? Muhammad's generosity to those who had opposed him and persecuted him has few parallels in history. Often, as after the First World War, vindictive peace-terms sow the seeds of future conflict. In the same way, if you have a victory in court or the boardroom, be careful not to perpetuate the struggle by your attitude toward those you have defeated. Generosity to those you defeat creates good relations. Muhammad reflected his belief in the mercy of God through his actions.*

day

317 Out Through the Door

The more he strives to injure me,
The greater is my clemency

—AL-HALLAJ (d. 922), A MUSLIM MYSTIC, WHO WAS EVENTUALLY IMPRISONED AND EXECUTED FOR HIS BELIEFS

When the Sandinistas gained control of Nicaragua, they tried to reconcile with former enemies. Tomás Borge, who had been imprisoned and whose wife was murdered, became Minister of the Interior. Visiting the main prison, he recognized two of his former guards. "Do you know me?" he asked. With downcast eyes, they refused to answer. "I am Borge," he said, "whom you tortured. . . . Now you will discover the full weight of the Revolution. . . . I forgive you. . . . Go on. Out through the door. You are free." Borge released some 5,000 members of the national guardsmen, saying, "We will never create a more humane society if we use hatred, if we answer abuse with vengeance." (From a Christian Aid bulletin.)

PRACTICE *Do you think those who have done evil actions should be set free? Amnesty is part of many peace agreements, but it is hard for those whose loved ones were killed to see their murderers walk free. However, one such person in Northern Ireland said, "If that is the price I must pay for peace, I am willing to do so." Peace requires sacrifices from many people. Consider the situations of conflict in which you are involved. Would the situation be resolved if you swallowed your desire for vindication and learned to live with your former enemy?*

Ahimsa

The law of love will work, just as the law of gravitation will work, whether we accept it or not.

—MAHATMA GANDHI, FROM *SATYAGRAHA*

Is nonviolence strong enough to transform the world? The nonviolent work of Gandhi and Martin Luther King has brought enormous benefit to thousands of people, but violence and terror seem to be on the increase. Gandhi himself never doubted the creed of nonviolence but was conscious that passive resistance too often masqueraded as nonviolence. Commitment to the struggle for truth (*satyagraha*) requires fearlessness, because fear distorts a person's judgment. Gandhi insisted that in its true sense, nonviolence "implies as complete self-purification as is humanly possible."

PRACTICE *As your heart becomes more peaceful, you become more aware of the violence and injustice in the world. The inner journey compels you to greater activity in the external world, but the attempt to apply the principles of peace in situations of conflict makes the inner journey even more essential. Nonviolence, as Gandhi said requires, as complete a self-purification as possible. Have you continued to grow more peaceful in your heart and in your life as you have pursued peace in the world? Gandhi's call is to do both.*

part seven

PEACE IN THE UNIVERSE

Many people find physical and spiritual refreshment in the appreciation of the natural world. In nature, you can find evidence of a Divine Presence. The sense of unity with all life creates a deeper reverence for our planet and a greater concern to protect the environment for our fellow human beings and all living creatures.

We are the flowers of a single garden,
The fruits of a single tree,
And the waves of one sea.

Beauty

In Nature we see God. . . .
Nature inspires devotional reveries.
In Nature is the essence of joy and peace.

—From the Sikh scriptures

Do you head for the countryside on the weekend? Although most cities provide parks for recreation, many people find stillness and renewal in the beauty of the wild. Great mountains give you a sense of your scale in the scheme of things. The peace of still water can calm both the body and the mind. Even a single flower can remind you of life's beauty and fragility. Sometimes people sense a living presence in nature, or "Mother Earth." If you feel nature ministers to your body and soul, then you also have a responsibility to care for and protect it.

PRACTICE *Sit quietly, and let your body and mind become still. Then picture a natural scene that helps you to be calm and lifts your spirits. Be aware of the beauty that surrounds you, the beauty of which you are a part, in your mind's eye. Reflect on this Native American Navajo blessing:*

Before me, beauty; Behind me, beauty;
Around me, beauty.
May I walk in beauty always
Beauty I am.

A Sense of Presence

Not in entire forgetfulness and not in utter nakedness, but trailing clouds of glory do we come from God who is our home.

—FROM "INTIMATIONS OF IMMORTALITY"
BY WILLIAM WORDSWORTH (1770–1850)

Have you sensed the mystery of life amid nature's grandeur? The English poet William Wordsworth grew up in the Lake District with its awesome mountains and still water. It was there he experienced a spiritual reality that he described in these words:

I have felt
A presence that disturbs me with the joy
Of elevated thoughts;
A sense sublime
Of something far more deeply interfused,
Whose dwelling is the light of setting suns,
And the round ocean and the living air,
And the blue sky, and in the mind of man.

—FROM THE POEM "THE PRELUDE"

Many people experience a sense of presence in the midst of nature. They often speak of a feeling of identity with the trees or the rocks and of a great feeling of gladness to be alive.

PRACTICE *We may be most aware of the hidden spiritual dimensions of life when we are in the presence of the awesome splendor and stillness of nature. Try to find time to spend by yourself in a scenic spot to discover if this is true for you.*

Love All God's Creation

It is God who sends rain from the sky, bringing forth buds and green leaves on every plant.

—QUR'AN: 6.95-99

For many people, the beauty of nature and a sense of presence point to the glory of God and an awareness that the whole of life should be lived in God's presence. "God is in the water, God is in the dry land, God is in the heart," said the Sikh Guru Gobind Singh (1666–1708). A Hindu scripture offers: "Salutations to God in the earth and to God in the plants." The Psalms see evidence of God in the wonder of the natural world and the provision of food and water for all animals. "You make the springs break out in the gullies. . . . The wild beasts drink from them. . . . The birds of the air nest on their banks and sing among the leaves." (Psalms 104.10–12.)

PRACTICE *If you are not religious, you may find talk of God off-putting. But you may still recognize a sense of uplift in the presence of nature's splendor. The novelist Fydor Dostoyevsky suggests your love for a particular flower or animal can grow into a universal love. "Love will teach us all things; but we must learn how to win love; it is got with difficulty. . . . Love all creation, both the whole and every grain of sand. Love every leaf, every ray of light. Love the animals, love the plants, love each separate thing . . . until you come at last to love the whole world with a love that will then be all-embracing and universal."*

day
322 Mother Earth

Our roots are deep in the lands where we live. . . . We walk about with great respect, for the Earth is a very Sacred Place.

—FROM THE SIOUX, NAVAHO AND IROQUOIS DECLARATION, 1978

Do you think of the Earth as a mother? In many Native American prayers, the image of Mother Earth suggests the sense of presence and the interconnectedness of all life. One example is this prayer of the Pawnee people:

Earth, our mother, breathe forth life,
all night sleeping,
now awaking,
in the east,
now see the dawn.

Earth, our mother, breathe and waken,
leaves are stirring,
all things moving,
new day coming,
life renewing.

PRACTICE *Do you find the image of earth as a mother helpful? It suggests that the earth provides and cares for you. It also suggests that just as a mother loves and cares for her children, so you should respect and care for the earth. It also implies our interdependence on other people and all life. Think of the different materials used to meet your needs. Think of the trees that supplied the wood for your chair and table and for the paper for this book, the materials used for the carpet or rug. Be grateful. Consider whether there are ways you could do more to preserve the planet for your children and their children.*

Hildegard of Bingen

The Earth is Mother of all that is natural,
Mother of all that is human.

—St. Hildegard of Bingen (1098–1179), mystic and environmentalist

Hildegard of Bingen has become a sort of patron saint of environmentalists. Hildegard became abbess of a monastery at age 38. She was a gifted musician, a biologist, and the author of a book about medicine. In her visions she spoke of seeing "the cloud of the living light." She saw men and women as equal in their work for God in the "creative greenness" of the Spirit, which made her unusual for the Middle Ages and gives her such contemporary appeal. She linked the importance of the environment with the recognition of the leadership role that women should play in society.

PRACTICE *Can you recall moments when you were full of the joy of being alive? At a time when many monks emphasized asceticism and suppressing bodily needs, Hildegard, with her mystic sense of the oneness of all life, affirmed the importance of the physical. "The body," she said, "is supported in every way through the earth. Thus the earth glorifies the power of God." She wrote:*

I am the breeze,
that nurtures all things green. . . .
I am the rain coming from the dew
that causes grass to laugh with the joy of life. . . .
I am the yearning for the good.

God in Everything

In that moment, I knew that I had my own special place,
as had all other things, animate and so-called inanimate,
and that we were all part of this universal tissue which was both
fragile and immensely strong, and utterly good and beneficent.

—AN ANONYMOUS MEMORY OF AN EARLY CHILDHOOD EXPERIENCE,
EDWARD ROBINSON, *ORIGINAL VISION*

Have you sensed a "presence" as you have watched the sunset or marveled at a great waterfall? The Ancient Egyptians worshipped Amen-Râ, the lord of all gods, as "the One who has made everything which has come into existence." Like many people who were dependent on nature, the Egyptians sensed a Divine Presence in all life. The same is true of the Celtic tradition of Christianity, in which there is renewed interest today. Hinduism also has kept alive the teaching of "ancient spiritual traditions in which human beings were looked upon as part of nature, linked by indissoluble bonds with the elements around them." (Dr. Karan Singh in *Replenish the Earth*, ed. Lewis Regenstein.)

PRACTICE *Try to feel your oneness with nature with the first verse of this Celtic chant,*

I am the wind that breathes upon the sea,
I am the wave on the ocean,
I am the murmur of leaves rustling,
I am the rays of the sun,
I am the beam of the moon and stars,
I am the power of trees growing,
I am the bud breaking into blossom.

A Petal of the One World Flower

Only through love and compassion is the protection of Nature possible.

—Sri Mata Amritanandamayi Devi

Everything that exists is a part of God, or the Universal Consciousness, according to the teaching of Amma, who has been given the name Mata Amritanandamayi, or Mother of Immortal Bliss, by her devotees. Regarded as an embodiment of the Universal Mother, Amma has physically embraced more than 21 million people in the past 30 years, holding them close to her loving heart. Her charities, which are based in Kerala in south India, have housed many homeless people. In the United States, Mother's Kitchen provides 40,000 meals a year. GreenFriends, which she has established to protect the environment, distributes and plants 100,000 saplings in Kerala every November.

PRACTICE *Amma emphasizes that we contribute to the beauty of life through the beauty of our lives. Comparing the world to "a big wonderful flower with many petals," she says the duty of each one of us is to protect the beauty and the fragrance of this flower. If even one petal is diseased, it affects the whole flower. There will only be real peace and unity in the world when everyone purifies his or her life. In your meditation, picture yourself as a petal of a lovely, sweet-smelling flower. As you do so, be aware of your own beauty and your contribution to the splendor and unity of all life.*

day 326 A Meditation on Walking

You, O God, are the Lord of the mountains and valleys. Open my eyes to see their beauty. In your power, in your thought, all things are abundant.

—A NATIVE AMERICAN SIOUX PRAYER

Do you remember the walking meditation described in the first chapter? The aim was to concentrate your thoughts on the act of walking so as to be totally aware of the present moment. As you walk through an ancient forest or in a mountain valley, you could practice that exercise in a relaxed way and benefit from the renewing energy of nature. Look at the trees. Consider their height and their age. They put the scale of human life in perspective. Consider the ancient mountains. Your life is but a moment in history, yet it is of profound significance, dependent on and the product of all that has gone before. The present moment is also a timeless moment.

PRACTICE *In the morning before I wrote this, I walked in still sunshine through a highland glen. No one was to be seen for miles, and yet I knew that before the roads were made on the other side of the loch, this had been the route drovers had followed with their flocks. Even before the valley was inhabited, the river had forced itself through the boulders on its way to the sea. On my way back, the first thing I saw in the loch-side shop was a plaque with these words: "He who sees nature as part of himself will take care of nature. He who sees himself as part of nature knows nature will take care of him."*

The Zen of Sport

If you do something real, something genuine in any sphere of life, it will live on after you, and that part of you will be eternal.

—KEN WALSH, CONTEMPORARY AUTHOR OF PRAYERS

Zen opens you to the present moment—to total awareness of immediate experience. I once received a book about Zen and snowboarding. Like skiing and mountaineering, snowboarding requires total concentration. Many outdoor recreations, if done properly, demand focused attention. If your thoughts wander when you are climbing a rock face, you and your companions may slip. If you start daydreaming when you are sailing in a storm, the boat may capsize. Sport may be physically tiring, but it clears the mind because you cannot concentrate if half your mind is replaying a difficult business meeting or planning how to cope with the next emergency at work.

PRACTICE *Do you see a link between recreation and spiritual health? Western society tends to isolate the spiritual from the other dimensions of life. Times of leisure should free you from demands of the clock and the usual pressures of day-to-day life. Sadly, much sport now exaggerates the competitive urge that dominates society. Leisure activities have become big business. Families often come back exhausted rather than refreshed after a day at a theme park. Reflect on how you spend your leisure. Do you use it as time to renew personal relationships and to stand aside from the routine and pressure of everyday living?*

day
328 The Dancing Nataraja

I find you Lord in all things and in all my fellow creatures,
pulsing with your life; as a tiny seed you sleep in what is small
and in the vast you vastly yield yourself.

—RAINER MARIE RILKE (1875–1926), AUSTRO-GERMAN POET

One of the best-known Hindu representations of god is the Nataraja, or Dancing Shiva. Shiva is represented with four arms dancing in a circle of fire. He is dancing in the heart of creation as he sustains all life. Hindu seers recognized that the same power that dances in the heart of the universe also dances in every human heart. Psalm 19 begins, "The heavens tell out the glory of God." It continues, "The law of the Lord is perfect and revives the soul." It testifies to the same life-giving power that sustains the world and renews the human heart.

PRACTICE *In your meditation, recollect moments of great beauty or peace that you have experienced in nature. Try to recapture the sense of exhilaration at the sight of a great waterfall or majestic sunset. Slowly internalize that experience. As you go deeper into yourself, you will sense a similar joy as you become aware that in the very depth of your heart you are sustained by the same power that is at the heart of all things.*

At One with Nature

For the earth forever turning, for the skies, for every sea;
For our lives, for all we cherish, sing we our joyful song of peace.

—WORDS BY KIM OLER FROM "MISSA GAIA"

Have you had a sense of oneness with Nature? Forrest Reid, writing early in the twentieth century, tells of a day when he realized how lovely the world is. "I lay down on my back in the warm dry moss and listened to the skylark singing. . . [It was] a passionate joyous singing. It was a leaping, exultant ecstasy. . . . The whole world seemed to be within me." (Forrest Reid, *Following Darkness.*) The sense of joy in nature became an inner experience as if the whole world was within his heart. Others have had similar experiences. This is how awareness of the beauty of nature can take you deeper into yourself.

PRACTICE *Have you tried painting a landscape or a vase of flowers? As your observe your subject closely, you take it into yourself and try to express your experience on paper. In the same way, awareness of the beauty of nature can illuminate your inner life. In meditation, try focusing your attention on a recollection of a place of beauty, particularly one you know and of which you have happy memories. Just sit still and let the beauty speak to you. Try not to think about it. Just be aware and sense your oneness with the world of nature.*

Do Not Harm the World

The field and the forest are the most beautiful and finest of the Houses of the Lord.

—Rabbi Abramtzi

Judaism has a special New Year of the Trees (*Tu B'Sh'vat*) when it is customary to plant saplings. There is a tradition that God showed Adam, the first man, all the trees of the Garden of Eden and said to him, "All that I created was for you. Do not harm or desolate the world: for if you harm it, there will be no one to fix it after you." This is true. Deforested soil can never again support a tropical forest or even grow crops for long, because most of the land's nutrients are in the vegetation, not the soil. Deforestation destroys indigenous people's livelihood and culture, erodes the soil, and can cause devastating flooding, as in Bangladesh.

PRACTICE *The next time you go for a walk in the woods, think about how precious the trees are. No wonder the Zorah, a Jewish mystical work, says: "If you cut down a tree before its time, it is as if you have destroyed a living soul." If you plant a tree, it is a gift to the next generation. Trees can also serve as a reminder of spiritual truths. The Psalmist compares the righteous to a tree with deep roots. The leaves and branches may be blown by the wind, but the trunk stands firm. So if you are deeply rooted in the spirit, you will retain your inner calm, even when you are ruffled by unexpected events.*

Come Back to the Woods Again

Come back, o tigers, to the woods again, and let it not be leveled with the plains. For without you, the axe will lay it low. You, without it, will forever homeless go.

—From the Buddhist Khuddakapatha

It is not only the next generation that benefits if you plant a tree. The prophet Muhammad, who emphasized the importance of planting trees, said, "Whoever plants a tree and diligently looks after it until it matures and bears fruit is rewarded. . . . Every fruit that a bird or a man or an animal shall eat will be counted to him as an act of charity." Muhammad also said that even when the world is about to end, "If any one of you has a palm shoot in his hand, he should plant it."

PRACTICE *Forests are important not only for human welfare, but as Muhammad recognized, they are vital for birds and animals. Tropical rainforests cover about 7 percent of the Earth's surface but contain two-thirds of all plant and animal species. They are in danger. Each year an area of rainforest the size of Pennsylvania disappears, threatening many species of animal and plant life. Besides supporting efforts to protect rainforests, make sure that the wooden items you buy are made from renewable forests. Human beings, as Islam teaches, do not own the Earth. It has been entrusted to them to take care of for the sake all life. You may like to recite this ancient Hindu prayer:*

May the axe be far away from you;
May the fire be far away from you;
May there be rain without storm;
Lord of Trees may you be blessed;
Lord of Trees may I be blessed.

day 332 Everything Is Sacred

This we know, the Earth does not belong to man. This we know, that all things are connected like the blood which unites one family. All things are connected.

—CHIEF SEALTH, A NINETEENTH-CENTURY CHIEF OF THE DUWAMISH PEOPLE

The testimony of Chief Sealth, a Native American chief, has become well-known because it expresses the sense that the earth is sacred. His words can help modern people understand the attachment of "first peoples" to the Land. He said, "Every part of this land is sacred to my people. Every hillside, every valley, every plain and grove, has been hallowed by some fond memory or some sad experience of my tribe. . . . Our bare feet are conscious of the sympathetic touch, for the soil is rich with life of our kindred."

PRACTICE *Can you recall some place where you grew up that evokes strong memories of its natural beauty? Perhaps the town where you grew up or a favorite holiday destination holds these memories. Many city dwellers have often lost this sense of place. Try to imagine the feelings of those who have always lived and tended one piece of countryside. They have been dependent on it for their livelihood and have cared for it. This will make you more sympathetic to first peoples and their distress at so-called development. They may teach you a new reverence for the whole earth.*

The Breath of Life

We are earthlings. The Earth is our origin, our nourishment,
our support, our guide. Our spirituality itself is Earth-derived.

—FATHER THOMAS BERRY, A LEADING ENVIRONMENTAL THEOLOGIAN,
FROM *CELEBRATING EARTH HOLY DAYS*, ED. SUSAN CLARK

You are probably well aware of the dangers of global warming and the greenhouse effect. The air, like the ocean and the soil, are not just the environment that makes life possible but also a part of life itself. James Lovelock, author of a book called *Gaia*, which is a Greek word meaning "Earth," says, "The air is to life what fur is to a cat and the nest for a bird. Not living, but something made by living things to protect against an otherwise hostile space. For life on Earth, the air is our protection against the cold depths and fierce radiation of space." (James Lovelock, *The Ages of Gaia*.)

PRACTICE *In an effort to conserve fuel during the Second World War, the U.S. government placed posters that read, "Is this trip necessary?" around the country. Perhaps you should have the same poster in your car. Burning fossil fuel for energy causes nearly half of all global warming. International action is necessary, but do you use more energy than you need? Walking is good for the body and spirit. It helps you to slow down and simplify your life. Using public transportation also slows you down, and is environmentally beneficial. Even small adjustments to your way of life are a sign of your concern for the health of the world.*

day 334 The Waters are Goddesses

The Lord is my shepherd; I shall want nothing.
He leads me beside waters of peace and renews life within me.

—BIBLE: PSALMS 23.1–3

How often do you use water during the day—to wash, to make yourself a coffee or a tea, to do laundry, to hose the car, to water the garden, to cook meals, and to clear up afterward? As you think of the many uses of water, you realize how difficult life is for those with little water. The Earth's limited supply of fresh water is a renewable resource, but only if it is properly managed.

PRACTICE *Think of the religious symbolism of water. Once, as I arrived at a remote Indian village, it started to rain heavily—the first rain for months. I was told it was a propitious sign of blessing on my visit. In Islam, ablutions are required before prayer. They not only refresh the body but also serve as a reminder of the need for inner purity when you approach God. Many Hindus, for whom the waters are goddesses, begin the day with a bath, accompanying it with the recitation of ancient scriptures. Christians use water in baptism as a sign of new life and of God's forgiveness. Let your mind be free, recalling images of water. How do they speak to your spiritual condition? The Bible says that God in his mercy sent rain on good and bad alike. (Matthew 5.45.) Yet humans in their selfishness do not share this gift.*

The Sacred Flame

O Fire, worthy of sacrifice, worthy of prayer,
May there be happiness in the dwellings of men and women

—BASED ON WORDS FROM THE ZOROASTRIAN LITURGY

For Zoroastrians, fire is the focus of worship, although it is wrong to speak of them as "fire worshippers." Zoroastrians see fire as a symbol of purity. Human beings need to be purified of selfishness in their use of energy resources, of which fire is a symbol. Many of the conflicts in the world are related to energy supplies. The situation may get worse as reserves of fossil fuel are used up. A concern for a peaceful world includes concern for equitable use of nature's resources.

PRACTICE *Fire is also important in Hindu worship. In some rituals, people stretch out their hands toward a sacred flame and symbolically transfer that flame to their hearts. Christians compare the Holy Spirit to fire, which purifies the soul and enflames the heart with love for God. As you sit quietly, think of past actions that you regret or of which you are ashamed, and visualize them being burnt to ashes by the fire of God's forgiveness as your soul is purified. Picture your heart as a smoldering fire, and feel the breath of God bringing it to life so it flames with the desire to worship and to serve others.*

Enoch heard a voice from the bowels of the earth, "Woe, woe is me, the mother of men; I am pained, I am weary, because of the wickedness of my children."
—SCRIPTURES FROM THE CHURCH OF JESUS CHRIST OF THE LATTER-DAY SAINTS

The protection of the planet requires international agreements. When the U.N. Charter was drafted in 1945, no one foresaw today's global threats to the environment. In recent years, efforts have been made to draft an Earth Charter. The United Nations has also encouraged religious communities to observe an Environmental Sabbath/Earth Rest Day early in June. A previous attempt to draft an Earth Charter began:

We have forgotten who we are
We have lost our sense of wonder
We have degraded the Earth
We have exploited our fellow creatures.

PRACTICE *When did you first become conscious of the threat to the environment? Have you thought of it as a spiritual issue as well as question of human survival? Many religions see the earth or life as sacred, especially those that speak of it as God's creation. A growing number of scientists emphasize the interrelatedness of all life and now speak of Earth as a living organism. James Lovelock said, "Most of us sense that the Earth is more than a sphere of rock. . . . We feel we belong here and that this planet is our home." Does this approach change your attitude to the environment? (James Lovelock,* The Ages of Gaia.*)*

Morning

Lord of land and sea
Reveal yourself to me
At the rising of the dawn
In the freshness of the morn

—David Adam, contemporary author of *Celtic Prayers*

Dawn and dusk are special moments when it is easy to sense a presence in nature. In almost every religion, these hours have been set aside as times for prayer. Dawn holds the promise of a new day, with its hopes and worries. Nature is still, and everything is fresh. To begin the day quietly helps you to live the whole day in tune with the rhythm of nature. If you begin your day in a rush, you may never have a chance to regain your equilibrium.

PRACTICE *Could you get up early one morning, so that you could watch the dawn? Find a quiet place and be aware of the stillness and sense of all life being renewed. You may like to read slowly this prayer by Masao Takenaka from Japan:*

Eternal God,
early in the morning, before we begin our work,
we praise your glory.
Renew our bodies as fresh as morning flowers.
Open our inner eyes, as the sun casts new light upon the darkness
which prevailed over the night.
Deliver us from captivity.
Give us wings of freedom like birds in the sky,
to begin a new journey.
Restore justice and freedom, as a mighty stream
running continuously as day follows day.
We thank you for the gift of this morning,
and a new day to work with you.

Evening

Abide with us in the evening of the day, in the evening of life, in the evening of the world.

—From the Lutheran Prayer Manual

Do you feel a sense of sadness and mystery as the day draws to a close? Does it remind you of your mortality—that your life too will one day draw to a close? Rabindranath Tagore captures this mood in these words: "The day is no more, the shadow is upon the earth. It is time that I go to the stream to fill my pitcher. The evening air is eager with the sad music of the water. Ah, it calls me out into the dusk. In the lonely lane there is no passerby, the wind is up, the ripples are rampant in the river. I know not if I shall come back home. I know not whom I shall chance to meet. There at the fording in the little boat the unknown man plays upon his lute."

PRACTICE *Imagine it is evening. You are at the sea's edge. It is a calm, breathless evening. Reflect on these words of William Wordsworth:*

It is a beauteous evening, calm and free;
The holy time is quiet as a Nun
Breathless with adoration; the broad sun
Is sinking down in its tranquillity;

The gentleness of heaven is on the Sea:
Listen! The mighty Being is awake,
And doth with his eternal motion make
A sound like thunder everlastingly.

Allow stillness to enter your body and your spirit. As you become still and go deeper into yourself, you will become aware that your life is linked to the mysterious chain of all life.

The Sea

If I dwell in the uttermost parts of the sea, even there your hand shall lead me and your right hand shall hold me. . . .
The darkness and light to you are both alike.

—BIBLE: PSALMS 139.8-11

Have you ever stood on a lonely seashore watching the waves? Did you sense your mortality as you reflected on the age-old movement of the waters? Watching the waves break on the cold grey stones, the poet Alfred Lord Tennyson (1809–1892), wrote "Break, Break, Break..."

I would that my tongue could utter
The thoughts that arise in me.

Another poet, Matthew Arnold (1822–1888), heard an "eternal note of sadness" in the roar of pebbles as the waves drew back. Long ago, the same sound made the Greek tragic playwright Sophocles (c. 496–c. 406 BCE) think of "the turbid ebb and flow of human misery." But to a person of faith, there is also a deeper note that speaks of God's abiding presence.

PRACTICE *The ever-changing beauty of the sea reflects the varying moods of human personality. There are times when all is quiet, but at other moments, the waves rise high and beat against the shore. However, even when the sea is most angry and wild, there is stillness in the depth of the ocean. Meditation will help you go deep beneath the ups and downs of your emotions to discover the stillness of your inner being. As you do so, you will find an inner peace that nothing can take away. You may also realize that even in the deep waters of life, God is present to uphold you.*

day 340 Mountains

To be fully alive is to have an aesthetic perception of life because a major part of the world's goodness lies in its often unspeakable beauty.

—REV. YUKITAKA YAMAMOTO, PRIEST OF THE SHINTO TSUBAKI GRAND SHRINE

Mount Everest was first climbed more than 50 years ago. Now it is almost a tourist attraction. You have to book several years ahead to climb it. In many traditional cultures, mountains (such as Mount Fuji in Japan) were sacred places and no one dared set foot on them. Before Moses climbed Mount Sinai to receive the Ten Commandments, he warned the people of Israel not even to touch the foot of the mountain on pain of death. The majestic solitude of great mountains was thought to be the abode of the gods and today they still can inspire awe, reminding you of human frailty and the amazing grandeur of the world.

PRACTICE *Many mountains are places of pilgrimage. On a bitterly cold morning, I set out in the brilliant moonlight to climb Mount Sinai with some friends. Snow and ice prevented us from reaching the summit, but we sensed the glory of the Holy One who was revealed to Moses at that place. With another group, in much hotter weather, I climbed nearly 4,000 steps to the beautiful Jain temple city of Shatrunjaya in Gujarat, India. The sound of temple bells and the chanting of pilgrims gives the place a peaceful serenity. However, no one, not even a priest, is allowed to stay overnight on the holy mountain. Even if you cannot travel to distant pilgrim sites, climbing a nearby hill as a form of meditation will increase your sense of wonder and reverence.*

The Stars

*Whoever you are: some evening, take a step out of your house. . . .
Enormous space is near. . . . The world is immense and like a world
that is still growing in silence.*

—RAINER MARIA RILKE (1875–1926), AUSTRO-GERMAN POET

Do you sometimes step outside on a clear night and gaze up at the starlit sky? To seafaring people, such as the Celts, the stars and the moon were friends who helped them navigate their way back home. For other people, the stars have provided signs of future events. Today perhaps your thought is of space exploration and the unimaginable vastness of space. This makes it more amazing that the life of each individual has profound meaning. What is your own place among the stars?

PRACTICE *As you sit quietly, relax your body and still your mind. Close your eyes, and picture a clear starlit night sky. Sense the beauty and the vastness of the universe. Is there life on other planets? We do not know. This makes the gift of life even more precious—for you and for other people. Consider whether you value that gift sufficiently. Does the way you live express your gratitude? Is there more you could do to ensure that other people and all beings enjoy this wonderful gift to the fullest?*

day 342 A Bunch of Flowers

Flower girl plucking petals,
Know in each petal life abides.

—GURU GRANTH SAHIB

Do flowers play a part in your life? We send flowers to express joy at a child's birth and to celebrate good news. We also send flowers to those who are ill and to the bereaved. Weddings are decorated with flowers and graves covered with them. Flowers speak of beauty, peace, and the harmony of the natural world, but they soon fade and so remind us that life's pleasures are transient and that life soon passes. Remembering our mortality encourages humility and a healthy perspective on the transience of life's achievements and disappointments.

PRACTICE *Choose some flowers as a focus for your meditation. Spend time arranging them and looking at them carefully. What do they say to you about how precious life is? Reflect on these words from a poem by the English poet Robert Herrick (1591–1674):*

Fair daffodils, we weep to see
You haste away so soon; As yet the early rising sun
Has not attained his noon.

I Saw the Cactus Bloom

The wilderness will rejoice and blossom. Like the crocus, it will burst into bloom; it will rejoice greatly and shout for joy.

—BIBLE: ISAIAH 35.1-12

Many flowers die in the fall, but bloom again in spring. Nature offers many signs that defeat and despair can be transformed. The Biblical prophet Isaiah compared the gift of the Spirit to water poured on dry land. For many Indians, the lotus is symbolic of something pure that has arisen from the mud. It suggests that human beings too can rise from murky circumstances to achieve great things. Truth and Love can purify each person and make him or her a thing of beauty.

PRACTICE *For your meditation, spend time looking at a plant or bouquet of flowers. Then read this poem by Chun-Ming Kao, which was written while he was imprisoned by the Communists. It is a message of hope that suffering will be transformed.*

I asked the Lord for a bunch of fresh flowers
but instead he gave me an ugly cactus with many thorns.
I asked the Lord for some beautiful butterflies
but instead he gave me many ugly and dreadful worms.
I was threatened,
I was disappointed,
I mourned.
But after many days, suddenly,
I saw the cactus bloom with many beautiful flowers,
and those worms became beautiful butterflies.

Teilhard de Chardin

I live at the heart of a single, unique Element, the Center of the Universe, and present in each part of it: personal Love and cosmic Power.

—TEILHARD DE CHARDIN (1881–1955), JESUIT AND PALEONTOLOGIST

Many scientists have experienced an intense sense of the wonder of the universe and of the divine presence in its midst. Teilhard de Chardin, a priest and scientist, said that life increases in complexity and consciousness as it evolves. Humanity is one peak in a process that moves through ever more closely knit social relationships and the integration of consciousness toward the Omega Point, which Teilhard de Chardin identified with Christ. Donald Nicholl suggests that the ultimate development of self-consciousness is a deliberate act of self-sacrifice on behalf of others, as shown in Jesus' self-offering at Calvary.

PRACTICE *Teilhard de Chardin used his evolutionary frame of thought to find meaning in suffering. "The world," he said, "is an immense groping, an immense search. . . it can only progress at the cost of many failures and casualties. Sufferers are not useless and diminished elements, but pay the price of universal progress and triumph." This does not reduce the pain experienced by those who suffer but may suggest it has a meaning. Through their sacrifice, life progresses toward the Omega Point. Does this evolutionary framework help to give meaning to your suffering or the work you do?*

Albert Schweitzer

Even ants and other insects will run away from danger. . . . They have intelligence and want to live, too. Why should we harm them?

—THE DALAI LAMA. INTERVIEW WITH
LEWIS G. REGENSTEIN IN *REPLENISH THE EARTH*

"Reverence for all life" is a phrase forever associated with Albert Schweitzer (1875–1965). A brilliant theologian and musician, Albert Schweitzer trained as a doctor and went as a medical missionary to French Equatorial Africa. There he devoted much of his life to the service of the sick and poor at Lambaréné Hospital. In calling for "reverence for all life," he wrote, "A person's religion is of little value unless even seemingly insignificant creatures benefit from it. To a truly religious person, life as such is sacred." He stressed that the commandment to love compelled humans to help animals and spare them suffering as far as possible.

PRACTICE *Some 80 years ago, Schweitzer warned of the damage that humankind's careless destruction of nature would cause. "Humans will end up by destroying the earth." (Ann Cottrell Free,* Animals, Nature and Albert Schweitzer.*) How careful are you to respect the life of plants as well as animals? Schweitzer said that if a farmer had spent the day cutting grass as fodder for his cattle, but on the way back wantonly cut off the head of a single flower growing at the edge of the road, he had injured life unnecessarily.*

Kindness to Animals

Surely we ought to show animals great kindness and gentleness for many reasons, but above all because they are of the same origin as ourselves.

—ST. JOHN CHRYSOSTOM (c. 345–407)

Holy people of many religions have shown deep sympathy for animals. Many saints lived as hermits in empty deserts or lonely forests. Birds and beasts were their only companions. St. Benedict (c. 480–c. 543), the founder of Western Christian monasticism, had a pet raven. The medieval Benedictine monk St. Meinrad was murdered by robbers in his cave. His ravens flapped their wings and made a commotion that helped villagers catch the thieves who had killed him.

PRACTICE *Do you have any pets? Pet owners often claim to know what their animal is thinking or saying. The legends about the friendship between saints and wild animals reflect the saints' respect for the holiness of all life. Their concern for animals was often in sharp contrast to the conventional views of their contemporaries. Reflect whether your treatment of animals fits in with the spiritual standards that you value.*

God's Family

All creatures are like a family of God and God loves best those who are kindest to His family.

—THE PROPHET MUHAMMAD

There are many stories of the prophet Muhammad's concern for animals. On one occasion, he entered a house and put down his cloak. While he was talking, a mother cat and her kittens made themselves comfortable on the cloak. Rather than disturb the cats, Muhammad took a knife and cut the cloth around the cats, leaving the cats a part of his cloak. The Qur'an itself says, "Whoever takes pity even on a sparrow and spares its life, God will be merciful to him on the Day of Judgment." Muhammad often rebuked followers who maltreated animals and insisted that the slaughter of animals should cause them as little suffering as possible. He said, "If you must kill, kill without torture."(Lewis G. Regenstein, *Replenish the Earth.*)

PRACTICE *Are you concerned about how the meat you eat has been produced? Some people are vegetarian because they object to the killing of animals for food. Anyone who has a sense of the unity of all life should ensure that if animals are slaughtered, it should be done with a minimum of suffering to the animals. Some methods of factory farming appear cruel, but producers respond to customer demands. Are you prepared to pay more so that animals suffer less? They too, as the Qur'an says (24.41), are God's creatures and each of them "knows its prayer and psalm."*

day 348 Cows

The cow is a poem of pity. . . . She seems to speak to us through her eyes: "You are not appointed over us to kill us and eat our flesh or otherwise ill-treat us, but to be our friend and guardian."

—MAHATMA GANDHI (1869–1948), *THE MIND OF MAHATMA GANDHI,* EDS. R.K PRABU AND U.R. RAO

Cows are regarded as sacred by Hindus. Mahatma Gandhi said that cow protection was "the most wonderful phenomena in all human evolution," as it took people beyond a concern for their own species and helped them to realize their identity with all that lives. "Protection of the cow," Gandhi said, "means protection of the whole dumb creation." The cow, whose many products are vital for Indian villagers, is like a mother who helps people think of God as a Mother who cares for them. Her life is simple but life-giving.

PRACTICE *Have you ever really looked into the eyes of a cow and seen her gentleness? Cows, which are allowed to roam freely in many parts of India, are tolerated even though they add to the traffic chaos. Despite his concern for the protection of cows, Mahatma Gandhi was clear that cow slaughter could never be stopped by law. "Knowledge, education, and the spirit of kindliness towards her alone can put an end to it." Even if blood sports are banned, cruelty to animals will only disappear when people sense the unity of all life. Gandhi agreed that it was sometimes right to put a sick animal out of its misery, but any of taking of life should be done with great reluctance.*

Take Care of the Insects

The person who looks on the creatures of the earth, big and small, as his own self, comprehends this immense world. Among the careless, the person who restrains himself is enlightened.

—MAHAVIRA JAIN (599–527 BCE), THE LAST TIRTHANKARA

I am a vegetarian. When I led a tour to Gujarat in northwestern India, I was pleased that all the hotels were vegetarian. This reflects the widespread influence of the Jain religion in the area. Jain monks take a vow to "renounce all killing of living beings." Their teacher Mahavira taught *ahimsa*, or nonviolence, to all beings. He carried a soft broom to gently sweep the path before him to avoid treading on any insect. He was also careful not to hurt insects that landed on him. Although Jainism is a small religion, its concern for the sanctity of all life has worldwide influence. Gandhi, who grew up in Gujarat, was influenced by Jainism.

PRACTICE *Are you too preoccupied with your own concerns to notice the pain of other living beings? Mahavira's wish to avoid killing was also an expression of his mindfulness and concentration. When he walked, he meditated with his eyes fixed on a space before him of the length of a man. "Looking a little sideward, attentively looking on his path," he walked so as not to step on any living being. Jainism, like Buddhism, emphasizes total awareness of the present moment. Much suffering to other people and other creatures is caused by heedlessness and hurry. Mahavira said, "Know other creatures' love of life, for they are like you."*

day 350

Birds' Hospital

May I always have a friendly feeling toward all living beings of the world and may the stream of compassion always flow from my being toward distressed and afflicted living beings.

—JAIN PRAYER

When a vulture was struck by her helicopter, Indira Gandhi, then Prime Minister of India, asked for the dazed bird to be taken to the Charity Birds' Hospital in Old Delhi run by the Jain veterinarian, Dr. R. K. Punshi. The vet treats all birds without charge, although this amounts to over six thousand cases in a year. Dr. Punshi explained his mission by saying, "All that breathes is precious. Who is to say the suffering of a sparrow is less worthy of solace than the pain of a man? The spark of life is no dimmer simply because it is encased in fur or feather."

PRACTICE *Do you agree with Dr. Punshi? Some religions teach that human life is more valuable than animal life, but those with a deep concern for animal suffering are usually also deeply sympathetic to human pain. The Jains have set up hospitals and welfare centers for humans in many parts of India. Their deep concern for the environment reflects a longing for a world without violence. That longing in turn springs from a peaceful and loving heart. As a Jain song puts it:*

May the sacred stream of amity flow forever in my heart.
May the universe prosper—such is my cherished desire.

What Does Dominion Mean?

In God's hand is the soul of every living thing
and the breath of all humankind.

—BIBLE: JOB 12.10

Do you think animals have rights as well as human beings? The Bible says that God, when he created the world, gave man "dominion" over fish, birds, and animals. This verse has often been used to justify ruthless exploitation of animals, but it immediately follows the verse that says that God created human beings in the divine image. In their rule over the animal world, they were meant to reflect God's loving care for creation. (Genesis 1.28.) The Bible also said that animals like human beings should rest on the Sabbath and it insisted that people should help an animal in distress—even if the animal belonged to an enemy.

PRACTICE *A concern for animal welfare is nothing new. Read this ancient prayer by St. Basil (c. 330–c. 379), a founder of Christian monasticism.*

O God, enlarge within us the sense of fellowship with all living things . . .
to whom thou hast given the earth as their home in common with us.
We remember with shame that in the past we have exercised the high dominion of human beings with ruthless cruelty, so that the voice of the earth, which should have gone up to you in song, has been a groan of travail.
May we realize that they live, not for us alone, but for themselves and for you, and that they have the sweetness of life.

day
352 Reconnect with the Natural World

I came to believe that there was One God with different names: Allah, Tao, the Creator, and so on. God, for me, was the Great Spirit in Whom "we live and move and have our being."

—JANE GOODALL, A CHAMPION OF THE ENVIRONMENT, FROM *REASON FOR HOPE*

Jane Goodall's detailed study of the chimpanzees with whom she lived in the Gombe preserve in Tanzania changed our understanding of humanity. Until that time, human beings were defined as "Man the Toolmaker"—but Jane Goodall observed one of the chimpanzees using pieces of grass to probe a termite nest. Then, she saw him modifying a twig to use as a tool. When she telegrammed the news to the famous paleontologist Louis Leakey, he said "either we must redefine man or accept chimpanzees as human." Besides her famous research, Jane, who has been upheld by her faith, has campaigned vigorously against cruelty to animals, which inflicts intense suffering and demeans humanity.

PRACTICE *In 1974, Jane Goodall was in Notre Dame in Paris. As she gazed at the great Rose Window glowing in the morning sun, the cathedral was filled with Bach's* Toccata and Fugue in D Minor. *The music seemed alive and possessed her whole being. In her endless campaigning for the environment, the memory of that moment has renewed her energy. Her message is simple. "Each one of us matters . . . and makes a difference. Each of us must take responsibility for our own lives . . . and show respect and love for living things and for each other. We must reconnect with the natural world and with the Spiritual Power around us." Have you made that connection? Do you feel your life can make a difference?*

Animal Welfare: A Moral Issue

The best and most experienced teachers do not talk of cruelty to animals. They talk of kindness to animals. We have a duty not only to refrain from harm but also to do positive good.

—CARDINAL HEENAN, FORMER CARDINAL ARCHBISHOP OF WESTMINSTER, ENGLAND, QUOTED FROM *COMPASSION FOR ANIMALS*, ED. ANDREW LINZEY

Concern about animal welfare is not sentimentality, but a profound moral and spiritual issue. John Austin Baker, a former bishop of Salisbury in England, said that it is based "on humility, reverence and awe in face of the mystery we call Life." He accepts that there may be times when it is necessary to take the life of an animal for food or for self-defense, or to save it suffering, but he warns how dangerous it is when we do this without any sense of the sacredness of life. Those who take animal life without any sense of compunction can come to see other people as vermin to be destroyed. "It is in the battery shed and the broiler house, not in the wild, that we find the true parallel to Auschwitz." (Andrew Linzey, ed., *Compassion for Animals*.)

PRACTICE *A Native American in a prayer of gratitude for food thanks God "for our animal brothers who gave themselves so that we should live." In ancient society, most animals were sacrificed to God before being eaten. This was an acknowledgment of the sacredness of life and a prayer that God would not be displeased by the taking of life. Do you give thanks if you eat meat or fish? Do you reflect that life has been taken to give you life? Remembering this should encourage you to live a life worthy of all that has been sacrificed for your welfare.*

The God of Hawks and Sparrows

Do you hunt the prey for the lioness
and satisfy the hunger of the lions,
when they crouch in their dens
or lie in wait in a thicket?

—BIBLE: JOB 38.39–40

A safari in Zimbabwe was one of the highlights of my life. From our shelter, we could see giraffes and zebras at the water hole. We watched herds of elephants. We saw monkeys playing in the trees. However nature is not only fascinating but also "red in tooth and claw." "God is the God of hawks no less than sparrows," wrote Oxford theologian Austin Farrer, "Of microbes no less than men." (Andrew Linzey, ed. *Compassion for Animals.*) Once, at an ashram in India, I expressed anxiety about all the mosquitoes—only to be told that it was their home long before I had come to stay!

PRACTICE *Awareness of the majestic beauty of nature together with the recognition that most life depends on the sacrifice of other lives may open your eyes to a new vision of the world. It is easy to assume that all other creatures exist for the benefit of humans, but a truer and more humble perspective is to recognize human beings' place in nature and to recognize the interdependence of your life with all living beings. If nature is held in trust by humans, then there is a responsibility to see that all beings fulfill life's purpose for them.*

What the Bear said to the Tiger

This is the sum of duty; do naught unto others which would cause you pain if done to you.

—From the Hindu epic, the Mahabharata, 13.114

Can we learn from animals? Many stories tell of their good examples. For Hindus, Sita represents the model wife. Abducted by the demon king Ravanna, she was eventually rescued by her husband Rama with the help of monkeys led by Hanuman. Hanuman wanted to destroy the demon guards, but Sita said, "No they were under the King's control and simply carried out their orders. Now Ravanna is dead, they will leave me alone." Sita then quoted the advice of a bear to a tiger. "You should not retaliate when another does you injury. . . . Even if those who do wrong deserve to be killed, the noble ones should be compassionate, since there is no one who does not transgress."

PRACTICE *To what extent do you think the agents of a cruel dictator are accountable for their actions? Those who resist are admirable, but most people fear for their livelihoods and indeed their lives. Ask yourself if you would have behaved any better in such a situation. Once a dictator is overthrown, we should not regard all the people of that land as enemies. Think about countries that were once regarded as enemies. Is that how you perceive them today? You can help eradicate bitter memories of the past through compassionate understanding.*

day 356 The Sword

All they that take the sword shall perish with the sword.

—BIBLE: MATTHEW 26.52

Stories about animals are often used to teach moral lessons. According to a traditional Jewish story, the otter complained to King Solomon, "Your majesty, didn't you decree that the wild creatures must live in peace? When I went to hunt for food, I asked the weasel to look after my young and he devoured them all," but the weasel said it was an accident. He heard the woodpecker pounding on the war drums and as he rushed to fight he trod on the baby otters. The woodpecker blamed the scorpion for swinging its javelin, but the scorpion said, "I was swinging my javelin because I saw the otter coming to devour my children." The king said to the otter, "The weasel is not guilty. He who sows death shall reap it."

PRACTICE *Fear breeds fear and violence breeds violence. This is the reason conflicts so often escalate from misunderstanding to confrontation. If you pick up a gun, it is more likely the other person will get a gun. The more guns there are, the more likely it is that one will be used. The person of peace tries to defuse a situation, even if means taking the blame or forgoing the right to own a gun. As you sit quietly, reflect if there are ways for you to diffuse a difficult situation. Is everyone waiting for someone else to make the first move? Could you initiate a process that will avoid confrontation?*

Ask My Donkey

We put bits into the mouths of horses to make them obey us. Likewise the tongue is a small part of the body . . . but no man can tame the tongue.

—BIBLE: JAMES 3.3–7

Once you realize that you are losing your temper, are you able to bring it under control? The Sufi holy fool Nasreddin was riding his donkey along a path when something startled the donkey. All of a sudden it was galloping at breakneck speed. Nasreddin's friends were astonished to see him speeding past. They cried out, "Where are you going so fast?" Nasreddin shouted back, "Don't ask me, ask my donkey." Like Nasreddin's donkey, arguments can all too easily gallop out of control. Fueled by anger, you end up saying something you regret.

PRACTICE *If you have had an argument recently, think back and ask yourself why the situation got out of control. Were you on the defensive? Why do you react to criticism? Were you hiding a mistake? Do you like everyone to think you are perfect? Was the other person under stress? Could you have been more sympathetic? If you give yourself time regularly to be quiet, to purify your negative emotions, and to let your heart become peaceful, you are better able to react calmly to life's up and downs.*

day
358

Be Kind to All Living Beings

I will mourn for the mountains because they have dried up: birds and wild animals have fled and gone.

—BIBLE: JEREMIAH 9.10

If a developer offered to build you a new luxury home and give you a large sum of money in exchange for your present house, would you accept it, even if it meant cutting down a local forest and disturbing the creatures that lived there? A medieval Irish saint, Kevin of Glendalough, lived in a tiny, uncomfortable cell. An angel is said to have offered to level some hills so that Kevin could build a fine new monastery. The saint replied, "I have no wish that the wild creatures on these mountains should be sad because of me." St. Kevin's concern for the animals grew from his closeness to God in prayer.

PRACTICE *The more you discover your inner self, the more you will feel at one with other living beings. A peaceful person avoids causing unnecessary suffering to any living creature. Such a person avoids damaging the environment, even if it means financial loss. Jewish rabbis taught that cruelty to animals is among the most serious of offences. A Hebrew proverb says: "The kind man feeds his beasts before sitting down to the table."*

Take Up Painting

Flowers appear on the earth; the season of singing has come,
the cooing of doves is heard in our land.

—BIBLE: THE SONG OF SONGS 2.12

Do you spend time sketching or painting? It can be a good way to relax and become more peaceful. It also helps you notice the intricate beauty of nature. Sri Chinmoy, a teacher of meditation who is also an artist and musician, has made millions of sketches of what he calls "dream-freedom peace-birds." These artistic works symbolize Sri Chinmoy's universal message of unity in multiplicity, harmony in diversity. Viewed individually, each bird is an emissary of peace, but also part of a wider movement.

PRACTICE *If you have not painted for a long time, why not give it a try? You could take a course, but if you wish to paint for relaxation, you may prefer experimenting by yourself. The end result is not as important as the process itself. Painting takes you out of yourself. Abstract dabbling—like a child playing with colors and paints—is a good way of freeing the mind to soar like a bird. Sketching a landscape or a flower helps you concentrate and observe the amazing and delicate beauty of the natural world.*

day
360 God's Indestructible Beauty

Joyless is the day's return
Till your mercy's beams I see;
Till they inward light impart,
Glad my eyes, and warm my heart.

—CHARLES WESLEY (1707–1788), METHODIST HYMN WRITER

Have you ever been confined to bed? Did you come to appreciate the beauty of a bouquet of flowers a friend or relative may have brought? Were you thankful to gaze out a window to see the trees and sky? Leonard Wilson said that he was sustained as a Japanese prisoner of war by a tiny window at the back of the filthy crowded cell. He could hear the song of the golden oriole and he could see the glorious red of the flame trees. "They conveyed something of God's indestructible beauty to my tortured mind." In the distance, he could see the top of Wesley's church and every morning he recited Wesley's hymn, "Christ whose glory fills the skies."

PRACTICE *When you are ill or bereaved, a bouquet of flowers is not only a reminder of a friend's concern but also a sign of the beauty of the world and of God's care for creation.*

What is enjoyment in this cell-like situation?
The flash of sunlight on a flower. . . .
A bird singing outside in the garden
All show forth the Glory of God. . . .
But first I have to learn
To recognize the moment of enjoyment.

—BRENDA DAWSON, FROM *ST. CHRISTOPHER'S IN CELEBRATION,*
ED. CICELY SAUNDERS

Animal Suffering

I shall become a savior to all those beings,
I shall release them from all their sufferings.

—The Bodhisattva's vow

A bodhisattva is someone who vows to become a Buddha in order to free all beings from suffering, no matter how great the effort. Mahasattva and two other princes were walking in a park when they saw a hungry tigress. One prince said, "She gave birth to seven cubs a week ago, but is too weak to feed them." Mahasattva thought to himself, "Now the time has come for me to sacrifice myself." Asking his brothers to leave, he resolved, "With deep compassion, I give away my body." Because the tigress was too weak to move, Mahasattva cut his own throat with bamboo and fell before the tigress, who devoured his flesh and blood.

PRACTICE *How much thought have you given to your moral responsibility toward the animal world? It is not suggested that you should follow Mahasattva's example! But Buddhists and Jains do not assume that human life is superior to animal life. Are you concerned how your food is produced? Commercially produced food may be less healthy, but your concern should be not only about your own health but also about the unnecessary suffering of animals in the interests of obtaining cheap food. The peace-loving person will be pained by the suffering of any living being. You may like to repeat the Buddhist verse:*

May every living being, forgetting none, be at peace.

day 362

Cosmic Revelation

The God who made the world and everything in it is the Lord of heaven and earth and does not live in temples built by hand. . . In him we live and move and have our being.

—BIBLE: ST. PAUL, THE ACTS OF THE APOSTLES 17.24–28

How big a role does nature play in your spiritual life? Father Thomas Berry, the most eloquent contemporary spokesperson for the aesthetic and spiritual importance of the natural world, complains that religions themselves sometimes divert attention from the cosmic revelation. "Because our sense of the divine is so extensively derived from verbal sources . . . we seldom notice how extensively we have lost contact with the revelation of the divine in nature. Yet our exalted sense of the divine itself comes from the grandeur of the universe."

PRACTICE *Does a visit to the country mean more to you than a place to get some fresh air and exercise? Nature can help you to recover your balance and feel a greater inner calm, but if it is to be a constant source of renewal for a peaceful heart, you need to be open to the sense of presence and wonder that it conveys. The natural and animal world can enhance your feelings of sympathy with all life and deepen your awareness of the Unity of all that is. It may even be a source of Divine Revelation. It is important not only to protect the environment but also to help others become aware of nature's rich significance.*

Spacecraft Columbia

Differences between people are a cause for celebration.

—Brenda Markland, Canadian physician, in *Visions of a Better World*, Brahma Kumaris

The seven crew members of the ill-fated Columbia spacecraft were people of different faiths, but they worked together for a common goal. Kalpana Chawla was a Hindu and a vegetarian; Rick Husband, an evangelical Christian; David Brown, an Episcopalian; William McCool, Roman Catholic; and Laurel Salton Clark, a Unitarian. Michael Anderson, a Baptist, had told his pastor, "Don't worry if I'm not coming back I'm just going higher." Ilan Ramon, who was Jewish, brought a Torah scroll that was used at a Bar Mitzvah ceremony in a concentration camp. He carried a drawing entitled *Moon Landscape* by 14-year-old Peter Ginz, who died at Auschwitz. Ramon said, "Space travel is what can happen when people make peace."

PRACTICE *If we could find the secret of peace, we could end the suffering and hunger of millions of people on earth and ensure that our precious planet is preserved in all its beauty for future generations. Frank Borman, commander of Apollo VIII, offered this prayer on Christmas Eve 1968 while in space:*

Give us, O God, the vision which can see your love in the world in spite of human failure.
Give us the faith to trust your goodness
in spite of our ignorance and weakness.
Give us understanding hearts and strength
to do what each of us can to set forward
the coming of the day of universal peace.

364 Planet Earth

I am flying above the Earth. How beautiful my planet is! It is a garden in full bloom. Human beings are beautiful. How kind and bright their faces are, how much harmony is in their souls!

—KIRILL EVGENYEVICH RODOV, RUSSIAN STUDENT,
IN *VISIONS OF A BETTER WORLD*, BRAHMA KUMARIS

The image of Planet Earth from space has been called a symbol for our age. David Brown, who was on the Columbia spacecraft, said "If I'd been born in space, I would desire to visit the beautiful Earth more than I ever yearned to visit space. It's a wonderful planet." Kalpana Chawla, a Hindu said, "The first view of the Earth is magical . . . in such a small planet, with such a small ribbon of life, so much goes on. It is as if the whole place is sacred. You get the feeling that I need to work extraordinarily hard along with other human beings to respect that."

PRACTICE *Kalpana Chawla gave this advice: "Do something because you really want to do it. If you're doing it just for the goal, and don't enjoy the path, then I think you're cheating yourself." You may not know the fruit of your actions. You may not see how your work contributes to the peace of the world, the relief of suffering, and the preservation of the planet. Your calling is to be true to yourself, to follow your chosen path. This brings integrity, wholeness, and a peaceful heart.*

Life Is a Magical Thing

There was a moth on board and it was just starting to pump its wings up. Life continues in lots of places, and life is a magical thing.

—LAUREL SALTON CLARK, A UNITARIAN CREW MEMBER OF THE COLUMBIA SPACECRAFT

The day before she died, Laurel Salton Clark sent an email from space, saying, "Hello from above our magnificent planet Earth. The perspective is truly awe-inspiring. . . . I have seen some incredible sights: lightning spreading over the Pacific, the Aurora Australis lighting up the entire visible horizon with the city glow of Australia below, the crescent moon setting over the limb of the Earth, the vast plains of Africa and the dunes on Cape Horn. . . .Mount Fuji looks like a small bump from up here, but it does stand out as a very distinct landmark. . . .Whenever I do get to look out, it is glorious. Even the stars have a special brightness."

PRACTICE *As seen from space, Planet Earth is beautiful and fragile. The earth we share with other people and other living beings is precious. All life is to be revered. The deeper you search into yourself, the more aware you become of your unity with all life. The exploration of outer space and of inner space both lead to a sense of unity and of oneness. Whether you long for a peaceful world or yearn for a peaceful heart, the quest is the same.*

Lead us from the unreal to the real;
lead us from darkness to light;
lead us from death to immortality.
Peace, peace, peace.

Sources

Adam, David. *Tides and Seasons: Modern Prayers in the Celtic Tradition*. SPCK, 1989.
Angelou, Maya. *On the Pulse of the Morning*. Random House, 1993.
Appleton, George, ed. *The Oxford Book of Prayer*. Oxford University Press, 1985.
Arnold, Matthew. *Empedocles on Etna*. Classic Books, 2000.
Ashwin, Angela, ed. *The Book of a Thousand Prayers*. Zondervan, 1996.
Batchelor, Mary. *Lion Prayer Collection*. Lion, 2001.
Belz, Peter, and Donald Reeves. *A Tender Bridge*. Cairns Publications, 2001.
Bernardin, Joseph, Cardinal. *The Gift of Peace*. Loyola Press, 1997.
Berndt, Hagen, ed. *NonViolence in the World Religions*. SCM Press, 2000.
Beversluis, Joel, ed. *A Source Book for the Earth's Community of Religions*. CoNexus Press, 1995.
Blanch, Stuart, and Brenda Blanch, eds. *Learning of God*. SPCK Triangle, 1985.
Blumenthal, David. *Facing the Abusing God*. Westminster/John Knox Press, 1993.
Boulding, Elise. *Cultures of Peace: The Hidden Side of History*. Syracuse University Press, 2000.
Bowker, John. *Problems of Suffering in Religions of the World*. Cambridge University Press, 1970.
Braybrooke, Marcus, ed. *1000 World Prayers*. O Books, 2003.
Braybrooke, Marcus. *A Wider Vision*. Oneworld, 1996.
Braybrooke, Marcus, ed. *Bridge of Stars*. Duncan Baird Publishers, 2001.
Braybrooke, Marcus. *Love Without Limit*. Braybrooke Press, 1995.
Braybrooke, Marcus. *Time to Meet*. SCM Press, 1990.
Braybrooke, Marcus. *What Can We Learn from Islam?* John Hunt Publishing, 2002.
Brittain, Vera. *Testament of Friendship*. Virago Press, 1987.
Brockman, James R., trans. *The Violence of Love: The Words of Oscar Romero*. Fount, 1989.
Brosse, Jacques. *Religious Leaders*. Chambers, 1991.
Burtt, Edwin A. *Teachings of the Compassionate Buddha*, 1989.
Buck, Pearl. *To My Daughters, with Love*. Buccaneer Books, 1996.
Cassidy, Sheila. *Sharing the Darkness*. Darton, Longman and Todd, 1988.
Carden, John. *Another Day*. SPCK, 1989.
de Carteret, Nikki. *Visions of A Better World*. Visions of a Better World Foundation, 1993.
Chang, Michael, with Mike Yorke. *Holding Serve: Persevering on and Off Court*. Hodder, 2002.
Cinquin, Emmanuelle. *Sister with the Ragpickers*. Triangle, 1982.
Clark, Susan, ed. *Celebrating Earth Holy Days*. Crossroad, 1992.
Clarke Wilson, Dorothy. *Take My Hands*. Hodder and Stoughton, 1963.
Cleary, Thomas, trans. *Immortal Sisters: Secrets of a Taoist Woman*. Shambhala Publications, 1989.
Cohn-Sherbok, Dan, ed. *Glimpses of God*. Duckworth, 1994.
Cook, Michael. *The Koran, A Very Short Introduction*. Oxford Paperbacks, 2000.
Cottrell Free, Ann, ed. *Animals, Nature, and Albert Schweitzer*. Flying Fox Press, 1989
Coward, H. and Cook. P. *Religious Dimensions of Child and Family Life*. Wilfrid Laurier University Press, 1996.
Craig. Mary. *Blessings*. Hodder and Stoughton, 1979.
Dalai Lama. *Ancient Wisdom: Modern World*. Little Brown and Co., 1999.
Dalai Lama. *The Good Heart*. Vintage/Ebury, 2002.
Davey, Cyril. *50 Lives for God*. Oliphants, 1973.
Dawson. Rosemary. *Something to Celebrate*. Church House Publishing, 1995.
Day Lewis, Cecil. *Requiem for the Living*, Jonathan Cape Ltd and Harold Matson Co., Inc.
Dominian, Jack. *Marriage, Faith and Love*. Darton, Longman and Todd, 1981.
Dominian, Jack. *Let's Make Love*. Darton, Longman and Todd, 2002.
Dunning, John H., ed. *Making Globalization Good*. Oxford University Press, 2003.
Enright, Robert D., and Joanna North, eds. *Exploring Forgiveness*. University of Wisconsin Press, 1998.
Espersen, E. *Meeting in Faith*. Sage International, Arlington, 1996.